The Science of Success in China

Modern China Series

The Science of Success in China

Zhang Xiuyu

North American Business Press

The Science of Success in China

ISBN: 9781948915144

NORTH
AMERICAN BUSINESS
PRESS

North American Business Press
Atlanta, Georgia
Miami, Florida
New York, New York,
Toronto, Canada

FIRST PRINTING, 2020

About Modern China Series

China, as one of the oldest civilized regions in the world, has emerged as something of a "new world" because it is working to embrace its own essence and heritage and link them to viable economic strategies. In the last 25 years, China has made tremendous strides by doing so. The country and her people have every right to take pride in these accomplishments. With these successes under their belt, many Chinese leaders and intellectuals anticipate continuing growth. China's plans and strategies, furthermore, are often based upon this premise.

There is tremendous interest in the US on the Chinese economy and business environment. China has emerged as a global superpower, and scholars and businessmen in the US are keenly interested in learning how this is going to continue to affect them and how they can do business with China. In response to growing interest from international and Asian scholars, North American Business Press is pleased to announce our Modern China Series (MCS) books, which is first of such series in the US and has garnered tremendous interest both in the US and around the world. With our first book reaching stores in September 2011, this initiative is aimed at developing relationships between NABP and Chinese scholars who desire to promote their academic and applied business writings to the rest of the world.

We have had an overwhelming demand for the Modern China Series from both authors who would like to publish in the series and people who would like to read the books. Currently, there are ten books published in the series and, additionally, we have a couple of dozen books that we are considering for the series. The books have been viewed by tens of thousands of people from the U.S. and the rest of the world.

We have published books relating to several areas revolving around the Chinese business environment. We have some books that focus on the best practices in marketing in China; some are related to "best practices" in doing business in China; and some on the outlook of the

Chinese economy. The market for the Modern China Series is huge. There are tens of thousands of scholars that are keenly interested in the continued growth of the Chinese economy and the implications that will have on the business world. Even more significant are the millions of businessmen that are interested in the impact that China will continue to have on the global economy. It is difficult to pin down the exact demand for the series, but it is very large.

We have big plans for growing the Modern China Series. This has the potential to one of the most significant economic/business series ever produced. We are very selective with the books that we will add to the collection, but we encourage any scholars who think they have unique and interesting perspectives on China to submit their books to us. From the readers' perspective, we are committed to producing high-quality books on a regular basis so that readers should expect a steady stream of insightful books to be coming out for many years to come.

This initiative is headed by Dr. Robert Tian, a renowned researcher and academic, who spearheads our efforts in partnering with foreign authors and administering day-to-day operations of this series. Dr. Tian, a Vice-President with North American Business Press and Editor of this series, spends much of his time in Beijing, Shanghai, and other Chinese cities, focusing on developing and managing our interests with authors and universities. Below is the list for the books we have published:

Enterprise Strategy: New Horizon authored by Zhang Xiuyu
Governance of Private Enterprises in Modern China authored by Zhong Qin
The Art of War and Enterprise Strategy Management authored by Fu Shouzhi
Marketing Issues in Modern China edited by Robert Guang Tian et al.
The Footprints of the Academician authored by Fu Zhouzhi
Marketing and Economics in Modern China (I) edited by Xiaoguang Qi et al.

Marketing and Economics in Modern China (II) edited by Wang Tianjin et al.
An Islamic Heritage in China authored by Ma Zhanming
China Environmental Anthropology authored by Wang Tianjin, Tian Guang, and Ma Jianfu
Can China Rule the New World? Authored by Tian Guang and Chen Gang
Critiques on Pan-marketization authored by Li Cunlin, Liu Hongfei, and Tian Guang
Economic and Economic Economical and Business Anthropology in China edited by Xiaoguang Qi and Tian Guang
China-Mongolia Economic Corridor authored by Eerdun Taoketao, Zhang Zhe, Wang Gang, and Wei Lisi
Anthropology of Chinese Foodways authored by Tian Guang and Chen Gang
Urbanization of Rural China authored by Li Taohong
Political Connection and Financial Fraud in China by Peng Jinqian
The Science of Success in China by Zhang Xiuyu

About This Book

By combining theory with practice, this book reveals the objective law of people's struggle for success. The steps to implement the objective law are as follows:

1) Fire the engine of success, cultivate a positive mental attitude, enhance personal enterprise spirit, and boost the confidence to win.
2) Set the compass for success, define a clear goal, and utilize your own strengths.
3) Hold the steering wheel to success and stay focused, control your attention, intensify your self-disciple, and manage yourself well.
4) Strengthen the propeller of success. If you want to achieve the ultimate success, you must strengthen the three propellers of success, namely, keep enthusiastic, devote a little more effort and do well in learning from setbacks and adversity.
5) Start the innovative machine of success, learn to think correctly, cultivate imagination and creativity, and organize a mastermind alliance.
6) Lay a solid foundation for success, keep healthy in body and mind, cultivate attractive personality, develop good habits, make a schedule and budget, and do a good job in teamwork.

Zhang Xiuyu's Achievements & Honors

Publications:

Full-crew Competition Management was published by the Reform Press in 1993. Yuan Baohua, the former director of the State Economic Commission of China, spoke highly of the new theory and wrote the title for the book.

The book titled "Meeting the Challenge: How can enterprises practice excellent internal skills?" was published by China City Press in 1996. It was highly praised by Yuan Baohua, the former director of the State Economic Commission of China, "it is well written, involving all the major issues of enterprise reform and management. An enterprise must both improve its external conditions and practice its internal skills in order to make great progress. Managers of enterprises should read the book carefully."

Zhang Xiuyu's Achievements & Honors

Enterprise Strategic Management was published by Peking University Press in 2002 as a textbook. It is not only very popular in China, but also quickly spread to the United States. It is well received and valued by the business, education and publishing circles of the United States.

How Can We Succeed was published by the Enterprise Management Publishing House in 2005.

Zhang Xiuyu's Achievement

Honors

At the special invitation of North American Business Press, I adapted the textbook Enterprise Strategic Management into Enterprise Strategy: New Horizon in English, which has been published in the United States.

The Path o
General in
ABW Theo
Peking Uni
This book c
systematica
concretely s
theory whic
Wang Hai, p
Star Group i
practice in l
employees t
Star Group a
and which h
correct in pr
characteristi
Group. The I
book has bee
United States

In 19
Excel
Comr

Zhang Xiuyu's Achievements & Honors

9, Zhang Xiuyu won the Award of Excellent Teacher and ent Educational Worker of Beijing Institute of Finance and erce Management.

Zhang Xiuyu's Achievements & Honors

In December 2008, Zhang Xiuyu won the Award of the 7th New Entrepreneurs of the Year in China.

Zhang Xiuyu's Achievements & Honors

In January 2009, Zhang Xiuyu won the Award of Outstanding Person of China's reform in 2008.

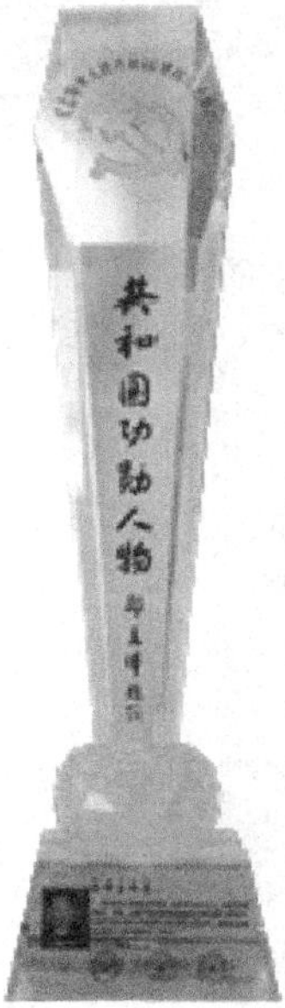

On the occasion of celebrating the 60th anniversary of the founding of the People's Republic of China, Zhang Xiuyu was honored as the meritorious person of the People's Republic of China and recorded in the Records of meritorious persons of the People's Republic of China.

Zhang Xiuyu's Achievements & Honors

Zhang Xiuyu's biography brief was edited into Who's Who in the World.

Zhang Xiuyu's Achievements & Honors

Zhang Xiuyu's Achievements & Honors

In May 2012, Zhang Xiuyu won the honorary title of Excellent Credible Entrepreneur in China.

Zhang Xiuyu's Achievements & Honors

On March 4, 2005, Zhang Xiuyu founded Beijing Chenggong Zhiyao Consulting Co., Ltd. at the age of 63 and started his second business to benefit the society. He created the first brand of China's success consulting industry, Key to Success.

Zhang Xiuyu has compiled 15 books, including many brand works. In management consulting, he has made more than 30 achievements, including many achievements on enterprise consulting. As a result, he has won many honorary titles, certificates and plaques from all walks of life.

Zhang Xiuyu's Achievements & Honors

The above are two ten-year strategic plans prepared by Zhang Xiuyu for China Banknote Printing and Mining Corporation.

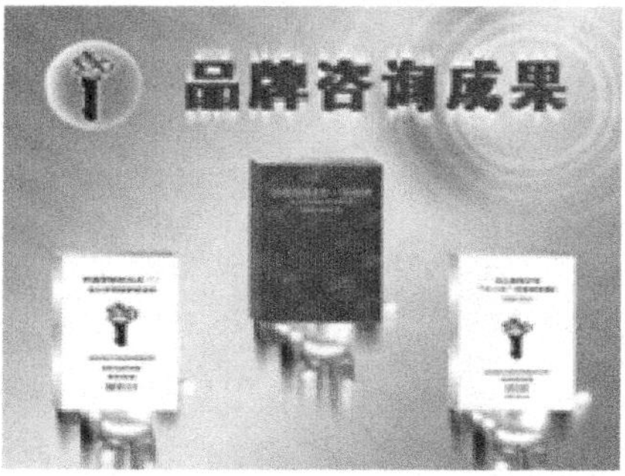

The above are the consulting report and the overall strategic plan during the Eleventh Five-Year Period prepared by the consulting team led by Zhang Xiuyu for Beiren Group Corporation.

Zhang Xiuyu's Achievements & Honors

The above are the eight consulting achievements prepared by consulting team led by Zhang Xiuyu for Beijing International Tendering Co., Ltd., including one overall strategic plan and seven schemes for the reform of the company.

Preface

Are you a successful person?

In the late 20th century, I dreamt of creating the science of success in China, establishing the career on the consultation for success in China, providing the best consultation services on the way to succeed for my clients and finally helping the organizations and individuals achieve success in their lives!

Science of success is a summary of the successful experience of thousands of successful people in all walks of life at all times and all countries. It embodies the quality of success of successful people in a centralized model. It is a powerful spiritual weapon for people to strive for success, an engine, a compass, and a strong backing to push the people to head towards success.

To start my career in the consultation for success, I will carry out success education and training, provide consulting services on success, and provide strategies for success and other intelligence services. In this way, I can provide the best consultation services on the way to succeed for my clients and help organizations and individuals achieve success in their lives.

My dream mainly consists of eight goals:

(1) Compile and publish “The Science of Success in China” as soon as possible.

(2) Make teaching courseware concerning the science of success.

(3) Select different types of units for the pilot project.

(4) Establish a consulting company specialized in the business on consultation for success.

(5) Set up the China Research Promotion Association on the Science of Success.

(6) Start a magazine or column titled Success or The Key to Success.

(7) Found the Chinese Academy of Success, and hold the national symposiums on the science of success and the lectures by successful people.

(8) Carry out international academic exchanges on the science of success.

Up to now, some of the goals as mentioned above are achieved, such as (1), (2), (3), (4) and (6), while some will proceed step by step, such as (5), (7) and (8). There is still a long way from fully realizing my dream, but I am firmly convinced that:

We will be able to accomplish anything that we can image and firmly believe! -- Napoleon Hill

As long as you intend to succeed, you are bound to make it! --Dale Carnegie

Where there is a will, there is a way. -- Mao Zedong

On the basis of studying, studying and mastering the spirit of science of success in the United States, it is a primary task to start the career of consultation for success by compiling the monographs or textbooks on the science of success in China as the fundamental teaching materials for carrying out the education, training, and consultation on science of success, in accordance with China's national conditions and characteristics. I started this work as early as the end of the 20th century and the beginning of the 21st century. After more than six years of hard work, my first book on the science of success in China, "How Can We Succeed?" was published by the Enterprise Management Publishing House in January 2005.

During the compilation of the book, the manuscript of the book was published continuously in the column "Wish You Success" set up by Shougang Daily at the special invitation of Shougang Daily. Moreover, a review on this book, "' How Can We Succeed?' assists you in attaining success", was published on Shougang Daily on April 29, 2005.

"Professor Zhang Xiuyu has been highly accomplished in the research on enterprise strategy, enterprise management, and other fields," the editor wrote in the book review, "Since science of success was introduced into China more than ten years ago, Professor Zhang Xiuyu has devoted himself to the research on the science of success. He is really an expert in the research of science of success. Recently, his book 'How Can We Succeed?' was published by the Enterprise Management Publishing House. It is of excellent guidance and benefits to those who intend to realize their goals and then attain success."

Since the publication of the book "How Can We Succeed?" I have been giving lectures in colleges and universities, industrial and commercial enterprises, research institutes, societies, associations, and other organizations nationwide in China, preaching the science of success to the leaders of enterprises, young and middle-aged cadres, teachers and students of colleges and universities, scientific researchers, college graduates as village officers, and laid-off workers and employee. When I was preaching the science of success, I was often asked by journalists, cadres, employees, and students, "Professor Zhang, are you a successful person?"

Every time I encounter similar questions, I will answer with a hearty laugh, "Whether I am a successful person is neither determined by you or me, but judged by the public according to my actual actions and effects. Just as the saying goes, practice is the sole criterion for testing truth."

So, am I a successful person? To answer the question raised by the audience, I have to show the photos that can reflect my practicee results and various honors given by society as follows.

Foreword

The career on consultation for success is a great and noble cause for the benefit of enterprises, institutions, and other organizations and masses from all walks of life, which originated from the United States in the 19th century, with a history of more than 100 years. However, in China, the science of success has just been introduced, and consultation for success is still an uncultivated land. In order to make the science of success popularize and develop rapidly in China, the primary task is to compile and publish a monograph or textbook on the science of success with Chinese characteristics to conform to the needs and habits of the Chinese people as soon as possible.

In order to achieve the goal, I spent six years learning and studying the science of success of the United States based on the ideas of Andrew Carnegie, steel tycoon of the United States, and initiated by Dr. Napoleon Hill. On this basis, I wrote the book "How Can We Succeed?" which was published by the Enterprise Management Publishing House in January 2005. It was the first time that I attempted to found the science of success in China, so that other scholars and experts may come up with valuable opinions in this respect.

Since "How Can We Succeed?" was published nearly fifteen years ago, I have gained rich experience in education, training, consulting, and company establishment over the years. On this basis and in response to the suggestions and requests from readers, I have re-compiled *The Science of Success in China*, aiming to reveal the laws of success to readers, introduce the principles, methods, skills and Examples of success, so as to inspire, guide, help and encourage more people to achieve success. On the occasion of the publication of *The Science of Success in China*, I would like to share the following four views with you:

1. Everyone wants to succeed

Everyone who is sound in mind expects to succeed; no matter it is an emperor, a president, or an ordinary person. It is the instinct, desire, and responsibility of humankind to seek success. We are born with the ability to succeed. Later, we gradually have the desire to succeed and undertake the obligation of succeeding in any work that we are busy with. Everyone expects to do their job well and to make it. Therefore, everyone has become conscious of success, whether they have realized it or not.

Then, what is success? There are several common arguments:

(1) "To make more money is to succeed." This view holds that you are successful as long as you can become a millionaire, a multimillionaire, or a billionaire.

(2) "To have high power is to succeed." This view holds that you are successful as long as you can keep a more top position with higher authority, such as being a county head, mayor, provincial governor, national leader, or chairman of the board of directors, general manager, or a schoolmaster, president and bureau chief, etc.

(3) "To win high reputation is to succeed." This view holds that you will make it, as long as you can gain a high reputation in China, in the whole world, and even in history.

There are many similar statements, but the above statements have significant limitations. It is mainly reflected in the following three aspects. First of all, it only lays stress on the forms of success but ignores the essential requirements of success. Secondly, it only emphasizes the manifestation of success in one aspect but neglects the indication of success in other dimensions. Thirdly, it obliterates the difference between justice and injustice, between benefit and harm, between the true, the good and the beautiful and the false, the evil and the ugly, and between an everlasting good name and an everlasting shame, making it more likely to mislead.

If someone becomes a millionaire, a multimillionaire or a billionaire, but spends the money indulging in eating, drinking, gambling and frequenting the brothels, and even violating the laws and discipline, or throw the money about or waste it recklessly, is it a success?

If someone has a high position and great power, but he abuses his ability to seek personal gain, engages in collusion between power and

goal, which is to enter an ovum containing micronucleus. The head of each sperm consists of 24 chromosomes, just as the micronucleus of the ovum contains 24 chromosomes. Each chromosome consists of closely linked colloidal beads, each of which includes hundreds of genetic factors.

All the genetic material and tendencies contained in the chromosome of the sperm are provided by your father and his ancestors; all the genetic content and tendencies contained in the chromosome in the micronucleus of the ovum are provided by your mother and her ancestors. The sperm and ovum represent the culmination of the victory in the battle for survival, which took place more than two billion years ago. When a particular sperm, which is the fastest and healthiest winner, is tied with the waiting ovum to form a tiny living cell, which is you who are going to come into the world.

Thus, you have been a champion, and you have inherited all the potential power and ability you need from the numerous past accumulations. Now, no matter what obstacles and difficulties there are in your life, they are inferior to those that you overcame when you were born! So, as long as you want to succeed, you are bound to be successful!

At the same time, the achievements of scientific research and the facts of human development history also provide potent arguments. According to scientists, the average person has about 100 billion brain cells. However, it is a pity that only 10% of these brain cells work for us and the rest 90% have been sleeping. Other scientists have pointed out that before their death, most people have developed only about 5% of their potential in their life, while the rest 95% of their potential has not been established. Great scientists like Einstein didn't use 15% of their brain cells. Dr. Otto, a famous American scholar, said: “The human brain seems to be a sleeping giant, and we all use less than 1% of our brainpower.” The memory capacity of a healthy human brain equals the knowledge contained in about 600 million books, equivalent to 1.2 million times the storage capacity of a massive computer. If we can use half of our brain's potential, we can quickly learn 40 languages, memorize a complete encyclopaedia and obtain 12 doctor’s degrees.

It can be seen from the above that no matter from the perspective of natural genetics or from the perspective of the acquired development concept, a person who wants to succeed and does his best will be bound to be successful.

3. Why can only a few people ultimately succeed?

There is no doubt that it is a correct argument that everyone is able to succeed. However, in fact, there are only a few ultimately succeeding. As for the reasons, people are not only different from each other in terms of family background, education level, physical condition, and other aspects, but everyone makes efforts in varying degrees. If some people have the right conditions and work hard, they will undoubtedly be able to succeed. But it is often the case that some people with poor conditions realize, while those with the right conditions fail, which indicates that some necessary conditions are required for success, but it is the individual's efforts that play a decisive role. The critical factor that affects the degree of the individual's efforts is not the intellectual quality of the individual but its non-intellectual quality. Such non-intellectual qualities include mental attitude, ideal, goal, will, confidence, determination, diligence, action, persistence, willpower, and so forth. A person who has a positive mental attitude, an ambitious goal, full confidence, and a strong will can create conditions even without any conditions and strive for success. On the contrary, a person with a negative mental attitude, no ambition, no confidence and weak will be unable to utilize the favorable conditions available, so it is less likely to achieve success. If you have excellent intellectual and non-intellectual qualities, no one can make it except for you. If you don't succeed in the end, the reason tends to be some shortcomings in your non-intellectual qualities, rather than those in your intellectual qualities. How to educate, cultivate and train these non-intellectual qualities is precisely what this book will reveal.

Here I want to emphasize that science of success is a branch of science. Science requires us to engage in academic studies in an honest and sincere attitude, and not to be lazy, hypocritical, or arrogant. Only those who aspire to success, study hard, be strict with themselves and practice seriously can achieve success. However, in real life, due to various reasons, only a few people can conduct themselves in conformity with these rules, which is also the fundamental reason why there are always a few successful people.

4. How can we succeed?

At all times and in all over the world, only a small number of people achieve their success, but success is an objective existence after all. Since it is an objective existence, there must be similar reasons for its existence, which means the necessity or regularity. That is to say, the reason why some people succeed is that they can handle affairs in conformity with the rules of success, whether they have realized them or not. In view of this, there are rules for success, which are created by thousands of successful people from all walks of life.

Since ancient times, people have been striving for success and studying the truth of success. Moreover, a great many famous remarks and proverbs are involved in sparkling philosophies about success. With the development of society, the competition in the fields of politics, economy, culture, and society is becoming more and more intense, while the public is required to master systematic and perfect philosophy of success so as to achieve greater success with high proficiency. Driven by such social needs, the science of success has come into being.

In the 19th century, Andrew Carnegie, the well-known steel tycoon of the United States, believed that his own success and the success of numerous inventors, entrepreneurs and politicians in the United States, such as Thomas Alva Edison, Henry Ford, Franklin Delano Roosevelt, Alexander Graham Bell, John Davison Rockefeller, Julius Roqenwald, all contained many valuable philosophies worth learning. Therefore, he is eager to find an appropriate person to study the success philosophy of celebrities in the United States. Furthermore, he believes that after the establishment of such science of success, his contribution to the world will be far more significant than his contribution to the world with material wealth.

Andrew Carnegie visited more than 200 young people in search of talents to explore the science of success, but he did not get satisfactory results. In 1908, 18-year-old Napoleon Hill visited Andrew Carnegie when he was studying at University, and he spoke highly of the philosophy of success proposed by Andrew Carnegie. Born in a low-income family, Napoleon Hill was a "disobedient child" when he was very young. His stepmother gave him love and courage to grow up and often blessed and encouraged him to strive for great achievements. It is she who inspires a troubled child to develop his personality, work hard, and become a cultured winner. After strictly investigating Napoleon Hill, Andrew Carnegie decided to entrust him with the task of establishing the science of success. He asked Napoleon Hill to visit 500 successful celebrities in the United States, summarize their philosophy of success, and create the science of success within 20 years. As expected, Napoleon Hill published a monograph The Law of Success, which clarified the philosophy of success of successful figures in the United States and laid the foundation of the science of success. Since then, people's consciousness of success has changed from unconsciousness to consciousness. Millions of people have consciously applied the science of success and achieved success in all aspects, which has played a vital role in the development of society.

Since then, Napoleon Hill has continued to explore success issues, diligently wrote science of success monographs, and imparted the knowledge on the science of success in the form of lectures and study classes. He received a Ph.D. and served as an adviser to two American presidents, Thomas Woodrow Wilson, and Franklin Delano Roosevelt, until his death on November 8, 1970. In August 1952, due to the long-term practice of the philosophy of success, Napoleon Hill changed from a young man with only $100 to a millionaire with a value of $400 million. William Clement Stone, the founder and President of Combined Insurance Company of America, met with Napoleon Hill, and immediately formed the Napoleon Hill Federation, devoted himself to the preparation of new books, the implementation of new training programs, and the promotion of the principles and skills of the science of success initiated by Napoleon Hill, which made the science of success spread throughout the United States and even the world. The Hills and their son decided to donate Hill's entire heritage to set up the

Hill Foundation to serve the cause of success forever. Dr. Hill is a model of experts in science.

This book focuses on how to educate, cultivate, and train people's non-intellectual qualities, especially on thinking and action. It believes that thinking and action are the secret to success. Without thinking, there would be no goal; without action, the goal would not be achieved. In this regard, as long as we make unremitting efforts to achieve a definite goal, everyone can be successful!

The science of success is a summary of the successful experience of thousands of successful people from all walks of life. It is a real reflection of the law of success of successful people and a powerful spiritual weapon for people to strive for success. Therefore, the science of success should not become the patent of a few rich people, senior officials, celebrities, and elites, but should be a talisman for millions of ordinary people to strive for success.

In the foreword of the first edition of his world-famous masterpiece Pushing to the Front, Orison Swett Marden, the founder of Success Magazine in the United States and the great tutor of the science of success, wrote: "for young people, the most ideal book should be like this - it must contain all types of specific examples, which can be used as the basis for the young to perfect themselves, and the material for them to motivate themselves. Its content must be positive, providing people with high energy and advice and inspiration. It must avoid falling into two extremes: just a pile of enormous materials, or only empty sermons. In addition, it must contain a large number of compelling examples of how those successful people overcome difficulties and ultimately achieve success."

Thus, it can be seen that Orison Swett Marden has proposed such high requirements for the books on the science of success that this book is far from meeting such needs. However, I regard the conditions proposed by Orison Swett Marden as my goal and try my best to get closer to this goal.

Zhang Xiuyu

January 30, 2019, Beijing

Table of Contents

Part I Start the Engine for Success

If a car wants to gallop, it must start the engine first, and then it can generate power so that it can arrive at its destination smoothly by authority. No matter how smart, knowledgeable, and experienced a person is, he must first have the motivation to strive for success and make unremitting efforts for success under the impetus of this motivation if he wants to grow up healthily and achieves success. Otherwise, he would be as useless as a car without an engine. In order to generate the motivation for success, people must first cultivate a positive mental attitude, enhance their personal enterprising spirit, and consolidate their confidence in the ability to win.

Part I Start the Engine for Success

Chapter 1 Cultivate A Positive Mental Attitude

Maxims for Success

Your mind has a secret invisible talisman. On one side is emblazoned the letters PMA (a positive mental attitude) and on the other the letters NMA (negative mental attitude). A positive attitude will naturally attract the good and the beautiful. The negative attitude will rob you of all that makes life worth living.—Napoleon Hill

Principles and Guidelines

A positive mental attitude is the most important one of the 18 principles of the science of success, as success can only be achieved based on a positive mental attitude and one or two of the other 17 principles. First, this section will explore the principle of positive mental attitude.

What is a positive mental attitude?

People may encounter all types of difficulties and setbacks in their growth, study, work, and life, such as disappointment in love, unemployment, disease, etc. Facing these problems in the course of life, different people will hold different attitudes, which will lead to different consequences. One attitude is to be in low spirits, to lose confidence, and finally to fail; the other is to find out the reasons, to summarize the lessons, to consolidate the confidence, to continue to move forward, as well as never to give up until you reach your goal. Thomas Alva Edison, one of the greatest inventors in history, is a model with the latter attitude. In order to invent the electric bulb, he made more than 10000 experiments and finally managed to create it. He believes that temporary setbacks are not equal to failure, but to the ladder towards the ultimate success. When people encounter problems, they will have their own attitude, which is known as a mental attitude. For the same problem, people may hold different mental attitudes, among which one type is a positive mental attitude, and the other type is a negative mental attitude.

A positive mental attitude refers to the act of recognizing that there are both good and bad aspects of things when they are checked but emphasizing the functional characters, so as to produce better wishes and results. When we look at the brighter side, good luck will come. A positive mental attitude refers to the correct, sincere, and constructive thought, behavior or reaction that anyone has in any circumstances or in any environment, which does not violate any law or human rights. It allows us to expand our hopes and overcome all the negative mental attitudes. Furthermore, it will provide us with spiritual strength, enthusiasm, and confidence to satisfy our desires. A positive mental attitude is an indispensable element of success, the basis of all success, and the essential principle in the science of success.

Different returns of two mental attitudes

Mental attitude, the invisible talisman, can produce two types of incredible forces, as it can not only enable us to gain wealth, and become happy and healthy, and live a long life, but also allow these things to get far away from us, or deprive us of everything that makes our life meaningful. Among these two types of forces, a positive mental attitude enables us to reach the summit of our life, and enjoy the happiness and beauty of life, while a negative mental attitude makes us in a bottom position in the whole life, tangled with numerous hardships and misfortune all the time. When we have reached the summit of our life, it will drag us from the summit to the bottom in case we are conquered by a negative mental attitude.

A positive mental attitude is the correct mental attitude. The right mental attitude always has the feature of positive energy, such as loyalty, honesty, hope, optimism, courage, creation, generosity, tolerance, wit, kindness, and high level of rationality. People with a positive mental attitude always have a more top goal, and continuously strive to achieve their goal. A negative mental attitude has the opposite characteristics to a positive mental attitude. Dr. Hill and President Stone, in the studies on the cases of numerous successful people for many years, have come to the conclusion that a simple secret that these successful people share is that they have a positive mental attitude.

Therefore, mental attitude is of considerable significance to the success of our career and life. If we keep a positive mental attitude, control our thoughts, and guide it to serve our definite goal of life, we can enjoy the favorable returns as follows:

(1) Have a sense of success and an environment for success.

(2) Be sound in body and mind.

(3) Receive independent financial income.

(4) Engage in a job that enables us to achieve our self-fulfillment.

(5) Be in a peaceful state in mind.

(6) Remove the fear and have firm confidence.

(7) Have long-term friends.

(8) Live a long life and a harmonious and balanced life.

(9) Get free from self-limitation.

(10) Have the wisdom of understanding ourselves and others.

On the contrary, if we hold a negative mental attitude and make it penetrate into our thoughts and affect our work and life, we may suffer the following consequences:

(1) Live a wretched and miserable life.

(2) Suffer physical and psychological diseases.

(3) Set limitations to make ourselves mediocre.

(4) Have fear and all destructive consequences.

(5) Restrictions in the ways we create to help ourselves.

(6) Fall into the situation where we have more enemies but fewer friends.

(7) Have all types of worries known to human beings.

(8) Be the victim of all adverse impacts.

(9) Surrender yourselves to the will of others.

(10) Live a meaningless and decadent life.

In this case, should we choose a positive mental attitude or a negative mental attitude? If we don't accept the former and hold on to it tightly, the latter will come to us automatically. There is no compromise between the two. Therefore, we must choose one of the two.

Efficacy of a positive mental attitude

William James, a famous psychologist, said: "the world is made up of two types of people, and one is those with a strong will, while the other is those with a weak will. When facing difficulties and setbacks, the latter always evades and hesitates to press forward. When faced with critical opinions, they are extremely vulnerable, so they may feel discouraged, while they have to wait for pain and failure, but those with a strong will not. From all walks of life, they may be manual workers or businessmen, mothers or fathers, teachers or else, or the elderly or the young, while they are all endowed with a strong innate character in their minds. The strong character refers to the inner courage to bear the external tests in the face of all difficulties."

As for the two types of people proposed by William James, as mentioned above, the first type holds a positive mental attitude, and the second one contains a negative mental attitude. So, why does a positive mental attitude generate such enormous power? In fact, a positive mental attitude does not have such magic power that it can create something out of nothing, create a job for the unemployed and generate billions of wealth for the poor, but everything is traceable, and ultimately, we have to depend on ourselves to achieve success. People with a positive mental attitude just adjust their mental attitudes in a timely manner, change their way of thinking and behavior, and analyze the facts based on what they really are. A person with a positive mental attitude doesn't deny the existence of negative factors, but he just learns not to let himself indulge in these factors. A positive mental attitude requires us to learn the way of positive thinking from every detail of our life, as positive thinking is a mode of thinking, which enables us to seek the best and most favorable results in the face of bad situations. That is to say, in the pursuit of a specific goal, there may be some hope for us even though we have difficulty in taking a step forward. It has been proved in many facts that when we look at the better side, we are more likely to make it.

In practical terms, we can predict whether a person will succeed in the future from the perspective of the current model of his or her thinking. What a person achieves will never exceed what he or she thinks. Those who have high aspirations are bound to achieve great success, while the desires of the ordinary people are merely limited to a small scale.

As the saying goes, thought is the precursor of action. If a person anticipates his success, he will carry out the operations that allow him to achieve success. As long as we adopt a positive mental attitude, all of us will ultimately succeed. Even if everything goes wrong, we will never give up easily and hold that we have nothing to do with success. We may encounter numerous setbacks, difficulties, and troubles in our lives, but as long as we uphold the sincere faith, confront the life, and firmly believe that good luck will come to us, we can come out ahead and solve the problems quickly. This applies to anyone on any occasion.

How can we cultivate a positive mental attitude?

We must cultivate a positive mental attitude so that our lives can develop according to their own intentions. Without a positive mental attitude, we would be unable to make great achievements. Thus, it is necessary to keep in mind that mental attitude is the only thing that we can fully master so that we should practice controlling our own mental attitudes, and guide our own actions with a positive mental attitude.

Then, how should we cultivate a positive mental attitude? Napoleon Hill summarizes the experience of successful people he has visited in his life and proposes 36 methods. Here, only the 18 practices that are the most important from my personal point of view are introduced as follows. If you want to learn all the ways, please read the original work Success Through A Positive Mental Attitude by W. Clement Stone and Napoleon Hill.

(1) Cut off all the relations with the failure in the past and eliminate all the adverse factors in the mind that run counter to the positive mental attitude.

(2) Find out what you want most in your life, make it your goal, and start to achieve it immediately.

(3) Determine the resources you need to achieve the goal, and make plans to obtain these resources, and make sure that your intentions are neither too excessive nor too insufficient.
(4) Concentrate all your thoughts on what you intend to do, and never leave any space for the blind and disorderly conjectures.
(5) Adopt various methods to cultivate a carefree mood by saying or doing something that makes others feel comfortable and doing one good deed every day.
(6) Make yourself understand that it's not the frustration that knocks you down, but the mental attitude you hold when you are faced with the disappointment, and train yourself to find out the positive side equivalent to the disappointment in each adverse situation.
(7) Make sure that you have developed the habit of continually endeavoring to do still better, and given play to such a practice with your love and enthusiasm. It's best to turn this habit into a hobby.
(8) Take the initiative to contact the person you offended in an unreasonable manner before and apologize to him sincerely. The more complicated this task is, the better you can get rid of your inner negative mental attitude after you apologize to the person.
(9) Get rid of your bad habits, give up one bad habit every day for a month in a row, and reflect on the results at the end of every week.
(10) Live in a way that applies to your physical and mental characteristics, and take exercises as much as possible to keep you sound in both body and mind.
(11) You should understand that love is the best medicine for your physical and mental diseases and that love will change and adjust the chemical elements in your body so that they can help you show a positive mental attitude and expand your tolerance. The best way to receive love is to give it.

(12) Increase your patience and embrace all things with an open mind. At the same time, come into more contact with people of different races and faiths to learn to accept the nature of others, instead of blindly requesting others to do what you want them to do.

(13) Reward those who have done good to you with what is worthy of equal or more value.

(14) Dispel the fear of old age. As time goes by, the intelligence will grow, which is bound to bring you something of equal or higher value.

(15) Be honest. You should show your true self whenever and wherever possible, as no one will believe in a liar.

(16) Please understand that you are the only one on whom you can rely at any time because you have a sound mind, the most valuable asset in the world, with which you can shape your own destiny.

(17) Believe in the existence of "infinite intelligence" in the universe, which will enable you to generate all the forces that are essential for you to master and guide your thoughts.

(18) Finally, act now! Insist on acting! Read and contrast the above items one by one once a week for six months in a row, and you will remold yourself thoroughly and become a new person.

In a word, as long as we genuinely cultivate our own positive mental attitudes, we will find that only one is the most important among all the people in the world, that is, ourselves. A positive mental attitude is the talisman and driving force for us to strive for success. With the cultivation of a positive mental attitude, we can always make sustained efforts with a higher goal, so as to achieve it.

Examples of success

Zhou Youguang: I am physically aged, but not mentally

On January 13, 2016, Mr. Zhou Youguang was 111 years old, living in a quality life equivalent to several lifetimes of others. Before the age of 50, he was engaged in both education and the economy. After the age of 50, he participated in the reform of Chinese characters and became a linguist. He is one of the leading researchers and makers of the Chinese Pinyin program. At the age of 85, he left his office and stayed in a small study, becoming an enlightenment thinker with a worldwide mind. In his 90s, he said that there would be one day more as long as he could live one more day. Zhou Youguang said on his 108th birthday: "My life started at the age of 80, and the previous years don't count for anything. In this case, I am 28 years old this year, so I have to continue to study at the age of 100." Since he came to 100 years old, he has been laughing at himself, "God is so busy that forgets me in the world."

In spite of this, he didn't waste that much time. Among his books, Bai Sui Xin Gao (Centenarian's Essay), Zhao Wen Dao Ji (Essay Collection), and Shi Bei Ji (Selected Essays) were published when he was 100, 104 and 105, respectively. "These books show that Zhou is always an inseparable figure and an important enlightenment thinker in the history of contemporary Chinese thought and culture," said Ma Guochuan, chief editor of Caijing Magazine. For this reason, since Mr. Zhou was 108 years old, scholars have spontaneously held symposiums for Mr. Zhou to celebrate his birthday, hoping to reach a consensus in the cultural and ideological circles and promote the progress of Chinese society. Ma Guochuan introduced that the theme of the symposium in 2016 was "towards the world, towards civilization," because one of Mr. Zhou's critical thoughts was that China must move towards modern civilization, as all countries are competing with each other on the same road. Even if we go on a detour for a while, we will ultimately march on the path of the universal civilization of mankind.

According to Liu Zhiqin, an expert, no one like Zhou Youguang at all times and in all countries has been able to publish new books after the age of 100. He is not only the only one in China but also the only one in the world.

Data source: Zu Wei. Zhou Youguang: I am physically aged, but not mentally. (Beijing Youth Daily, 2016-01-11.)

94-year-old Qin Yi wrote and starred in her new movie, The Beautiful Kokonor Lake

In 2015, Qin Yi, 94, appeared in Shanghai with the film, The Beautiful Kokonor Lake, which she produced, wrote, and starred in. Qin Yi, looking refreshed with her silver hair, denied that The Beautiful Kokonor Lake was her last movie, and said that "this is not my last one. I am still preparing a new script." Claiming that it is never too old to act, Qin Yi said that "I have new inspiration and new creative enthusiasm every day, and all these inspirations and enthusiasm come from my life." Qin Yi has long been known as a renowned landmark figure in the history of Chinese films. "I have been working for more than 80 years, but I have been intended to do something more for Chinese films," she said with a smile. In recent years, Qin Yi has not retired from the movie stage due to her old age and occasionally stars in some film and television works. But in September 2014, when Qin Yi decided to set foot on the Qinghai-Tibet Plateau for the new film, she shocked every one of the camera crew. In the movie The Beautiful Kokonor Lake, Qin Yi is responsible for producing, writing, and starring in the movie. When asked why she devoted so much to the film, Qin Yi introduced that she was moved by the people and deeds at that time, "I was deeply impressed when I first knew it in a news report, while I couldn't forget it for several years. Now I finally have the chance to make it into a film."

The Beautiful Kokonor Lake takes the construction of the Qinghai-Tibet Railway as the background of the times and recalls the story of 30 years from the perspective of Mei Xinyi, the heroine of the film. In the movie, Qin Yi plays the 60-year-old Mei Xinyi at the age of 93. Moreover, Qin Yi is so confident that she has to act the leading role across the age limit of 30 years and to play in emotional scenes with an actor in his 30s from the Xinjiang Song and Dance Troupe in the film. She said, "I didn't make up much, just wearing a headgear with black hair. Even the wrinkles on my face were similar to those of the character. Anyway, as an actress, I must act my role well." In her 90s, Qin Yi went climbing the Qinghai-Tibet Plateau in person without a stand-in and insisted on the location shooting for a month. In this regard, all the people in the film crew were anxious about her health. Qin Yi, who had been engaged in the War of Resistance Against Japan, said: "during the Defense of Sihang Warehouse in Shanghai on August 13, 1937, in the War of Resistance Against Japan, I worked in the front line as a medical worker, carrying the stretchers and carrying the sick and wounded on the back. Shooting is the same as fighting. As long as the director yells 'Cut!', I will stand in the fire and jump in the water. No matter how many difficulties we encounter during the shooting, it will be the most significant victory as long as we manage to shoot the scenes well."

It took more than a decade to shoot The Beautiful Kokonor Lake, from preparation to startup to post-production. And during this period, the crew also encountered some financing difficulties and did not have the first investor until the crew shot in Qinghai Province. Hence, the crew finally went to the Qinghai-Tibet Plateau to start shooting before the mountain pass was sealed. Although there is unparalleled natural scenery in the film The Beautiful Kokonor Lake and some stunts are used to support some disastrous scenes that are extremely difficult to get a view, and the actors act well in their scenes concerning emotional activities. Thus, the film is entirely worth seeing. However, compared with those eye-catching films that cover a budget of hundreds of millions of Yuan at present, the investment in the movie at an amount of over twenty million Yuan is not worth mentioning. However, it deserves to be said that Mao Amin, who sang the theme song for the film, offered to be a volunteer for the film. As a screenwriter and actor of the film, Qin Yi did not take any payment for it, and said, "and Tong Ruixin doesn't take any money. As long as we save a little bit and suffer a little more, we can spend the major funds on post-production."

When the film The Beautiful Kokonor Lake was submitted for approval, the review took merely two hours, which originally used to last for twenty days. Qin Yi said, "most of today's films are about fighting, romance or pursuit of excitement, while there are few concerned about the inner world. This film is not only artistic but also enables the viewers to reflect on something. It should be released in all the cinemas." For the external rumors that The Beautiful Kokonor Lake was her last film, Qin Yi did not agree, “It is not my last work, while I am preparing for a new script. What I see and hear in daily life can all be regarded as the right theme. Art comes from life, so the excellent screenwriters and actors should go deep into life.”

Data source: Xiao Yang. 94-year-old Qin Yi wrote and starred in her new movie: This is not my last film. (Beijing Youth Daily, 2015-06-25.)

Zhang Xiuyu : Sixty years old is a young age

How do you think about 60 years old? The traditional concept is that 60 years old is old age, representing the terminal point for life and work. But I argue that sixty years old is a young age, representing the beginning of a second venture. Why do I say that? Let’s take a look at a poem and an essay I wrote on my 60th birthday:

Tribute to Sixty

——Thoughts on the 60th birthday

Sixty years old is a young age, a golden stage of life, the beginning of a second venture, and the starting point of the second youth.

Sixty years old is a young age

According to the research results of cytology, embryology, genetic engineering, neurology, genetics, and other theories, scientists have shown that people can live to 150 years old. 60 is less than half of the life span, so those aged sixty years old should be at a young age.

In 1990, it was found in the fourth census of China that there were 6,434 people aged over 100 years old. Among them, the oldest was 136 years old. Compared with the results of the third census, there were 2583 more centenarians in China.

The above facts show that it is entirely possible that people can live to 150 years old, which was proposed by scientists. According to the report of the Reuters on May 12, 1993, a world organization that closely monitors the population trends said that, in 1993, the world's population reached 5.5 billion, among which there were about 40,000 centenarians. The centenarians account for a tiny proportion of the world’s total population, but the census data of all countries in the world reflect that people's life expectancy is longer and longer and that the number of long-lived people is on the rise.

The historical materials of the history of scientific development also prove that the golden age for people to achieve significant scientific research results tends to be between sixty and seventy years old. For instance, from 1987 to 1989, the average age of the world's Nobel Prize winners was 60 years old in physics, 61.6 years old in medicine, 65.7 years old in literature, and 73.3 years old in economics. It can be seen that the age between 60 and 70 years old should be the golden stage of life.

So, the former British Prime Minister, Margaret Thatcher, said, "the real life begins at the age of 65." The age of 60 should represent the youth of a man, and a golden age of life, a time when we can continue to make great achievements, which should be warmly praised. Any view that 60 is the end of life is not only against science but also extremely harmful.

Chapter 2 Enhance the Personal Enterprising Spirit

Maxims for Success

Personal enterprising spirit refers to the ability to do what needs to be done without being reminded by others. Although this is the most excellent quality among various personalities of mankind, it tends to be neglected. Donate a little more to cultivate your personal enterprising spirit, since you are not waiting for things to happen, but take the initiative to trigger them. —Napoleon Hill

Principles and Guidelines

Andrew Carnegie, the founder and first generation of master of the science of success, and Steel Tycoon of the United States, once told Napoleon Hill that "Two kinds of people will never make great achievements, among which one kind is those who will not take the initiative to do something unless he is asked to do it and the other is those who can't do well even if he is asked to do it. Those who do not need to be urged will take the initiative to do what should be done, and those who never give up halfway are bound to achieve success." These people understand that they should devote a little more, and do more than others expect. In other words, such people are possessed with a personal enterprising spirit.

What is a personal enterprising spirit?

"Enterprising spirit is a scarce virtue, which can drive a person to take the initiative to do what he should do before being told to do it," Napoleon Hill told us.

Hobart, another master of the science of success, gave a more detailed description of the enterprising spirit:

What is an enterprising spirit? Let me tell you that it is to take the initiative to do what to be done. Next to what you take the initiative to do what should be done, it is to do it immediately when someone tells you how to do it.

Inferior people only do what they should do when they are kicked from behind, and such people have been working hard most of their lives while complaining about their bad luck.

Finally, there are much worse people who will never do what they should do. Even if someone runs to him to show how to do it and completes it together with him, he will never do it. He is unemployed most of the time, so he is vulnerable to discrimination unless his father is wealthy. But if this is the case, the God of fate will also hide and wait patiently in the corner of the street with a big stick in hand.

Which type of the above-mentioned persons do you belong to?

It can be seen that personal enterprising spirit is the electric generator that transforms people's imagination into action, is the power to stick to the activities to the end, and is also an essential element to achieve the goal. In a word, the personal enterprising spirit is actually a kind of power for us to motivate ourselves. As long as we are granted such power, we can transform many dreams, ambitions, hopes, desires, goals, and other inner pursuits into practical actions, and we can hold on these pursuits to the last until we realize our own pursuits.

Main traits of the personal enterprising spirit

In countless people who have made extraordinary achievements, they have some traits in common. One of the essential matters we need to do now is to reflect on whether we have these traits and think about the appropriate ways to increase and intensify these traits.

- Determine a definite goal.
- Continuously strengthen the motivation of establishing a goal.
- Establish a mastermind alliance in order to obtain the power to achieve the goal.
- Independent personality.
- Have the will of self-discipline.
- Have the perseverance based on the will to win.
- Develop a lively, open, and restrained imagination.
- Develop quick and precise decision-making habits.
- Give opinions based on facts rather than subjective guesses.
- Get into the habit of demanding a little more from ourselves

- Cultivate the ability to stimulate and control enthusiasm.
- Cultivate the habit of paying attention to details and keeping improving.
- Develop the ability to listen to critical opinions but not to lose our temper.
- Familiar with ten primary motivations.
- Develop the ability to focus on one task at a time.
- Develop the ability to take more responsibility for our own actions.
- Have the mind to bear all the burdens for the faults of our subordinates.
- Be patient with our subordinates and friends.
- Keep a positive mental attitude at all times.
- Develop the ability to use self-confidence.
- Cultivate the habit of carrying it out to the end.
- Develop the habit of emphasizing quality rather than speed.
- Cultivate an honest and trustworthy attitude.

There is no doubt that many of these traits are familiar to us. Some people may think that they already have these traits. However, the essence of these traits of success is that they are all closely related to each other so that we can't just play one of them and ignore the others. Imagine: if a person does not use confidence via his personal enterprising spirit, how can he play the role of confidence? And how can a person give play to the role of personal enterprising spirit in the absence of a definite goal? Obviously, we can't separate them. However, the power source that can start the acts of success is the personal enterprising spirit, while the mainline that can connect the above traits of success is also the personal enterprising spirit. In view of this, cultivating the personal enterprising spirit is the first step to translate different expectations into reality.

How can we cultivate the personal enterprising spirit?

Personal enterprising spirit is the most exciting and mysterious force that inspires us to move forward. It exists in the life of each of us, just like our abilities to protect ourselves. It is the never-ending self-driving force of the enterprising spirit that motivates the people to head towards their own goals. Then, how can we cultivate our personal enterprising spirit?

First of all, we should never feel satisfied.

"If a person is satisfied with his current situation, he will stagnate," said Robertson, a master of science of success, "Of course, people should not be disappointed and dissatisfied with their own destiny, but they should never feel satisfied." Life is like climbing a mountain. We must have the ambition to reach the top of the hill, or we will never be able to reach the top. If someone does not feel satisfied, he may look around and then find many opportunities for development. These possibilities seem to be vague at the outset, but they come from dissatisfaction. It can be seen that if you are dissatisfied, you will have a dream, and then turn the dream into a goal and then into action. If you can stick to the action to the end, you will be bound to achieve success.

For a person who is satisfied with the status quo, he does not have any better ideas and better wishes, while he does not know that it is because of dissatisfaction that the great elite of mankind is created. Only the unsatisfied passion can enable us to develop the enterprising spirit that changes the status quo and encourage us to pursue perfection, which is not only the ultimate power source for people to strive for success but also the mystery of human progress. Dissatisfaction can encourage people to change from weak to strong, from failure to success, from suffering to happiness, and ultimately from poverty to wealth.

Second, we should have our own dreams.

Hope is the raw material of success. It can be transformed into confidence, and then into determination, which can be finally put into practice. Hope comes from our dream and sprouts from our imagination. If we have a dream, it is still valuable even if it is far from being realized, because the dream allows us to see many possible opportunities, which are difficult for others to access.

In childhood, people are full of childish dreams. Andrew Carnegie, the steel tycoon of the United States, talked about his hopes and aspirations to his 9-year-old brother Tom when he was fifteen years old. He said that if they grew older, he would establish an Andrew Carnegie brothers company to make a lot of money so that he could buy a carriage for his parents. They played the game supposing everything every day, which naturally enabled them to keep many dreams in their hearts. When an opportunity approaches, he will seize it in reality and turn his dream into reality.

Thirdly, we should have an ambitious goal.

Johann Wolfgang von Goethe, a great thinker, and poet said: "the most important thing in a person's life is to set an ambitious goal, and then to achieve it with enough talent and strong endurance." In real life, many people do simple and ordinary things all their lives. They seem to be very satisfied, but in fact, they are fully capable of accomplishing more advanced things. Their expectations are very low, so it is impossible for them to create a great cause from scratch. That is to say, and the narrow life goal limits them to establish a grand goal.

Ambition can lay a solid foundation for a beautiful life. It urges us to finish the goal and helps us resist the temptations that are enough to destroy our future. Only with the encouragement of great goal and the persistent pursuit of a meaningful life can we make great achievements in the world. Only those who are not satisfied with the status quo, pursue perfection and keep improving will become winners.

When someone asked the secret of success for a highly paid professional manager in the United States, he replied, "I haven't succeeded yet! No one will truly succeed, as there is always a higher goal ahead." Only unimportant people will argue that they are winners, while the truly great people have never reached their goals. As great people make progress, they will set increasingly higher standards for their lives. As they broaden their horizons, their enterprising spirit will gradually grow.

Finally, we should have an indomitable willpower.

We always plan our future life, but if we don't make unremitting efforts to turn it into reality, these plans will always stay as plans, while we are forever engaged in idle theorizing. Imagine that without the hard work of the construction workers, the blueprint of the architect would always be empty talk. Therefore, to make our dream come true, we must accomplish the following three tasks. First of all, we need to make our goal concrete; second, we need to focus on it and do our best; third, we need to make our goal come true. In this process, all the necessary conditions depend on ourselves, rather than anyone else. No matter where we are and how much wealth we have, only our persevering willpower can turn our ideal into reality.

Examples of success

The enterprising spirit leads the blind professor Yang Jia to a bright world

According to the standard issued by the World Health Organization (WHO), there are 45 million blind persons in the world. According to the survey of the China Disabled Persons' Federation, there are about 12 million visually disabled persons in China. Among the visually disabled persons, Yang Jia, a blind professor at the Chinese Academy of Sciences, is undoubtedly a leader. At the age of 15, she was admitted to Zhengzhou University from Changsha among various competitors by virtue of her strong initiative. When she was 21, she came to Beijing and stepped into the gate of the University of Chinese Academy of Sciences. When she was 37, she eventually entered Harvard, one of the world's top universities, becoming the first blind student at Harvard. Nowadays, she is not only teaching and educating people, writing books but also holding social positions in a number of international and domestic organizations, active outside the campus and among healthy people. Over the years, she has enjoyed the confidence and success in the bright world, as well as tasted the pain and hesitation in the dark world. However, she has eventually discovered the channel between the two worlds and let herself go and come as she likes. "What everyone has at the moment is won by their own strength. Every step they take is closely bound up with the path to be taken in the future, and there is no difference between a healthy person and a disabled person," she said.

She is blind in her eyes, but she has an extremely strong enterprising spirit and self-confidence, and her heart is filled with light.

The youngest university teacher

In 1978, the national college entrance examination system was restored, and the teacher said to Yang Jia, who was still in the first grade of high school, "You can have a try, just like a test." Unexpectedly, she really stood out from the thousands of college candidates and got the admission notice from the English Department of Zhengzhou University. With the notice, Yang Jia was a little confused. After all, she was only 15 years old. The assistant principal of the school thought that she was too young to go to college and that she would not be late to go to university one or two years later. However, she, together with her family, decided to accept the challenge for an entirely new environment.

For Yang Jia at that time, Zhengzhou was a completely strange city. Most of her classmates were six or seven years older than her, or even ten years older. They all managed to enter the university after experiencing the ten years of turbulence, so that all of them cherished the opportunity to learn on campus, thus sparing no effort to engage in academic studies. Maybe because Yang Jia was born to refuse to concede defeat, or was deeply affected by the atmosphere on campus, she scored far ahead of all her peers in the English Department, making many of her seniors who once didn't take her seriously feel ashamed of their inferiority. Her foreign teachers were amazed at her excellent English listening and writing skills, but they didn't know that the candles on her bed lit up until the second half of the night every day. Because of her academic excellence, Yang Jia was appointed to the faculty ahead of the job assignment on graduation. At the age of 19, she became the youngest college English teacher at Zhengzhou University. Standing in front of her students who are almost the same age or even older, she tasted the self-confidence and delight brought by imparting knowledge for the first time.

However, Yang Jia did not feel satisfied with this, and it had always been her dream to take up advanced studies in a higher institution. Two years later, she was admitted to the University of

Chinese Academy of Sciences, which nurtured numerous scientists and attracted her to learn knowledge assiduously.

Yang Jia was one of those who were born to be a teacher. Before she graduated from the University of Chinese Academy of Sciences, she was often assigned by her teacher to take over classes. The students liked her way of lecturing, and presented flowers to her, which invisibly increased the burden on other teachers. At the age of 24, she once again became the youngest lecturer in the University.

She suddenly went blind at a young age

Before the age of 29, Yang Jia was the favorite of the god, with an intelligent mind, elegant temperament, a tall figure, and an enviable job, and she had never felt any disappointment from her life. However, misfortune does not stop because of the favor of the god for her.

Yang Jia was responsible for teaching the course of English writing, which was usually taught by foreign teachers. However, the leaders of the University expected to train their own writing teachers, so Yang Jia was assigned to teach English writing. She taught the students for a total of eight semesters, receiving favorable results.

The students were often asked to write in class, and Yang Jia often had to correct their compositions after class. However, she found that when she checked the students' compositions, her eyes felt a bit of strain. Then, she first skipped some lines when reading the text in class, and when she read the words in the book, she could see clearly at first sight, but the words looked vague when she read them again. And after she blinked, her eyes seemed to be fine again. At first, she used a pencil to read and make notes. Later, she decided to use a pen as the color of the pencil was too light to see. At last, she couldn't see the carbon ink clearly. Unconsciously, the darkness devoured her little by little, and she finally was unable to see anything.

After the examination of Tongren Hospital, it turned out that she had macular degeneration in both eyes, while there was no therapy to cure, and she would lose her sight sooner or later. When hearing this, she was totally confused. Standing on the platform in the morning, she could still calm down. Although her eyes were blurred, she still gave lectures as usual. Chalk and students made her feel that she had not been abandoned by the bright world. In the afternoon, she ran around among different hospitals and doctors with her parents, but in return, she was disappointed again and again. At that time, she knew that the illusion would eventually be shattered.

A person who suddenly goes blind, just like a child at a loss, is suffering and wandering in two worlds. They not only cherish the past days but also fear the existing reality, which is a psychological process that is difficult to endure. In the days of seeking medical treatment, Yang Jia contacted many people with poor eyesight and felt that they could understand each other. And for a time, she even relied on that circle so much that she was reluctant to step out.

Youngest blind professor

However, it is a confrontation of the survival of the fittest. She is aware that she must face reality and defeat the cowardly her. After suspending the teaching for half a year, Yang Jia reappeared on campus. She found that in the new world that she was not familiar with, and that her pursuit, her class and her students had remained unchanged, while only the way she got along with them and communicated with them changed. She urged herself to learn the new way as soon as possible.

Everything has to start all over again. After decades of walking on her legs, she has to learn to take a step again. With long legs and arms, she used to be a member of the women's volleyball team when she was a student, and she loved to take strides when walking. In the past, she didn't think much of the curb, the edge of furniture, and the thermos bottle on the office floor. But now she has suffered a lot from all of these. She had also been stabbed in the eye by an untrimmed branch and had to wear glasses to prevent further injury.

She also needs to change the way she reads and learn to use her fingertips to touch the point-like characters, not only in Chinese but also in English. There are few blind schools specialized for the blind adults in the society, so she has to study on her own, and visit teachers everywhere and get some advice by phone. She gave full play to her hearing ability. She bought cassettes one by one to record the English programs of the radio and collected all kinds of materials available. She didn't lower her teaching standards because she couldn't see. In the end, she was still titled the youngest associate professor of the college.

After going blind, Yang Jia also published several books, including A Course Book of English Writing for Postgraduates and A Course Book of English Reading for Postgraduates, which were designated as the textbooks for postgraduates by many colleges and universities. Her tutor and mentor, Professor Li Pei, who is known as the first person in the field of Chinese Applied Linguistics, spoke highly of her and wrote the preface for her works. Unfortunately, the changes did not change the trajectory of her life but made her life more profound and meaningful.

"He who knows others is learned; He who knows himself is wise. He who conquers others has power of muscles; He who conquers himself is strong." This is Yang Jia's favorite maxim. In order to teach the course and compile the textbook, she gets up early every day, listens to the English news of the day, and goes to bed late at night. She has a strong ability to accept new things. Moreover, she has surfed the Internet via a voice system to send and receive e-mails online, scan and read articles, and grade students' electronic text assignments. The computer has become another pair of eyes for her to be concerned about the world.

Strive for a world-class university

Yang Jia has always been proud that her school is the cradle of Chinese scientists, where the strong academic atmosphere has always inspired her to keep forging ahead. Yang Jia is excited by the University's proposal to build itself into a world-famous and first-class institution of higher learning in Asia. As a member of the university, she is eager to experience what is a world-class university in person.

Yang Jia's standard has always been to study at the best university. In 2000, as a senior visiting scholar sent by the Chinese Academy of Sciences, she passed the examination with excellent results and entered John F. Kennedy School of Government, Harvard University , a famous institution in the United States, to study for the Master of Public

Administration (MPA). At that time, there was no relevant course in China, and the MPA program of John F. Kennedy School of Government ranked first in the United States and even in the world. Yang Jia became the only blind student from abroad in the history of Harvard University.

John F. Kennedy School of Government is an international college at Harvard, where the students come from all over the world and compete fiercely with each other. For Yang Jia, there are so many books that she has to read because the opportunity is rare. She took a dozen courses, far beyond the requested number of courses by the university. Studying for a degree at Harvard is not an easy task for anyone. For Yang Jia, it takes her several times the energy as ordinary people. In class, she and her classmates listen and take notes together without any special care. After class, she will scan hundreds of pages of materials assigned by her teacher, and then listen to the computer reading disks one by one. The software she used in China can no longer match the number of materials she read and the speed of her reading. So she taught herself the latest voice system software in the United States. Thus, her schedule has been arranged tightly.

Eight credits are required to obtain an MPA degree from John F. Kennedy School of Government, while Yang Jia not only got 10 credits within one year but also excelled in all subjects. One of the courses is the Art of Leadership offered by David Gergen, a top professor at Harvard University. Yang Jia, with her outstanding performance and a paper entitled On Deng Xiaoping's Art of Leadership, was favored by Professor Gergen and obtained the highest score A+ in the School. According to the regulations, professors in John F. Kennedy School of Government are not allowed to give such high scores, but Yang Jia has created another miracle in Harvard with her strength and personal charm.

At the graduation ceremony a year later, when the host called the name of Yang Jia, thousands of teachers and students at the venue stood up to applaud the great blind student, while the applause lasted for a long time. The scene made Yang Jia deeply feel that it was worth undergoing the hardships in the past year. In a letter to Deng Pufang, chairman of China Disabled Persons' Federation, the head of John F. Kennedy School of Government wrote that "In doing so, we all affirm not only the great achievements she has made but also the beauty and wisdom of the country she represents, as well as a series of important thoughts."

Cycle of life

After returning to China, Yang Jia offered two new courses, Economic Globalization and Art of Communication, at the University of Chinese Academy of Sciences, both of which were offered by the top professors at Harvard University. Yang Jia has obtained their special permission and is expected to create her independent brand by combining the examples in China with the introduction of Harvard courses. In terms of teaching form, Yang Jia also adopted the model of the world-class university for reference, opened her own class and invited experts from different fields to her class. She believes that interdisciplinary communication enables people to view the issues from a more comprehensive perspective. These two new courses have a good response. In this regard, the University also proposes to take her courses as the content of distance education and further promote them to universities nationwide.

The new research direction does not affect Yang Jia's contents of regular teaching, while she is also responsible for the English courses of the postgraduates and doctoral students. Moreover, Yang Jia also finds pleasures in a busy time in teaching. Writer Liu Heng once wrote an article for her, while the article described her life as a process of reading, teaching, listening, and writing and back to teaching, which may be a cycle that she is destined to experience in her life.

The past painful days have passed, and she no longer cares about that. Except for her eyesight, she has no longer felt that she is different from anyone else, and the sufferings have made her work much harder to approach her dream. She has been awarded the title of Advanced Workers in succession, and the Fourth Youth of the Year Beijing. Since 1997, she has also served as vice-chairman of China Association of the

Blind and vice president of Association of the Blind of Beijing Disabled Persons' Federation, devoting her wisdom and strength to solve the difficulties of the blind truly. After learning about Yang Jia's deeds, Li Lanqing, then Vice Premier of the State Council, wrote to Chen Zhili, then minister of education, and spoke highly of her optimism, self-confidence, self-improvement, patriotism and professionalism.

Lu Yongxiang, President of the Chinese Academy of Sciences, wrote in a letter to the Party committee of the University of Chinese Academy of Sciences: "I am very happy to read from the Science Times that Yang Jia has returned from Harvard, and I am moved by her perseverance and pursuit of excellence. From here, I can see the spirit of contemporary Chinese youth again."

Yang Jia has a clear idea about all of this, as what everyone has at the moment is won by virtue of his own strength. Every step he takes is closely related to the path he will take in the future. There is no difference between a healthy person and a disabled person. She wrote passionately:

I can't see the flowers, but I can smell the fragrance; I can't read the books, but I can acquire the knowledge; I can't see the sunlight, but I can also shine; I can't see the distance, but I will go out of myself; I can't see you, but I want you to understand the beauty in me!

Data source: Anonymous. Blind professor, Yang Jia: After the age of 29, she exceeded her limitations and took the road with ease and pleasure (The People's Daily, 2012-07-10.)

Zhou Wenqian: Snake queen from the mountains

In Dalu village, Fuzi Town, Lingshan County, Qinzhou City, Guangxi Zhuang Autonomous Region, China, an ordinary peasant woman raised thousands of cobras and became an expert on acquiring wealth in a few years. She is Zhou Wenqian, known as "snake queen in Lingshan" by the local people.

She saw a business opportunity when going out to work

Zhou Wenqian was born into a poor family. In order to let her three younger brothers go to school, she went out to work after graduating from junior high school as the eldest. In 2003, Zhou Wenqian and her husband went to work in the chicken farm around the county town of Lingshan County. When they were free, they would buy some eggs from the chicken farm and sell them in the villages and only made a few cents for an egg. Once, when it rained and the road was slippery, Zhou Wenqian fell to the ground with her bicycle, while the eggs all got broken on the ground.

In the chicken farm, there are many pipped eggs that can't hatch and chickens that can't survive, which will be thrown away. Zhou Wenqian felt pity to throw them away and then used these things to raise dozens of pigs. However, when the pigs become full-grown and ready for slaughter, the price in the live pig market declined, and she could only break even after the past year of hard work.

However, the stubborn Zhou Wenqian did not feel discouraged. Once, she helped the chicken farm to deliver a batch of pipped eggs to a customer in Wuli Town. Only then did she know that the pipped eggs are the best feed for snakes. A bright idea suddenly came to her mind that she could make use of her convenience in the chicken farm to collect piped eggs and sell them to the customers who fed snakes as the forage.

However, at that time, she didn't make much money only by selling the eggs as feed. The customers who sold snakes told her that a Ptyas mucosus, weighing 2.5 kg, could be sold for six or seven hundred yuan, while the investment cost was not more than 100 yuan. In this way, the profit of a snake is equal to the income of a month when she works from dawn to dusk. Zhou Wenqian suddenly came up with the idea that she could feed snakes by herself.

From the monthly salary of 400 Yuan to the annual income of 3 million Yuan

No sooner said than done. In 2006, Zhou Wenqian borrowed 5,000 yuan and bought 2,000 snake eggs of pyyas mucosus and cobras. For the insufficient part, she exchanged pipped eggs with snake farmers. According to snake farmers' method of hatching snakes, Zhou Wenqian took care of the eggs even in the smallest details day and night. In less than three months, the snakes grew as thick as a child's arm. At that time, Zhou Wenqian was happy to feed and clean snakes every day. She also observed and recorded the changes in snakes.

In two months, the snakes could become grown up and sold, but fate played a cruel joke on Zhou Wenqian. It was on May 12, 2008, that a heavy earthquake took place in Wenchuan, Sichuan Province. Zhou Wenqian's snake farm was also suffering from a disaster like a violent earthquake, as she found that all the snakes were eating all the time contrary to their usual behavior, but they stopped eating a few days later, lying on the ground motionlessly one by one. Zhou Wenqian and her husband were panicked, while they didn't know what was wrong with the snakes.

After checking, they found that the snake farm was not disinfected thoroughly. Zhou Wenqian quickly gave injections to the snakes one by one, but it was too late. At last, only dozens of more than 1000 snakes survived, while the nearly 200,000 yuan that was about to be made became a floating smoke. Looking at the empty snake farm, Zhou Wenqian wept bitterly.

It is said that women will get energetic after a good cry. Zhou Wenqian thought that, compared with the people in the earthquake-stricken areas in Wenchuan County, the earthquake in her snake farm was nothing serious, and that she could start her business all over again. So Zhou Wenqian dried her tears and borrowed money to buy back some snake eggs. This time, she and her husband concentrated on learning technology from the books and computers and fed the snakes in strict accordance with the procedures. With more contact with snakes, she gradually mastered their habits and eating patterns, as well as the prevention and treatment technology of disease prone. As a result, they took fewer detours.

Hard work has not yet brought wealth to the family, and the unfortunate once again came to the family. One day in 2009, her husband, Ning Defu was accidentally bitten by a cobra and couldn't move on the spot. At that time, the situation was critical. Ning Defu was sent to the hospital in Lingshan County town for emergency wound treatment and then sent to Fangchenggang City overnight for injection of antitoxin serum. For days and nights, Zhou Wenqian stayed by her husband's side, but she didn't go to sleep once until her husband was really out of danger.

Everything comes to him who waits. In 2010, the first batch of snake eggs and snakes were eventually grown up and ready for sales, and thus they had an income of more than 80,000 Yuan. With this successful experience, Zhou Wenqian's way of raising snakes has finally become smoother and smoother, and the scale of the snake farm has been continuously expanding. In 2011, Zhou Wenqian's snake farm started turning a profit. After that, the Wenqian farm in Fuzi Town, which she founded, expanded from 140 square meters to more than 1,700 square meters, and the number of snakes stored increased from more than 1,000 at the beginning to nearly 10,000, and the annual income increased from zero to 3 million Yuan. It has become a large-scale farm in Lingshan County, which integrates snake feed processing, incubation, and reproduction of snake eggs, production and sales of meat snakes and breeding snakes. In the 1st Snake King Contest in Lingshan County, her cobras and pyyas mucosus won the first and second prizes respectively. Therefore, Zhou Wenqian, known as Snake Queen in Lingshan County, became famous overnight.

It is really good when everyone becomes rich

According to Zhou Wenqian, artificial snake farming is a good project for rural entrepreneurs to become rich. She said: "every part of the snake is valuable, as the snake skin can be sold as medicine, and the snake meat is very popular in Guangdong and other places. In the future, snake venom extraction can be developed. In this way, it is no problem that several hundred Yuan can be made from a snake. Manual snake farming has a history of more than 20 years in Lingshan. In the early 1990s, due to the immature raising technology, the survival rate of snakes was very low, and little progress was made in the snake farming industry." Zhou Wenqian said that the snake raising technology is mature now, and she would like to share her own methods of snake raising with the villagers.

She has established the Wenqian snake industry breeding base in Fuzi Town, Lingshan County, and driven the masses to acquire wealth by raising snakes in the pattern combining the base with farmers. No matter what difficulties and problems the farmers met when they were feeding the snakes, she was always available on hand and she was willing to teach all of the techniques involved in snake raising to the farmers. Zhou Wenqian and her husband also gave lectures in the snake raising training classes in their village and other towns several times. Zhou Wenqian, with her own courage, wisdom and mind, made a great contribution to the people becoming rich and striving for a better-off life.

Zhou Wenqian was titled the snake queen in China

From August 28 to September 8, 2012, Grudge Match, a program on CCTV-1, recorded a series of inspirational programs of labor competition in Deyang City, Sichuan Province. Two contestants in Lingshan County, snake queen Zhou Wenqian and snake expert Liang Wei, took part in the Snake King Contest, won the first place and the title of Star Worker.

The players in Lingshan County are the red flag team, and those in Chengdu are the golden drum team. In a joyful atmosphere, the two teams came on the stage with their own snakes. In the four parts of Snake Driving by Snake King, Snake Dancing by Snake King, Snake Distinguishing by Snake King, and Snake Venom Extraction by Snake King, Zhou Wenqian and Liang Wei from Lingshan County were brave but not reckless, and skillfully drove the snakes. According to the regulations of the contest, they let the snakes accomplish the specified walking route and actions based on the wishes of the players, and won the warm applause and cheers from the audience

Finally, Zhou Wenqian and Liang Wei from Lingshan County won the first prize in the contest, becoming Snake King in China and winning the title of Star Worker.

Data source: Sun Zhiping, Xiong Hongming, Zhong Qun. Lingshan County, Guangxi Province: Snake Queen out of the mountains. (http://www.xinhuanet.com/, 2013-05-28.)

26-year-old millionaire: He was worth tens of millions Yuan two years after graduation

It is not uncommon for college students to start their own businesses, but legends always emerge. Every time we hear that a college student has become a millionaire or a multimillionaire in just a few years, we often only pay attention to the amount of his wealth, but seldom try to decipher the password of his success. Wu Lijie, in this case, started his own business four years ago and graduated from university just two years ago.

From a poor college student who originally owed more than 10,000 Yuan of tuition fees to a company boss with tens of millions of assets, how will he inspire us?

When an empty bottle has a dream, it will be motivated to start a business

In the early 1980s, Wu Lijie was born in Taishun County, Wenzhou City, Zhejiang Province. His home is deep in the mountains, and he has to climb over many mountains to the town. It is so steep that the drivers from other places dare not drive along the dangerous road on the edge of the cliff. When he was a child, he never walked out of the mountain. His family was very poor, but he fell in love with painting. He didn't do well in his academic studies because he was addicted to his own hobbies. In 2000, he failed to be admitted to the Central Academy of Fine Arts and finally was admitted to the Fashion Design Department of Zhejiang Sci-Tech University.

When receiving the letter of admission, Wu Lijie was not very happy and wanted to return to the high school for the senior class, since he had been dreaming of being admitted to the Central Academy of Fine Arts and become a well-known painter in the future. But his father's words could not allow him to criticize his life: “You should feel fortunate that you can still go to school in such a poor family! Your tuition fee of 10,000 Yuan is paid by your elder sister! Besides, at your age, it's an empty bottle, so it is the same whether there will be mud or gold in it. As long as you study on a firm footing, you will always harvest a lot. Never dream of loading gold in the bottle from the very beginning!" Under the strict guidance of his father, Wu Lijie had to enter the Fashion Design Department of Zhejiang Sci-Tech University.

Wu Lijie is most interested in painting sketches, oil painting, and other artworks, but his major was fashion design. Then, his daily tasks were merely to draw the costume charts and design fashion styles.

In the beginning, Wu Lijie was just a very ordinary student on campus, while the only difference between him and other students was that he didn't engage in empty talks. Instead, he had been wondering whether he could make some economic benefits by learning to draw costume charts like this every day. Once, he thought that many painters made a living by selling their paintings. Could he make money by selling costume design drawings?

Hangzhou is a fashionable and leisurely city, where fashion stores and fashion companies can be seen everywhere. It has been in extremely fierce competition in all the industries that rely on costumes. So, it's not easy for Wu Lijie to make money with just a few costume paintings. In his first summer vacation at University, he spent almost every day in the streets of Hangzhou. He visited hundreds of factories under the hot sun with a package of well-designed costume paintings. Moreover, he said that he could design clothes and wanted to work on holidays to earn his tuition fees whenever he met a person. However, no one pitied him. After two months, he got nothing.

He has a dream and achieves nothing, but in many cases, his self-encouragement in the diary has become the greatest driving force for Wu Lijie to start his own business. With his own efforts, in the first semester of the sophomore year, his painting won an award in the 2nd Melatonin Cup CCTV Fashion Design Competition. After that, he has won many awards in the "China Cup" International Fashion Design Competition. Since then, his excellent works can often be found in the show window of the university, and he has gradually become a celebrity on campus.

To make encouragement a habit will strengthen the courage to struggle

After his works won prizes, Wu Lijie changed his strategy from the promotion of his works everywhere in the past to focus on one company. In November 2001, he chose an influential clothing company in Hangzhou to sell his costume paintings. The boss chose eight from more than 30 samples of costume styles he brought and paid him at fifty Yuan per picture.

It was only four hundred Yuan, but it made Wu Lijie feel that his pocket was so heavy that it seemed to be loaded with tens of thousands of Yuan. That night, he had a good sleep.

While Wu Lijie felt excited, the boss of the clothing company thought that it was a big bargain to buy eight pictures for 400 Yuan. The boss found that the costume paintings drawn by Wu Lijie were all well designed when he took them back to the company and that the pictures were increasingly creative. Moreover, he believed that Wu's works could even compete with those of the designers in his company. At that time, if they hired a fashion designer in Hangzhou, the annual salary would be RMB five to six hundred thousand, at least. So, the company quickly agreed that Wu Lijie could work for a monthly salary of 600 Yuan. Subsequently, Wu Lijie used the same stupid method to start a part-time job in another three companies. In this way, his monthly income reached more than 2,000 Yuan in his sophomore year. There is no doubt that it is not easy for students to earn money by taking part-time jobs.

In January 2002, Wu Lijie worked for a foreign brand clothing agency in Hangzhou. The boss asked him a difficult question when they met for the first time, "Mr. Wu, you are a designer, but I hope that you can understand the ways of marketing better. If you know nothing about marketing, how can you design some products that can be favored by the market? So, how can we develop this French clothing brand in the Chinese market?" This question baffled Wu Lijie at that time. Fortunately, the boss was also very considerate, and encouraged him, "I'll give you one week. In the week, you can make a plan, and I believe you can perfectly accomplish the task!"

Ultimately at a loss, Wu Lijie had to go back to university. He decided to discuss the countermeasures with his classmates and consult his teachers. In the University, he is a poor student but moved his classmates and teachers with his talent and diligence. Therefore, all of them supported him and encouraged him to take a part-time job while studying. A week later, he came back to the company with a well-thought-out plan in mind, and told the boss, “Boss, I have two suggestions for marketing. First, European clothing sold in China should be appropriately reduced according to the figure of Chinese people. For example, this newly imported French suit, which is fully applicable to the European style, and there are slits at the back of the suit. But it would be better if we make all these slits into a lithographic one, and make the waistline more inside. You see, the suit I'm wearing now fits me better. Second, we can hire professional models to take photos of the revised costumes, make the photos into albums and then distribute them to consumers.”

The boss felt delighted to hear Wu Lijie’s plan, “Well done! Your suggestions take into account the details!” The boss readily agreed to employ him and entrusted him with full responsibility for the corresponding operation. Next, Wu Lijie began to make a costume album for that company. It was his first order, so he took it very seriously and intended to set up his brand of picture album making on this occasion. When he solicited businesses with his well-prepared albums in other companies, he got instant results. The first company where he took a part-time job would like him to make a clothing album and offered a price of 40,000 Yuan. It was extremely low compared with the market price, as the latter was set at 80,000 Yuan, at least. It was a whopping price for Wu Lijie. So, why can Wu Lijie accomplish it?

Wu Lijie went to the female models in the college to take photos of the clothes so that he could save half of the cost. In addition, he could design clothes on his own, and the profit of this part is completely a net profit for him. So, he made a picture album with a low price and made a profit totaling 20,000 Yuan from it.

In this way, Wu Lijie made some money while attending the classes on campus. He lived a hectic life, but very passionate. One day, one of his close friends advised him, “So bro, there are at least 4,000 clothing companies in Hangzhou now, but there are few design companies that are specialized in providing services for fashion brands. Don’t you find any business opportunities in it? Now you always take part-time jobs among different companies, but I believe it would be better if you could set up a brand company to serve them.” Wu Lijie was suddenly enlightened when hearing that, and then he decided to accept the advice of his friend.

In the summer vacation of 2002, after finishing his sophomore year, he rented a studio outside the university. Then, he registered with another two classmates to Hangzhou Huatai Clothing Brand Planning Co., Ltd., with a registered capital of 200,000 Yuan, of which he has a 75% share. The core business of their company is to design clothing, arrange stores, and make image albums for clothing companies. Next, the knowledge he obtained in class and the experience he acquired from part-time jobs enabled him to work as a fish in water. After entering the junior year, he made image albums for more than 50 clothing companies in half a year. He could earn at least several thousand Yuan or even ten thousand Yuan from each order.

The more professional it is, the better it will be. Growth is more important than success.

A steady stream of orders soon made Wu Lijie worth millions of Yuan. When he graduated from university in July 2004, he had served more than 200 clients and made nearly 3 million Yuan within two years since he started his business. However, during this period, he also deeply realized what was busying himself with benefiting other people. If he designed a popular clothing style, the manufacturer could make hundreds of thousands or even millions of Yuan, but he could only get tens of thousands of Yuan. Hence, he felt that he could no longer suffer losses like this.

In view of this, Wu Lijie managed to register with Howen Clothing Co., Ltd. in France via one of his friends, but many of his college classmates were worried about where to go after graduation. Then, he began to recruit a large number of employees with great ambition. He thought that it was merely a small-scale business to design works and make picture albums. Besides, he had so much cash on hand at that time, so he decided to run a factory to produce clothes and leather goods directly. In a few days, he recruited more than 100 employee and many of them were his college classmates.

Soon, Wu Lijie put all the 3 million Yuan earned from designing into the factory. However, what was unexpected was that he did not know what to do, although he was quite familiar with how to design. At the end of 2004, within less than three months, his factory suffered a heavy loss due to improper management.

In this occasion, Wu Lijie contracted the factory to another person in early 2005, so that he could save his principal. Finally, they agreed that Wu Lijie was responsible for design and promotion, while the other side was responsible for producing clothes based on the requirements. After abandoning the production, Wu Lijie began to concentrate on marketing. To quickly develop the market, he rented the top floor of Qianjiang Hotel to plan large-scale investment meetings many times. In the end, he sold a total of 100,000 garments in the year of 2005, with a net profit of 3,500,000 Yuan. Escaping from the crisis, he said with emotion: “We have to learn to give up some, as we can not take things all of a lump. It is impossible that a man can make all the money in hand. Then, we should try our best to do what we are most specialized in, while the other money can be made by those who are specialized in other fields.”

The thrilling entrepreneurial experience made Wu Lijie increasingly bold and stable to struggle. In May 2006, he began to march towards the leather market and set up his third company, Peason Leather Co., Ltd. At this moment, he went for the boss of the first company where he took a part-time job at the university and put forward the idea of the joint operation. He could be responsible for technology, and the boss could invest in the joint development of the market nationwide. He believed that his design technology was very excellent, and the other side was a brand product agency that had been operating for many years. Especially, the agency had a mature and extensive network in the market and social relations. In this way, with the help of the agency's sales network, Wu Lijie has sold the clothing and leather products that he designed and produced to 15 provinces in China.

Today, Wu Lijie, who owns three companies, is worth more than 10 million Yuan, but he is very modest, "Compared with Li Ka Shing, I am far from a successful person. Besides, my dream was to be a painter, but now I am a fashion designer and businessman, so I have not yet realized my dream. In fact, I think growth is more important than success. Success is only a result of glory, which will fleet. But growth is a long process, as there are a large number of experiences, twists and turns, and so on, and we need to learn to control it all our lives."

Data source: Anonymous. 26-year-old millionaire: He was worth tens of millions of Yuan two years after graduation. (Hc360.Com, 2008-08-25).

Chapter 3 Confirm the Confidence to Win

Maxims for Success

As long as you are confident, you can move a mountain. As long as you believe that you can succeed, you will achieve success. The way to test your confidence is to see if you apply it when it's most challenging, especially when it's most needed. —Napoleon Hill

Principles and Guidelines

A positive mental attitude is the first step to success; a personal enterprise spirit is the engine towards success, and the confidence to win the fundamental guarantee to success. In all the principles of success, self-confidence is an essential component and an essential condition to make all the great achievements. To change your life, you must first confirm your confidence to win. The power of confidence will never be used up. It is a kind of resource that can be recycled endlessly. Only when you make full use of the power of confidence and get rid of all the constraints in your mind can you be urged to complete the plan, achieve the goal, accomplish your wish and finally achieve success.

Confidence can defeat all difficulties

Confidence has such amazing power that it can change the bad situation and bring an incredible happy ending. Those who are full of confidence can never be knocked down, and will ultimately become the conquerors of life.

Confidence is the antidote to the toxin, impossibility. Self-confidence with a sense of direction enables us to be powerful in each of our ideas. When you have strong confidence to push the wheel of success, you can have a meteoric rise and climb the mountain of success. Helen Keller, a famous American woman writer, overcame the triple pain of the inability to see, hear or speak. She devoted her whole life to social welfare and was called Wonder Woman. Her life is undoubtedly the best confirmation of this line.

When Helen Keller was born, she was a normal baby. She could see, listen, and babble. But a disease made her blind, deaf and dumb when she was only nineteen months old. The physiological upheaval has greatly changed Helen Keller's character. If she didn't feel satisfied with anything, she would knock and beat at random, and savagely grab food with her hands and stuff it into her mouth. At that time, if someone tried to correct her, she would roll on the ground, shouting without thought of others, as rude as a tyrant. In desperation, her parents sent her to a school for the blind in Boston and hired a female teacher to take care of her.

Fortunately, little Helen Keller met a great angel of light, Johanna (Anne) Mansfield Sullivan Macy, in the tragedy of darkness. From then on, Ms. Anne Sullivan's struggle with the little girl who suffered the triple pains began. When Helen Keller washed her face, combed her hair, and ate with a knife and fork, Ms. Anne Sullivan had to teach her while fighting with her. Helen Keller, a stubborn and opinionated girl, resisted her strict education by crying, screaming and other ways. However, relying on self success and the tools of reshaping destiny, self-confidence, and love, Anne Sullivan finally awakened Helen Keller's sleeping power of consciousness. Self-confidence and self-love come into being in the heart of the young Helen Keller, and thus she can be freed from the hell of pain and loneliness, and finally head towards the light in the struggle.

Helen Keller once wrote: “on the night when I first realized the existence of words, I lay in bed in an excited state. At that time, for the first time, I hoped that it would soon be dawn. I guess no one else could feel the joy of my time.” Although Helen Keller is still blind and deaf, she has learned to communicate with the outside world by using fingertips instead of eyes and ears. When she was a teenager, her name had been known all over the United States, and she became a model for the disabled.

It is impossible that the young Helen Keller has no sense of inferiority. Fortunately, since she was a child, she has set up a strong confidence in her heart and transcended her inferiority. After the young

Helen Keller became famous, she did not become complacent. She continued to receive education assiduously. In 1900, Helen Keller studied the finger speech method, convex characters, and vocalization, and gained more knowledge than ordinary people by these means. Finally, she was admitted to the Radcliffe Institute for Advanced Study, Harvard University. The first sentence she said was, “I'm not dumb anymore!”She was extremely excited to find that her efforts were not in vain. Four years later, as the world's first blind and deaf person who received a college education, she graduated with outstanding results.

Helen Keller not only learned to speak but also to write on a typewriter. She has a keen sense of touch. She could know what the other party is talking about just by putting her fingers gently on the person’s lips. She can “appreciate” music by putting her hands on the wooden parts of the piano and violin. If you ever shook hands with Helen Keller, she can recognize you by memory when you meet and shake hands with her five years later, knowing that you are beautiful, healthy, weak, funny, bright, or full of complaints. With her strong belief, Helen Keller finally conquers herself and embodies her value. Although she didn't make a lot of money or become a politician, she achieved much more than the rich and politicians. After the Second World War, she made speeches in Europe, Asia, and Africa, which aroused the public's attention to the disabled.

At that time, Helen Keller suffered a lot, but she was able to overcome it and project light to the world. What does it say? It shows that confidence is the No. 1 chemist. When confidence is integrated into thoughts, people will immediately pick up this shock subconsciously, turn it into an equal amount of spiritual power, and then transfer it to the field of infinite wisdom so as to promote the materialization of the ideas of success.

It can be said that if you have doubts, you will fail, but if you believe in victory, you will succeed!

What is confidence?

Confidence is a state of mind and a positive attitude. Confidence can endow the people with the driving force, life, and the action to think. It is also the starting point of all the approaches to accumulate wealth, the root of all miracles, and the mysterious and magical power that cannot be analyzed by all scientific laws. Confidence is the only comfort when you are frustrated, and the only way for human beings to control the universe's infinite intelligence. In a word, confidence is life, strength, miracle, and the foundation of creating a career and achieving success!

Confidence is the generator of success

Behind every successful person, there is a huge force, confidence, which supports and pushes them to their goals. Confidence is an essential condition for making all great achievements, which is of great significance to those who are determined to achieve success. Confidence can promote people to release infinite enthusiasm, energy, and wisdom in the subconscious and then help people to obtain huge wealth and achievements in a career. In this regard, confidence is compared to the engineer of a person's psychological architecture.

The human mind is a complicated machine, and the power of the machine comes from outside the mind. To reach and gain this powerful force, we must open the door of confidence, and It is our desires and motives that open the door of confidence. There is no other way. In addition, the opening range of the door depends on the intensity of such desire and motive. Only with a strong desire can we fully open the door of confidence.

The power of confidence is inexhaustible, as it is a type of resource that can be recycled endlessly. Everyone can easily gain confidence but does not need to pay any fee. As long as you want to use confidence, you can use it in freedom.

The ways to gain confidence

As long as you have such a faith that you can achieve success, you will be bound to succeed. The more confident you are, the more likely you will be to succeed. Those who will hold on to the last and refuse to accept anything impossible prefer to achieve success, rather than those who are lacking in confidence and improperly belittle themselves. To confirm the confidence to win, first of all, you must become confident. The ways to gain confidence are as follows:

First, you need to know the exact goal of your life that you have the ability to achieve. Then, you should ask yourself to make unremitting efforts, persevere, and work towards this goal. In addition, you should take action right away.

Second, you need to know that the dominant thought in your mind will eventually turn into the external substantive action and that it will gradually turn into the material entity. As a result, you need to spend some time every day thinking about what you want to be, so as to depict a clear picture in your mind.

Third, with the help of self-suggestion, you need to show the desires that you adhere to in your mind to support yourself to achieve the goal. Therefore, you need to spend about 10 minutes every day asking yourself to improve your self-confidence.

Fourth, you should never stop trying to achieve the definite leading goal in your life, until you develop enough confidence to achieve the goal.

Fifth, you must never engage in any activities that are not beneficial to the public. Only when you have goals that are good for people, for yourself, for the country, and for society, you can get help from others, making it more likely to achieve success.

Examples of success

Zhang Haidi: Write her life with her strong mind

On May 9, 1983, the Central Committee of the Communist Party of China approved the Report on further learning and publicity activities for zhang Haidi from the Secretariat of the Central Committee of the Communist Youth League and the Shandong provincial Party committee to the Central Committee of the Communist Party of China. Then, the CPC Central Committee issued the Decision on learning from

Zhang Haidi. Party and state leaders inscribed an inscription for Zhang Haidi, calling on the whole people to learn from the disabled and outstanding communist Youth League member. Zhang Haidi is an exceptional representative of a new generation of young people who grew up with the support of the party and the people. Zhang Haidi's lofty thoughts, indomitable spirit, and exemplary actions have aroused substantial repercussions in society.

Remarks by Zhang Haidi

"When we are alive, we must work for the people and be beneficial to society. I will leave the light in the world like a shooting star."

"I have to spend every minute of every day in pain, but others can not see it. Because it's too painful, it is far beyond the imagination of ordinary people. I have been ill for 41 years, and I can live to this day. To a large extent, I am supported by my mind. The most important thing for a person is thought. I have the courage to aspire to a new life. I have been sick since I was five years old. I am not only alive but also working. I can't live without accomplishing anything. When I am alive, I will learn and do more for the masses. Since I am a shooting star, I will leave the light to the world and dedicate everything to them."

"In the road of life, anyone will encounter difficulties and setbacks, and it depends on whether you can overcome it. If you defeat it, you are a hero and the strong one in life. If you want to struggle, your inner strength is eternal, but it will not last long if you always rely on others to move forward. Even if you fall a hundred times, you should stand up one hundred times. In a dilemma, you should establish your confidence, believe that everything will be the history, and encourage yourself to overcome difficulties with an optimistic mental attitude. As is known to all, genius is born in pain!"

"It's not terrible to fall ill. What's terrible is that the person lost the courage of life. As long as you bravely overcome difficulties, you can create a beautiful new life. Life is short. If you want to make your life meaningful, you should dedicate your last light and heat to the party."

"I have high ideals. I don't want to be such a boring person that I attempt nothing and accomplish nothing. If I don't learn more, I will feel uncomfortable. Then, I am willing to dedicate my life to my desired career. Although I have difficulties in walking, I have been so optimistic for many years, full of passion for a better life."

A girl who fell into oblivion with two-thirds of the body moved China in 1983

Zhang Haidi could not receive formal education at school or enjoy a normal life as a healthy person. But she taught herself the courses from primary school, middle school, university to postgraduate studies, translated a large number of English novels, and learned traditional Chinese medicine on her own for free acupuncture treatment for others. When the contemporary youth began to think and fret about the meaning of life, she made a sonorous answer with her words and deeds.

On February 24, 1983, at Beijing Railway Station, Train No. 298 from Jinan stopped in the winter night with the first light of morning. When the train door opened, a wheelchair was laboriously moved out, on which sat a 28-year-old disabled girl.

At that time, few people in Beijing knew Zhang Haidi, but with long fashionable hair, a pair of black-framed glasses as an intellectual and wathet blue turtleneck, she was still eyecatching among the people with green military uniforms and blue overalls. Zhang Haidi did not expect that in another ten days, her story, image, and voice would be spread all over China. She would be able to be compared with Lei Feng and be known and admired by the youth all over the country for a while.

An article that was neither significant nor time-effective appeared on the headlines of The People's Daily

After Zhang Haidi arrived in Beijing, the Propaganda Department of the Communist Youth League Central Committee arranged her to settle down in the Evergreen Hotel of the Central School of Communist Youth League of China. According to Wei Jiuming, then head of the Propaganda Department of the Communist Youth League Central Committee, Wang Zhaoguo, then the first Secretary of the Communist Youth League Central Committee, Hu Jintao, executive secretary, and several other secretaries paid a visit to Zhang Haidi. Hu Jintao asked the

Propaganda Department to help Zhang Haidi settle down and get well prepared for the event.

Although Zhang Haidi was in Beijing for the third time at that time, unlike the previous two for medical treatment, this trip had a special meaning for her life. After discussion, the Secretariat of the Central Committee of the Communist Youth League elected her as an advanced model of the youth in China and planned to publicize her and her deeds to the youth nationwide.

On August 16, 2009, in the office of Shandong Branch of the Xinhua News Agency in Jinan, Song Xiwen, a retired journalist over seventy years old, described how Zhang Haidi and her deeds were discovered while stroking the yellow issue of The People's Daily. In November 1981, song Xiwen, who was in charge of the rural report at that time, was on the bus to Donga County for an interview. He heard that Li Xia, a photographer from Shandong Pictorial, said that they were photographing a girl recently. She was exceptional and had a severe disability since childhood, but she taught herself acupuncture, foreign language, and radio, and then treated the people in the neighborhood free of charge. When hearing that, Song Xiwen was interested in the girl, and the next day, he asked Li Xia to go to Shenxian County, Liaocheng, where the girl lived.

The row of small bungalows next to Shenxian County Cultural Center has been demolished, but some old traces can be seen from the photos taken by Li Xia. Zhang Haidi lived in a low dormitory, but the interior furnishings were elegant in a Western style. At that time, her wooden bookshelves were full of biographies and professional books, and beside her bed was a double-speaker recorder and an accordion which was seldom seen in the county town.

In Song's impression, Zhang Haidi is like the hostess of a cultural salon in a small county. Before her story was reported, many young people gathered in her tiny room, where there were workers, doctors, teachers, and unemployed young people. Zhang Haidi could play the accordion and sing very well. And many young people borrowed books from her room, discussing what they have learned and known and contemplating the meaning of life.

After nearly ten days of interviews, Song Xiwen wrote an article, The paralyzed girl Lingling is as warm as a fire. In the article, he mainly used Zhang Haidi's childhood name, Lingling, and depicted the story that Zhang Haidi was physically disabled, but worked hard and cured the sick. “At that time, I thought that I could write a story for the girl, but I didn't expect to have such an impact.”

After the manuscript of the Xinhua News Agency was issued, this article that was neither significant nor time-effective appeared on the headlines of The People’s Daily. Letters from all over the country were continuously sent to Liaocheng. Other news media went to Liaocheng to interview Zhang Haidi. Some units began to invite Zhang Haidi to deliver speeches. However, Zhang Haidi became a well-known model among the people a year later.

A girl who fell into oblivion with two-thirds of the body taught the courses from primary school to university on her own

At the end of 1982, the Communist Youth League elected a new Central Committee of the League. Because of the situation at that time, the new leading group expected to find a typical example that can be seen and learned by the young people in the new era.

Wei Jiuming recalled that from January 7 to 22, 1983, the National Conference on Workers' Ideological and Political Work was convened. The Deputy Secretary of the Communist Youth League of Shandong Province told him about Zhang Haidi’s story. After investigation, Wei Jiuming wrote a written report to the Secretariat of the Central Committee of the Communist Youth League. After repeated discussions, the Secretariat of the Central Committee of the Communist Youth League finally agreed that Zhang Haidi would go to Beijing as a typical example of advanced youth.

When Zhang Haidi just settled down in the Evergreen Hotel of the Central Committee of the Communist Youth League, Guo Meini, a journalist from China Youth Daily, interviewed her in Shandong, paid a visit to her with an acupuncturist.

When the girl who helped Zhang Haidi to push the wheelchair took off her clothes, Guo Meini described that her heart was suddenly shrinking. She saw that Zhang Haidi's spine was twisted on the back in the shape of S, while on both sides of her spine were long scars left by four major operations. The doctor who examined Zhang Haidi gave an acupuncture treatment with a silver needle from her feet up, including the abdomen and cardia. However, Zhang Haidi didn't perceive anything until the doctor reached the location of the second thoracic vertebra. The doctor could not help sighing that Zhang Haidi was the most severely disabled patient that he had ever treated. Zhang Haidi completely supported her life with her strong willpower.

However, Zhang Haidi was severely disabled with high paraplegia when she was five years old. She never received formal education on campus. But she taught herself the courses from primary school, middle school, university, and graduate studies on her own with her tenacious willpower. Her parents were transferred to the Shanglou Village in Shenxian County. She taught herself traditional Chinese medicine science to treat the villagers free of charge. She treated more than 10,000 people with acupuncture free of charge, becoming a well-known village doctor far and near. In Shenxian County town, she could not find a job for a while. Alone in her room, she studied how to draw paintings, play the instruments, and learn English, Japanese, German, and then popular Esperanto. In addition, she translated an English novel of 130,000 words. In Shenxian Chengguan Hospital, even if she could not control her defecation, she retained that hard-earned job by drinking no water in the daytime. Then, she could retain her hard-earned job with a monthly income of 25 Yuan by taking a lot of painkillers. Zhang Haidi once said, “no one will condemn me for lying down to eat and drink, but it makes no sense living in this way.” She said she intended to do something for the society and be a useful person for society.

As Guo Meini put it, in the early 1980s, young people just came out of the Cultural Revolution. At that time, they did not receive a good education or acquire useful skills, but they had to face difficulties and setbacks in entering a higher school and getting a job. Under the general trend of reform and opening up, they were most concerned about what to do in the future. Zhang Haidi is exploring the meaning of life with her actions while answering the questions of the times. It is accidental but inevitable that Zhang Haidi came into the sight of young people.

Her suicide, which was ignored by the media in the past, made her closer to the frustrated generation of young people

On March 1, 1983, five days after Zhang Haidi came to Beijing, the article titled The Pillar of Life, written by Guo Meini and Xu Jialiang, appeared on the headlines of China Youth Daily. It is worth mentioning that it was not until the publication of The Pillar of Life that Zhang Haidi's suicide was first disclosed, although the media agencies in Shandong and even in China had interviewed Zhang Haidi and reported her story many times in the previous year.

At the age of 17, Zhang Haidi returned to Shenxian County from Shanglou Village, where her parents were transferred. Her experience as a barefoot doctor in the village made her confident in her future. However, when looking for a job in Shenxian County, she was snubbed and discriminated against at all places. In winter, Zhang Haidi sat in a wheelchair and crowded in front of the county labor bureau to wait for recruitment. It was so crude that the employers told Zhang Haidi that so many healthy people had not yet got a job. Zhang Haidi's begging was coldly rejected. While her parents went on a business trip to Liaocheng, Zhang Haidi took a lot of sleeping pills.

Zhang Haidi recalled that after taking the pills, she thought of the beautiful scenery in the countryside, the villagers she had treated, and Pavel Andreevich Korchagin. She said hastily, "Help me, please! I am still young. I'm still useful. I want to live!"

Guo Meini said, before interviewing Zhang Haidi, other media agencies had never reported the episode, and she also learned it from the recording of Zhang Haidi's speech. Zhang Haidi said, "I told some newspapers about this, but they didn't write it. Maybe some people think it's a disgrace."

Guo Meini recorded Zhang Haidi's suicide with her consideration. She said that she wrote about Zhang Haidi's victory over pessimism, recognition of her responsibility to society, and firmness of her belief in life. It would be more helpful to the young people in the early 1980s who suffered setbacks from the Cultural Revolution. According to Guo Meini, after her article was published in the newspaper, many readers wrote in their letters and told her that it was Zhang Haidi's suicide that made them feel that Zhang Haidi was not as challenging to reach as the previously publicized figure. Moreover, they thought that she had wavered and had some shortcomings so that they felt her a real person and thus believed in her. She is a living person in reality, not a God.

For the reasons why Zhang Haidi can be favored by the young people in the new era, one is that she looks fashionable and has an independent character. Later, A Ying, a writer who worked with Zhang Haidi and Shandong Writers Association, told such a story. When Zhang Haidi delivered a speech in Beijing, she was accused of her long hair. At that time, long hair was associated with the capitalist class. When she fell sick in hospital, a leader in charge of women's work visited her in the hospital and advised her to cut her long hair short when seeing her long hair. But Zhang Haidi did not want to get her hair cut. Later, when she took part in an activity in the Great Hall of the People, she tied her hair with a handkerchief, but she quietly pulled the handkerchief off the moment she entered the conference hall.

After that, Zhang Haidi, who had been a low-key person for some physical reasons, took the initiative to fade out of people's sight. Zhang Haidi recalled many years later that she had intended to refuse the invitation for the trip to Beijing because she preferred to do some reading, work, and study with her friends in her room. Later she thought that if she had to go, she would come back soon.

Data source: Liu Dili. The young woman in the wheelchair: write her life with her strong mind. (Beijing Youth Daily, 2009-09-17.)

"Queen Worker" Wu Shihong

Dwick Duggan, a former president of the American Football League, once said: "if you think someone will knock you down, you will be knocked down. If you believe that you can stand to the last, you will stand to the last. If you want to win, but you do not believe in yourself, you will never defeat others. If you think you will fail, you will fail. Therefore, looking at the successful examples of the world, I find that all victories start with the will and confidence of the individual to strive for victory. All wins derive from what you keep in mind. If you think you are superior to your opponents, you are superior to them. Therefore, you have to think about the benefits and have faith in yourself so that you can win. In life, the strong are not necessarily the winners, but sooner or later, victory is exclusive to those who are confident." Wu Shihong is a confident woman.

To be a successful person!

Wu Shihong, born in the 1960s, was a nurse of Beijing Chunshu hospital. She was of the origins of Manchu, Mongolian, and Han nationalities. As Wu Shihong put it herself, she had nothing but to live humbly in her teens. "I was lifeless, and I couldn't even have enough to eat and wear. I was so far away from legend and glory that you couldn't associate me with them."

From 1979 to 1983, Wu Shihong had leukemia. All her hair was almost lost as a result of repeated chemotherapy. After recovering from leukemia, Wu Shihong suddenly realized that her life could only be started again because there might not be enough time left in her life. Maybe it was from then on that Wu Shihong came up with the idea that she would be a successful person. The stubborn Wu Shihong started a new life with her tenacious willpower. With only one radio, she spent a year and a half learning Xu Guozhang's three-year English course and got the stepping stone to a new life.

In 1985, she read the recruitment notice of IBM in the newspaper, so she prepared to apply for the company via a foreign service company. Before that, the foreign service company had recommended many candidates to IBM, but they were not hired. Wu Shihong did not receive high education or work in a foreign company, but she had a belief that she would never allow anyone to stop her from any gate.

Wu Shihong came to the five-star Great Wall Hotel. She summoned up her courage and walked into IBM's agency in Beijing.

Wu Shihong successfully passed two rounds of written tests and one oral test. At last, the examiner asked her if she could type. She answered immediately, “Yes, I can!” “so how many characters can you type in a minute?” “What’s your standard?”

The examiner told Wu Shihong a standard, and Wu Shihong immediately promised that she could. She looked around and found that there was no typewriter in the examination room. As expected, the examiner said that she would try typing again when she was admitted next time.

In fact, Wu Shihong had never been in contact with a typewriter. After the interview, Wu Shihong rushed back and bought a typewriter with the 170 Yuan she borrowed from her relatives and friends. At that time, she had been typing day and night for a week, her hands were so tired that she could not even hold chopsticks for dinner, but she miraculously typed as many characters as the professional typist. Several months later, she paid off the debt, which was a burden on her, but IBM didn't test her typing skills anymore.

Wu Shihong became one of the most ordinary employees in the world-famous enterprise.

“I will be capable of managing anyone in our company.”

In the early years when Wu Shihong worked for IBM, she did some low-skilled work, such as making tea and pouring water and doing some cleaning, which was utterly physical work. She once felt extremely inferior, and it was even an extravagant hope for her to touch the fax machine, which represented high technology in her mind. She was only relieved to be in such an environment that she could dress warmly and eat her fill.

However, this inner balance was quickly broken. Once, Wu Shihong came back with a flat car, which was loaded with office supplies she had bought. She was stopped at the gate of the building by the doorman, who deliberately asked to check her employee’s card in a foreign enterprise. Wu Shihong had no card, so she had to be stalemated at the gate. People in and out of the building looked at her with peculiar eyes. Seeing that, she was thoroughly humiliated in her mind, but she had no way to vent it. Wu Shihong secretly vowed that such days would not last long and that she would never allow others to block her outside any gate.

Wu Shihong's sensitive mind was heavily hurt in another incident. At that time, a senior female employee from Hong Kong frequently drove others to do things for her, and Wu Shihong was naturally requested to run errands for her. One day, the female employee said to Wu Shihong angrily, "Juliet (English name of Wu Shihong), if you want to drink coffee, please tell me!" Wu Shihong was completely surprised and did not know what she was talking about. The female employee shouted directly in her face, "If you want to drink my coffee, please close the lid every time!" Wu Shihong suddenly realized that she was regarded as a thief who often drank her coffee. It's an insult to her personality. Wu Shihong shuddered like an angry lion, and she thoroughly vented the depression at the bottom of her heart. Afterward, Wu Shihong secretly vowed to herself that she would be capable of managing anyone in the company someday in the future.

Inferiority can overwhelm a person like a mountain, or generate powerful power like a propeller. Wu Shihong wants to change the status quo and liberate herself from the bottom. Then, she spent six more hours working and studying than others every day, so she became the first to be promoted to business representative among the employee of the same batch. Then she was selected among the first batch of local managers, and then the first general manager of IBM in South China.

Enrich herself on the basis of practice

Wu Shihong started at the bottom of IBM and had been promoted repeatedly for her outstanding sales performance in the 12 years until she became the general manager. When Wu Shihong was the general manager of IBM in South China in Guangzhou, she once managed a company with more than 200 employees. In the company, she needed to care about not only the sales performance of an industry but also all the affairs relating to personnel and finance. And she must have insight into market opportunities and trends. It is far from enough to depend on the marketing personnel to seize the market, but some unique strategies are required. Otherwise, the company would forever stagnate in the thinking pattern of the marketing personnel. The marketing personnel believe that it is more likely to sell their machines in the industries with larger funds, while the strategic thinking is concerned about whether a market is dominated by microcomputers or medium-sized computers, and whether there will be problems in the follow-up development and growth potential of a market, although it seems quite bustling. However, Wu Shihong was struggling to find proper solutions to such questions, so she began to dip into some books on market analysis very seriously.

Wu Shihong always enriched herself on the basis of practice, analyzed and solved problems in her own way, and dissected the situation and strategy of IBM China at that time. At that time, IBM did not pay too much attention to the market but focused on major clients to conduct marketing strategies from top to bottom according to the pyramid structure. It is because Wu Shihong's best use of the situation that IBM's products could occupy a leading position in the Chinese market.

Choose Microsoft to realize her dream

On February 5, 1998, after more than five months of two-way selection, Wu Shihong faxed the signed agreement to Microsoft headquarters. The superior of Microsoft told Wu Shihong that she was born for Microsoft and that Microsoft was always reserving a seat for her. Wu Shihong chose Microsoft because it was in line with her dream either to make a Chinese company go global or to lead an international company to the Chinese market. After choosing Microsoft, Wu Shihong said she would face three challenges. First, she should perform the duties of the general manager and do a good job in all aspects. Second, she must get to know the company, its employee and products as soon as possible. Third, she was worried about whether the employee in Microsoft China would accept her and whether Microsoft would accept her.

After joining Microsoft, Wu Shihong had been busy with recruiting the people of ability and training the personnel. Wu Shihong attributed her greatest achievements after she came to Microsoft China to the discovery of a large number of local management and business elites, which also built a solid foundation for Microsoft China's road to the future. Wu Shihong said that in the future, Microsoft would concentrate more efforts to reshape its image and communicate effectively with people from all walks of life. Wu Shihong was ready to take on the new challenges with great momentum.

However, as Wu Shihong embarked on her ambitious program to reshape Microsoft China's corporate image, a bad fortune came to her. The antitrust lawsuit against Microsoft in May 1998 obviously exacerbated the contradiction between Wu and Microsoft executives and made Wu further reflect on her choice. Owing to the Big Stick Policy executed by Microsoft in China, on the one hand, it made part of Chinese users feel nervous, while on the other hand, because of the media's fueling the incident, it also aroused the universal anti-Microsoft campaign from the subconscious. It can be said that Wu Shihong at that time was best with troubles internally and externally. On June 18, 1998, Wu Shihong decided to resign as general manager for personal reasons.

Realize her ambition in the national industry

The press had always been keen on where Wu Shihong would go after resigning from Microsoft. The public was concerned about what would happen to Microsoft without Wu Shihong, where Wu Shihong would go after leaving Microsoft, and whether there would be a better opportunity for her in the industry.

On October 11, 1999, Wu Shihong had been waiting for the day for a long time. In the afternoon of the same day, a number of journalists gathered in Kempinski Hotel, and TCL held a grand press conference here to welcome Wu Shihong to join TCL. Wu Shihong was luckily chosen by TCL, a famous home appliance enterprise in China, and entrusted with the important positions of Managing Director and Vice President of TCL Corporation, and President of TCL Information Industry Company Limited. Thus, Wu Shihong began to realize her ambition in the national industry.

Wu Shihong is always excellent. She is adept at exercising leadership and analyzing and summarizing so as to find the corresponding path. She believes that in the fierce competition, enterprises with weak vitality will die out. In particular, the IT enterprises in China should deal with the problem in the persons in charge of marketing and technology, respectively, and strive to learn the specific market rules and management. For example, many enterprises in China have been developing at high speed for quite a long time and developing into a large scale, but they could not support their operations all of a sudden. The reason for this is that they don't grasp the market rules or are poorly managed.

Put her heart and soul into everything

Wu Shihong's experience is to put her heart and soul into everything that she is engaged in, and not to constantly be distracted to check whether there are any other opportunities around while working. Everything she does, she should have a short-term goal on to what extent she should make efforts at least. It's when she accomplishes the on-going task that she will look up in the distance. If she has been double-minded to look for any shortcut and opportunity, she will find that she has nothing better than others in front of every opportunity that she desires. The only way to close the gap is for her to redouble her efforts.

Data source: Xiao Wei. Women's Capital. (Beijing: Jiuzhou Press, 2002.)

A boy with no arms could play the piano with both feet

Just a few days after the Spring Festival in 1998, Liu Wei played hide-and-sake with three friends around his house. Unexpectedly, an accident happened.

It turned out that the place where they played hide-and-sake was a power distribution room that was illegally constructed. The low and loose brick wall made Liu Wei fall on the 100kV high-voltage line, suddenly getting in a dead faint. According to the doctor's diagnosis, Liu Wei's double-arm muscles were all necrotic due to electric shock, so he had to have an amputation of both upper limbs as soon as possible, or his life would be hardly saved.

Five days later, Liu Wei came to his senses and knew nothing about what had happened. Naive Liu Wei thought that he was just suffering from a serious illness, and then his hands would be reset after he recovered in hospital.

His mother tried to hide the truth, but it was impossible to hide it again and again. She finally told her son the truth. After knowing that he lost his arms, Liu Wei became very depressed and dazed all day, unwilling to take a step out of the ward. What made him more miserable was that he could no longer go back to a normal life, go to school or play with his friends.

He was skilfully enlightened by the unarmed painter to light the light of life

Just when Liu Wei was so disillusioned that he even thought of going to die, a painter like Liu Wei, who lost his arms, walked into his world and re-lit the light of life.

In 1978, Liu Jingsheng was injured by high-voltage electricity at work at the age of 26 years old, while his arms were also highly amputated. After a difficult trough period, Liu Jingsheng could not only take care of himself but also write and draw with his feet and mouth. His works have been exhibited in the United States, Japan, Austria and other countries, and he has held individual exhibitions in Hong Kong, Shenzhen and other places. He has become an accomplished calligrapher and painter.

No one knows more about Liu Wei's pain after losing her arms than Liu Jingsheng. After meeting with Liu Wei, Liu Jingsheng did not talk too much to comfort Liu Wei, but showed him with concrete actions, as he folded up the quilt and wrote with his feet.

A living example showed to him that Liu Jingsheng could still live without his arms. Liu Wei had been plagued but was suddenly enlightened when seeing Liu Jingsheng fold up the quilt and write. Liu Wei had refused to eat and drink for several days before, but he eventually got out of the dilemma. He began to comanage with the follow-up treatment of the hospital, doing rehabilitation exercise in the rehabilitation center while practicing wearing socks, brushing the teeth, washing the face and writing with his feet. But if you write with your feet, you have to practice in an abnormal sitting position. Once you sit for a long time, you will have pain in your waist and back. Whenever Liu Wei felt a pain in his back, he would intend to loaf on the job. When he couldn't stand it, he thought of giving up. At this time, Liu Wei's mother always went out of her way to encourage him. At that time, there was a game hall on the fourth floor of the rehabilitation center. My mother bought some game coins to ask him to play games in the room. Others played games with hands, but he played with his feet. He was addicted to playing games, which allowed his toes to be fully exercised and then helped him learn to write quickly.

He joined the disabled swimming team and won the gold medal

The athletes in the disabled swimming team in Beijing were disabled in varying degrees, but Liu Wei was the most wounded. He had no arms, and it was tough for him to learn to swim. He practiced swimming thoroughly with the parts below his waist, so he was much harder and tired than others.

At the beginning of speed training, Liu Wei often swam the slowest among the players. But he refused to concede defeat, so he had been encouraging himself to catch up with other teammates. Without hands, he strengthened his legs and bit the rope with his teeth, and then tied plastic around his waist to keep balance. Under the high-intensity training, he made rapid progress.

In 2002, Liu Wei won two gold and one silver medals in the 2002 China Swimming National Championships for the Disabled. His dream is to attend the 2008 Beijing Paralympic Games. Just as he was actively preparing for the Games, a sudden illness came to him.

Long-time and intensive training led Liu Wei to burn himself out, and he suffered from a disease called anaphylactoid purpura, which is a severe disease of low immunity. If Liu Wei continued to practice like this, he would get in mortal danger. Three months after meticulous treatment, Liu Wei once again recovered from illness but had to give up swimming. At that moment, Liu Wei was at sea again.

He learned to play the piano with his feet to realize his dream of music

In the senior year of high school, Liu Wei was imbibed in all kinds of songs that he downloaded from the computer. After madly fascinated with music, Liu Wei had the impulse to compose music, so he bought all kinds of books on music theory, and studied them day and night. His mother searched for a music teacher for him. With the help of Liu Jingsheng again, Liu Wei met Mr. Zhong, an independent music producer. Mr. Zhong told him to learn to play the piano before learning to compose.

Liu Wei, who lost both hands, had never touched the piano before, let alone played it. But he was so eager to do well in everything that he didn't want to give up his music dream so easily. So he challenged his limits and learned to play the piano with his feet.

Soon, Liu Wei's mother helped him contact an official in a university for the disabled. The music teacher there clearly told Liu Wei that no one in history played the piano with feet, and then no teaching materials were available for reference. No one else taught him how to play the piano with feet, so he taught himself. He could not find the fingering of tips, and he created it by himself. Liu Wei firmly believes that there are only things that you cannot imagine, yet nothing you cannot achieve.

However, when Liu Wei sat in front of the piano, he found that playing the piano with his feet was much more difficult than he thought. The piano is high, and there was no space to support his feet. And his legs were entirely suspended. He would get exhausted after practicing playing the piano for a long time. His parents made a wooden shelf for Liu Wei to put his feet as high as the piano so that it would not be so hard that his feet can be put on the shelf.

However, after that, all kinds of problems appeared again. For instance, his great toes are short and wide, and the piano will be keyed if it's a little askew. But after a period of practice, Liu Wei had been able to play the standard notes in his unique way, which was rather difficult for him.

Training the skills to play the piano with toes, he accompanied Andy Lau

During that period, Liu Wei became obsessed with practicing playing the piano with his feet. He had been studying and exploring how to play the piano by the piano all day long except for having dinner. He practiced for seven or eight hours every day and made progress every day. After more than two months of hard practice, he finally mastered the way of toe fingering he created and could perform harmony with his left and right feet. Three months later, he played the first complete piece, Edelweiss. Six months later, he played the MARIAGE D' AMOUR as fluently as those with the certificates of Piano Grade 7. On April 29, 2008, Liu Wei, as a special guest, participated in the recording of the program Olympic Songfest. At that time, Andy Lau was deeply moved by Liu Wei's performance. After Liu Wei finished the performance, Andy immediately ran to hug him. Later, Liu Wei played Let It Be, one of Andy Lau's songs. Accompanied by the piano sound, Andy Lau sang with the audience on the spot.

Liu Wei was learning to sing and learning how to produce music in Mr. Zhong's studio. Liu Wei said it was just the first step for him to play the piano. Next, he would become a musician. So he would begin to learn to compose music and write lyrics and produce the songs that belonged to him.

Data source: Li Ping, Chen Wen. The armless boy could play the piano with both feet. (Beijing Broadcasting and Television Weekly, 2010-03-18).

Part II Set the Compass of Success

With the driving force to strive for success, we must also apply these forces in the right direction to achieve the goal of success. To achieve success in the right way, we must set the compass of success and find our goal. In other words, we need to determine a clear goal and manage our strength.

Goal enables us to shift our focus from work to achievements in work

Jean-Henri Casimir Fabre, a French naturalist, once did a study on the caterpillars. These caterpillars march in long lines on the trees, led by one caterpillar and followed closely by the rest. Fabre put a group of caterpillars on the edge of a large flowerpot so that they meet head to tail and form a circle. These caterpillars, like a long procession, have no head or tail but are continuously crawling along the edge of the flowerpot. Fabre put some food beside the caterpillar group to tempt them. If they want to eat food, they must be disbanded and not crawl one after another.

Fabre predicted that the caterpillars might soon get tired of the meaningless crawling and turn to food, but the caterpillars did not. Out of pure instinct, the caterpillars walked along the edge of the flowerpot at the same speed for seven days and seven nights until they starved to death. These caterpillars abide by their instincts, habits, traditions, precedents, and experiences, but they finally come to nothing, although they exert themselves to the utmost.

Many of those who fail, similar to these caterpillars, believe that they make some achievements as long as they are busy all the time, and that work itself is a success. They confuse the difference between work and achievements at work. In fact, no work itself can guarantee success. To make a task make sense, you should move towards a clear goal. In other words, the measure of success is not how much work has been done, but how many achievements have been made.

The goal helps us avoid this. If you have a clear goal and regularly check the progress of the work, you will naturally shift the focus from work itself to achievements in work, so as to achieve the goal by sparing no effort to make enough achievements. With the realization of one goal after another, you will further develop a higher goal and realize a larger ideal.

Criteria for a clear goal

A person without a goal is like a ship without a rudder. He will drift forever and only fall into a world of disappointment, frustration, and failure. Even if he has a goal, but if it is a vague goal, it is also difficult to reach the destination, so that he can only linger in where he is originally located forever. A journalist asked Lewis Walker, the former president of the American Association of Financial Advisers a question on what factors led to the inability to succeed. Walker answered that it was an ambiguous goal. The journalist asked him to explain in detail, and he answered, "I asked you a few minutes ago: what's your goal? You said that you hope to have a cabin on the mountain one day. It is a vague goal. The problem is that the one day you said is not a specific day, and then it is less likely for you to succeed."

"If you really want to buy a cabin on the mountain, you must first find the mountain, learn about the present value of the cabin that you prefer and then work out how much the cabin is worth in five years in consideration of inflation. Then you have to decide how much to save each month so as to achieve the goal. If you do, you may be able to buy a cabin on the mountain in the near future. But if you just have an empty talk, your dream will never come true. A dream is pleasant, but if it is an obscure dream that does not have a practical action plan, it can only be a delusion." So, Napoleon Hill tells us that the goal must be long-term, specific, ambitious, and concrete.

The goal must be on a long-term basis

If you don't have a long-term goal, family problems, diseases, traffic accidents, and other situations out of control may become the setbacks that you can not overcome and may even lead to the complete failure of actions. If you have a long-term goal, you will regard every setback as the stepping stone for you to make constant progress no matter how serious it is, but never as a stumbling block. The experience of countless successful people has proved that as long as you work hard towards the set ambitious goal every day, you will be able to achieve your goal that you have dreamed of.

Goal must be definite

As you know, if we find a magnifying glass and a piece of paper, we will put the magnifying glass against the sun, and shine the focus of the sunlight on the paper, the paper will be burnt with the heat of the sun after a period. On the contrary, if the magnifying glass is moved back and forth between the sun and the paper, the sunlight can also shine on the paper, but the paper will never blaze out because the sunlight cannot be focused on a point.

In the same way, no matter how much ability and talent you have, if you don't manage it or focus it on a specific goal all the time, you will never be able to achieve success. When an experienced hunter discovers a group of prey, such as birds, rabbits, and deer, he does not shoot at the whole group of prey, but at one of them. Only in this way can he shoot at the targeted prey and hunt many preys. If he doesn't aim at the specific prey but shoots blindly at the whole group of prey, he will be bound to gain nothing even if he is able to fire at the target from a distance and a hundred times without a single miss. Therefore, one of the art of goal setting is to focus the goal on a specific pursuit.

Goal must be ambitious

An ambitious goal will inspire the people to make some innovations so that they are likely to make outstanding achievements. The ambitious goal is a powerful driving force in our lives, which promotes our personality and urges us to forge ahead. In addition, the ambitious goal broadens our horizon, develops our capabilities, and awakens our potential. Therefore, we will feel that there is a new power whirling in the blood, a vigorous passion surging all over us. It can not be seen from those narrow ambitions and dirty motivations. Only an ambitious goal can enable us to be suddenly enlightened from the bottom of our hearts, to recover our self-consciousness fully, as well as to overcome all the cowardly and inferior ideas in our minds. Thus, we will obtain endless courage and strength.

If a low-level goal is set, it will be a drag on our capabilities, and then our capabilities will keep up with the low level. A goal without any challenge will be a devastating blow to the ability to act because our capabilities and the whole body and mind are oriented by the goal. When you have an ambitious goal, you are promising to make great achievements. The people who have made the most contributions and have the best value in the world are those who have lofty ideals and ambitious goals. It is true at all times and in all countries.

Goal must be refined

Another aspect should be paid attention to in the setting of a goal. That is to say, the goal must be specific. Goals should be visible, measurable and achievable. If you set an ambiguous goal that can not be measured, it will reduce your enthusiasm. The reason is that the goal is the source of the driving force. If you don't know how much you've moved toward your goal, you will get discouraged and even completely quit. Napoleon Hill once gave a real example to show what the result would be if a person could not see his distance from the goal.

On July 4, 1952, the California coast was shrouded in fog. On Catalina Island, 21 miles west of the coast, a 34-year-old woman waded into the Pacific Ocean and began swimming toward the California coast. That morning, the sea was so cold that it froze her body. And the fog was so heavy that she couldn't even see the boat escorting her. Fifteen hours later, she was both tired and numb with cold. She knew that she could not swim anymore, so she asked others to pull her on board. Her mother and coach were in another boat, telling her that the coast was close and encouraging her not to give up. But she looked out to the coast of California and saw nothing but fog. She was not pulled onto the boat until 15 hours and 55 minutes from her departure. A few hours later, she felt much warmer and then began to feel the blow of failure. "To be honest, I'm not making excuses for myself," she told the reporter without hesitation. "If I saw land at that time, maybe I could hold on to the last moment." She was only half a mile off the coast of California when she boarded the boat. Later she said it wasn't fatigue that made her give up halfway, but it was that she could not see a target in the fog. Two months later, she successfully swam across the same strait and swam about two hours faster than a man. She is a skilled swimmer, but she also needs to see the goal so as to exert the utmost effort to

Chapter 4 Determine the Goal

Maxims for Success

You have to know what you want to pursue in your life and make up your mind to get it. Focus on your goal with all your heart, and you will be bound to succeed. Think about and plan the goal you desire and do not mind any other distractions. It is the formula that all successful people abide by. —Napoleon Hill

Principles and Guidelines

A positive mental attitude is the foundation of building a building of success, and a clear goal is the masonry to build the building. Your past or present situation does not count, but what you want to achieve in the future does count. If you don't have a desire for the future, you will never be able to accomplish anything great.

You will not succeed without a goal

As we all know, if we want to drive a long way, we must first determine the destination and take the map with us before we depart. When we buy a flight ticket in an airline, the airline will be unable to issue it if we do not specify the destination. However, in real life, only a few people know what they want in their life and have feasible plans to reach a goal. These people are leaders from all walks of life, and they are all successful and have not spent their lives in vain. According to the statistics of the U.S. Department of Labor, only three of every 100 Americans can live an economically carefree life to some extent when they are 65 years old. 97 of every 100 Americans aged 65 or above must support themselves by their monthly social security benefits. Only five of every 100 Americans who work in highly-paid industries, such as lawyers and doctors, do not have to rely on social security benefits when they are sixty-five years old. The reason why so many people can't achieve what they desire that they have never set up a definite goal of life. Thus, Napoleon Hill tells us that you will not succeed without a goal.

A goal is a real determination to achieve what you desire. The goal is much better than fantasy because it is within our reach to be achieved. Without a goal, nothing can happen to you, and no steps can be taken. If you don't have a goal, you can only linger on the journey of life, and you will never get anywhere. So, you need to give a specific range for where you want to go. Your past or present situation is not critical, but what you want to achieve in the future is the most important.

Goal is the masonry to build the building of success

Goal is not only the ultimate outcome that an individual pursues but also a milestone on the road of success. It plays an important role in the whole journey of life, which is mainly manifested in the following aspects:

Goals can motivate us

After a goal is determined, it works in two aspects. On the one hand, it is the basis for people to make efforts, while on the other hand, it spurs on people to move forward. Goal gives people a visible shooting target, and people will have a sense of achievement in their attempts to achieve these goals. When you achieve one goal after another, you will gradually alter your way of thinking and work, and then you will become increasingly enthusiastic.

Goal enables us to see our mission

Many people in the world do not feel satisfied with their lives and the world around them. According to the survey, about 98% of those who are not satisfied with their situation do not have a clear picture of their favorite world. Nor have they set a goal to improve their lives and a goal of life to give an impetus to themselves. As a result, they have no choice but to continue to live in a world that they have no intention to change.

According to Napoleon Hill, a doctor has done a lot of research on the common features of the elderly living to the age of over 100. The results show that these long-lived people have nothing in common in the diet, sports, control of alcohol, and tobacco consumption. But they have something in common in their attitude towards the future, as all of them have a definite goal of life.

Making a life goal may not enable a person to live to be 100, but it will undoubtedly increase the change of his success. If a man does not have a goal, he may achieve nothing. As a trade tycoon put it, an ordinary employee with a goal in mind will make such excellent achievements that he will be remembered by history. But a person who has no goal in mind can only be an ordinary man.

Goal enables us to reach our potential

Many years ago, it was reported in a newspaper that 300 whales suddenly died. These whales were trapped in a bay when they were chasing sardines. Frederick Brown Harris said: "these tiddlers lead the giant in the sea to die. The whales die because of chasing slight profits, and consume their huge power in vain for an insignificant goal."

A person without a goal, like a whale in the story, has tremendous power and potential, but they focus on simple things, which make them forget what they should do. To put more bluntly, we must focus on the goals that we have the advantage, and that will pay off to reach our potential. The goal helps you focus. When you keep working on your strengths, they will develop further and finally enable you to achieve your goal.

Goal enables us to make provisions for bad times

A successful person always makes decisions in advance instead of remedying it afterward. They make a plan ahead of time, rather than wait for instructions from anyone else. They don't allow others to manipulate their work in the process, as they have set their own goals and plans. As the old saying goes, those who do not plan for the future will find trouble at their doorstep. Those who fail to plan in advance will not come to a perfect end.

Goal enables us to make provisions for bad times, forcing us to break down the tasks that we should complete into practical steps. To make a road map leading to success, people must set a goal first. Benjamin Franklin, an American inventor and statesman in the 18th century, said, "I always believe that a person with ordinary ability will be able to accomplish great deeds if he has made an excellent plan."

Goal enables us to have a clear idea about the order of priority

Setting a goal helps us have a clear idea in the order of priority among routine affairs. It is likely for us to get caught up in the everyday affairs that have nothing to do with our ideals. A man who forgets the most important things is bound to be a slave to trifles. A wise man once said, "wisdom is the art of knowing what to ignore." That's the truth.

Goal enables us to grasp what we have now

A successful person is able to grasp what he has now. You can only achieve your goal through your efforts at present. As Hilaire Belloc put it, "when you dream of the future or regret the past, what you only have will be gone from your hand."

The goal is targeted at the future and is to be realized in the future, but it enables us to grasp what we have now. The reason is that any big goal is composed of a number of tiny goals. To achieve an ambitious ideal and goal, we must prepare and achieve a great many tiny goals. Each big goal is achieved based on the realization of several tiny goals. Therefore, when we focus on the work at hand, we will understand that all the efforts are to pave the way for the realization of the future goal. Therefore, we should cherish the present, grasp what we have now, do a good job at work at hand and then head toward success step by step.

Goal enables us to assess our progress

Those who fail have a common problem that they seldom assess the progress they have made. Most of them may have no idea about the significance of self-assessment or have no way to measure the progress they have made.

The goal offers us a crucial means of self-assessment. If you have a concrete goal, which can be seen and touched, you can measure the progress that you have made so far by measuring the distance between your current status and the ultimate goal, so as to enhance the confidence to achieve your goal constantly, and then finally achieve your goal.

complete the tasks she is able to complete. Therefore, when setting a goal, we must specify it.

Determine the specific goals

Excellent organizations have set long-term goals for the next ten to fifteen years. Managers often ask themselves, "what do we want the company to look like in 10 years?" and then plan and make arduous efforts on this basis. The new factories are not to meet the needs at present but to meet the needs in five or ten years. Each research department should also conduct research on the needs in five or ten years. An organization should meet its needs.

In the same way, individuals should also make a plan for five to ten years and determine their goals. Then, which goals should be determined? It is based on the following two steps:

First, divide your ideal into work, family, and social intercourse. Then, you can avoid conflicts and enable yourself to face up to the full view of the future.

Second, find your own answers to the following questions.

What do you want to accomplish?

What do you want to be?

What can satisfy you?

Here is an example of an individual's 10-year plan:

Work plan in ten years

(1) What income level do I want to achieve?

(2) What level of responsibility do I want to take?

(3) How much power do I want?

(4) How much prestige do I want from my work?

Family plan in ten years

(1) What standard of living do I want my family to achieve?

(2) What kind of house do I want to live in?

(3) What type of trips do I like?

(4) How do I want to raise my children?

Social plan in ten years

(1) What kind of friends do I want to have?

(2) Which club do I want to join?

(3) What leading positions do I want to take in the community?

(4) What social activities do I want to take part in?

Finally, it should be pointed out that a person's achievements will be somewhat smaller than his original ideal. So when determining the future goal, his vision should be broader.

Ways to set and implement a goal

It should become a lifestyle to set and implement a goal, which is roughly based on the following six steps:

Determine the goal and the starting line

Some people still can't find their way or even lose their way with the map and compass in their hands. The reason is that they don't know where they are now. Maps and compasses work if you make clear where you are.

For the same reason, when setting and implementing a goal, we should not only make clear our goal but also our starting line. Without a goal, there is no way forward. Without a starting line, you would be unable to plan your itinerary.

Express the goal plainly

People need something to give them clear guidance and help them focus on their goals. But it can only be provided by yourself, while others can not do it for you.

The best way to focus on a goal is to articulate your life goal. When expressing the goal, you should base yourself on your dreams and beliefs. In view of this, you will be able to set such a goal that is lofty, ambitious, specific, and feasible.

Decompose the overall goal into several specific goals

Once you have made your goal in life, you can make long-term and short-term goals. The goal may involve all aspects of life, while it depends on what you want to achieve, such as personal development, professional achievement, economic income, family responsibility, interpersonal relationships, good physical conditions and so forth. In order to facilitate the implementation of the goal, you should pay attention to the following aspects:

1. The goal in life should be as grand as possible

The loftier the goal is, the greater the progress people will make. An ambitious goal can stimulate people's maximum potential and promote them to make great achievements. The first reason why a person is great is that he has a grand goal. Why can a grand goal make people great? The reasons are as follows. A grand goal is to do great things, take into account more people and more matters, and solve more problems in a larger scope. If they want to solve major problems and serve many people, they have to be equipped with excellent skills. And they may even surpass their own gains and losses and make great sacrifices in some aspects. In this process, they are naturally recognized and respected by society and the people, and thus become mighty.

2. The goal in life does not need to be detailed and accurate

A big goal in life is a noble ambition in life, which might request you to struggle for ten, twenty years or even a lifetime. However, it is difficult to precisely refine such a big goal, especially for young people who are lacking in successful experience and social experience. With the increase of successful experience and the realization of phased goals, you will stand higher, while it may become gradually definite to establish a big goal in life.

Therefore, the goal in life does not need to be detailed and accurate, as long as you have a clear direction and a rough idea about the specific ideal, such as becoming an outstanding scientist, entrepreneur, or politician to change the world.

3. Short and medium-term goals should be motivational, practical and feasible

Psychological experiments have shown that things that are too difficult and easy are neither challenging nor stimulate people’s enthusiasm for action. The short and medium-term goal is the guide of practical action, and if it is lower than your standard, it will be unable to motivate you. But if it's out of reach, you can't come up with a practical plan, or you can not see the desired result in the next one or two years, it will dampen your motivation, and play a negative role in your action.

So, how can we master an appropriate level? It's completely different from person to person. Due to the disparity in personal conditions, we must set a short and medium-term goal, which is not only higher than our standard but also basically feasible, in accordance with our qualities, experience, personality characteristics, environmental conditions, and other actual conditions.

4. Short and medium-term goals should be as specific and time-limited as possible

Short and medium-term goals are targeted at the next three or five years, or one or two years, and some short-term goals may even be targeted at the next three months. If such a goal is not specific and clear, it means that you do not have a clear goal. Only the specific and clear goal with a time limit is of great significance to guide the actions and motivate the people. Otherwise, it is inevitable for anyone to behave in a lax and undisciplined way. Then it will be far from success or even excellence.

Do it now

When you have determined your goal in life and carefully set specific goals for each stage, you will achieve nothing if you do not take action. Without an action, anything will be an empty talk. You can head toward your goal step by step and finally achieve success only when you make unremitting efforts. There is something in common among the people who have made brilliant achievements in the world, as they have set definite goals, and they are unbending in the struggle, hold on their goals to the last and never give up until their goal is reached.

Regularly assess the implementation of the plan

Regularly assessing the progress is of equal importance to doing it now. With the progress of the plan, we sometimes find that our short-term goal does not make us close to the long-term goal, or we may find that the original goal is not so realistic, or we may feel that one of our long-term goals does not conform to our ideals and our ultimate goal in life. In any case, we need to make adjustments. The more unfamiliar a person is with creating a goal, the more likely he is to misestimate it, and the more necessary it is to re-assess and adjust the goal.

Celebrate what you have achieved

Finally, take a moment to celebrate what you have achieved. Napoleon Hill has always believed in the reward system. When we make the expected achievements, we should reward ourselves. For instance, we can be slightly rewarded for a tiny prize and greatly rewarded for a grand prize. But we must not reward ourselves before we accomplish the task. When we have made a great achievement, we must enable us never to forget the celebration in our life, so as to constantly enhance our confidence to achieve the goal and strive for success.

Examples of success

Haier's success stems from Zhang Ruimin's dream

Where Haier's success comes from, on the surface, is the brand strategy, diversification strategy and internationalization strategy that Haier has implemented for many years, but the deepest reason is Zhang Ruimin's dream that the products that he has made can be in great demand in the German market and the world market one day.

Have a dream due to stimulation

In 1984, Zhang Ruimin, 35 years old, went abroad to Germany for the first time. He sighed when seeing the huge gap between China's economy and Germany's. Especially when one of his German friends jokingly told him that the best-selling goods made in China in Germany were fireworks and firecrackers, Zhang Ruimin felt his heart bleeding. At that time, Zhang Ruimin had a dream that the products he made could be in great demand in the German market and the world market one day.

In the same year, Zhang Ruimin was transferred as the plant director of the Qingdao Refrigerator Plant. Since then, he has embarked on a road of serving the country with industry and realizing his dream.

Begin to realize the dream in predicament

On December 26, 1984, Zhang Ruimin took over Qingdao Refrigerator Plant reluctantly. When he arrived at Qingdao Refrigerator Plant on his bicycle, he felt heavy to take office as plant director. At that time, he was greeted not only by a thick pile of transfer reports but also by a loss of 1.47 million Yuan and a stinking factory area. In such a nearly ruined enterprise, Zhang Ruimin, who was called by the Japanese as a person cold outside and warm inside, began his way to realize his dream.

1. Set up rules: Start with the rule that no urination is allowed anywhere in the workshop

According to the general rule, a new official applies strict measures. After Zhang Ruimin took over the Qingdao Refrigerator Plant, it seemed that he ought to take some measures that could get quick results, such as focusing on production, emphasizing efficiency, and adjusting the leading group. But after analyzing the situation of the enterprise, Zhang Ruimin decided to start from establishing the basic order and the trust relationship in management. He abandoned all the rules and regulations which existed only in name, and formulated 13 simple rules, including no urination in the workshop, no working late and leaving early, no drinking during working hours, no looting of factory materials and so forth. These rules may seem ridiculous now, but at that time, many people could not abide by these tules in the Qingdao Refrigerator Plant. After these 13 disciplines were made public, there was no defecation in the workshop, but some workers may urinate in the workshop from time to time. And even part of workers would take the public assets of the enterprise at will. So Zhang Ruimin asked his subordinates to post the thirteen rules on the door of the workshop, and once again stressed the punishment measures on those who violated the rules. Unexpectedly, the next day, a worker swaggered into the workshop and left with a box of the workshop's pieces of stuff. Two hours later, Zhang Ruimin posted a notice on the bulletin board to dismiss the worker.

Then, the workers learned that the new director took the rules seriously. In a short time, these thirteen rules were executed without fail, which laid a solid foundation for the formulation of the subsequent twenty-two rules, thirty-three rules, and even the well-known Haier's corporate culture. Zhang Ruimin knows that as long as the workers are willing to abide by these thirteen rules, it will be an easy task for them. For a reason, it is the best way to establish rules and establish a trust relationship in management by starting from the simple and practical rules.

2. Emphasize quality: Defective products are waste

After that, the rules and orders were gradually established, and the output of the enterprise gradually increased, but the quality problems arose repeatedly. At that time, in the 1980s, refrigerators were still in short supply in China and customers could only by a refrigerator with the refrigerator coupon. And only a few of every 1,000 urban residents had a refrigerator at home. In this context, the ordinary household electrical appliances enterprises with proper production lines would try their best to manufacture refrigerators, while those with no production lines had to try their best to import spare parts and assemble them for sales. All of these enterprises aimed to make immediate benefits. For a while, numerous refrigerators were on sale in the market, but the good ones were mixed with the bad ones. However, Zhang Ruimin calmly analyzed the market trend at home and abroad, and believed that the shortage of refrigerators would not last for a long time. In the future market competition, product quality is of uppermost priority. He told his employees many times that the quality of products and services should be the priority among priorities if they wanted to win in the market. Therefore, he decided to focus on the quality-based battle in advance. Then, the widely known incident took place that Zhang Ruimin smashed 76 unqualified refrigerators. From then on, Zhang Ruimin's idea that defective products are waste gradually became the quality consciousness that has been deeply ingrained in the minds of the Haier people and laid a foundation for Haier's concepts. For instance, the user is the god of the enterprise, the enterprise sells its reputation, and excellent products are manufactured by excellent people. It also makes it possible for Haier to carry out the Six Sigma quality management and brand building strategy. Haier's quality awareness has also extended to the service sector, creating a “one-stop international star service” with Haier’s characteristics.

3. Make the brand famous: Brightening the West after brightening the East

From 1984 to 1991, many products in China were in short supply. Unlike the short-term behavior of some enterprises that produce whatever sells well, Haier only focuses on making refrigerators. At that time, Zhang Ruimin did intend to make more money but did not want to have more than he could do. He wanted to make the refrigerator product a famous brand first, and then make use of the brand effect to carry out diversified operation, which was brightening the West after brightening the East. Zhang Ruimin implemented the brand-building strategy, focusing on the quality and top-quality products while strengthening the promotion of the brand image. In Haier, the investment in brand image building is far greater than that in product promotion. It turned out that Zhang Ruimin’s brand-building strategy was a correct strategy. When Haier refrigerator was rated as Famous Trademark of China, many refrigerator brands that were older than Haier refrigerator had disappeared, while some enterprises that had been larger than Haier in scale could be no longer found in the market.

Accelerate the pace of realizing the dream on the way

Since 1991, with Haier's loud brand effect, Haier has embarked on the most basic road of modern enterprise development and expansion to realize diversified expansion with capital operation, thus speeding up the pace of realizing the dream.

Haier's diversified development process through capital operation reflects Zhang Ruimin's contingency management taking objective factors into full account. Zhang Ruimin believes that in the world, enterprise mergers can be divided into three stages. First of all, when the capital stock is dominant and the technology does not take the lead, big fish will swallow little fish and the small-scale enterprises will be merged into large-scale enterprises. Secondly, when the technology exceeds the role of capital, it is the fast fish that eat the slow fish, which means that the enterprises with the leading technology innovation ability will defeat the enterprises with the backward technology innovation ability. Finally, in the 1990s, there was a mode of powerful combination, which means that the sharks ate sharks.

Zhang Ruimin is well aware of China's national conditions. In China, it is impossible for big fish to eat small fish, slow fish or sharks. In China at that time, due to the political system, as long as the fish is still alive, it is impossible for you to eat it. You can eat the dead fish, but eating the dead fish may make you suffer from diarrhea. What if you want to eat fish but don't want to eat dead fish? Zhang Ruimin found a space between living fish and dead fish, eating the shocked fish. The shocked fish are those enterprises that have better hardware facilities but worse management and other software facilities. Zhang Ruimin was confirmed that it is possible to manage these enterprises well with Haier’s management ability and corporate culture. From 1991 to 1998, according to the idea of eating shocked fish, Haier successively merged 18 enterprises, including Qingdao Hongxing Electric Appliance Plant. They sent three employees to each of the combined enterprises. Among the three employees, one was responsible for the overall operation, one was responsible for product quality and the rest was responsible for business management so that all the eighteen enterprises could cease to lose and begin to turn out a profit.

Realize the dream in the triumph

The Haier brand was built, and the scale and strength of Haier were expanded. Zhang Ruimin was finally able to realize his dream that his products would sell well in the German market and the world market someday. From 1998, Haier began to implement the internationalization strategy.

Zhang Ruimin designed an unconventional idea for Haier's internationalization strategy, difficult at first and quite easy afterward. In other words, developed countries are the first choice both for export and for factory building abroad. It's out of common sense because when exporting products, ordinary enterprises prefer to export to countries that are behind their own countries first. Even if they export to countries that are more developed than their own countries, their products are sold at a low price for the purpose of earning foreign exchange through export. Haier not only exports to developed countries first but also sells its products at a high price for the purpose of building a famous brand through export. It is said that Zhang Ruimin views everything from a different perspective, but in fact, it is not true. Zhang Ruimin has his own analysis ideas. It is difficult to export products to developed countries first, but once they consolidate their position in developed countries, it will yield twice the result with half the effort by exporting them to developing countries. As for the higher price, first of all, it comes from self-confidence in the quality of Haier's products. Second, it is to break the impression that the products made in China are cheap in the minds of foreigners. In fact, as early as Haier developed the market in China, Zhang Ruimin adopted the strategy that difficult things go first and quite easy afterward. In other words, it first occupied the market of Beijing, Shanghai and other developed cities, and then established brand effect in the developed cities, then took advantage of the situation to promote to the ordinary cities. In the end, it received favorable results.

Haier's internationalization strategy has gone through two processes: the internationalization of Haier and the internationalized Haier. Haier's internationalization is that after becoming a famous brand in China, Haier vigorously develops its export business and makes its brand widely known. The premise is that Haier has become a very competitive exporter in China, and that the standards of its products can meet the requirements of international standards, and that the products are very competitive in the international market. As a German dealer said, "I'm afraid that we can not stop Haier from entering the German market, because its quality has conquered us. Our curiosity also makes us make mistakes. We can't believe that a product made in China dares to be priced at the level comparable to that of the West. Once it enters the inspection procedure, we have no reason to refuse it, because its products are excellent.

The internationalized Haier refers to the construction of Haier's branch in foreign countries. It is no longer a Haier product made in China, but a Haier product designed, produced, and sold locally. In this way, it is a localized Haier product. Since Haier built a factory abroad, the international Haier has been questioned by many people, and even many people argue that Zhang Ruimin is winning a reputation at a loss in business. Yesterday's success doesn't mean tomorrow's success, but we should believe in Zhang Ruimin's talent for contingency management for many years.

Data source: Zhang Yanning. A pioneering hero. (Beijing: Enterprise Management Publishing House, 2003.)

Zhang Xiuyu : Why do I choose enterprise strategic management?

I have taught philosophy, political economy, labor economics, personnel management, enterprise management, administrative management, and talent science, etc. in 1997, I chose to engage in strategic enterprise management. Why do I choose it?

First, this is an excellent opportunity to carry out business management training in an all-round way in China.

Second, discipline is a critical discipline, known as the study of monarchy in the field of business management. It has a high market demand in the future.

Third, only a few scholars engage in this field in China, and there are fewer experts. Thus, it is promising to make some achievements in this field.

Fourth, my interest, temperament, wisdom, knowledge, experience, and insight are suitable for studying this discipline.

Last but not least, I have the confidence, determination, persistence, and willpower to win. I will be able to practice and summarize again and again. And I will never give up until I achieve my goal, I will never give up.

Results: Based on years of practical experience in teaching, scientific research, training, and consulting, I compiled the textbook strategic enterprise management, which was published by Peking

University Press. The textbook has been published in three editions, printed for more than 20 times and sold for more than 100,000 copies. The textbook is not only very popular in China, but also quickly spread to the United States. It is well received and valued by local business, education and publishing circles. At the invitation of North American Business Press, the English version of the book, Business Strategy: A New Perspective, has been published in the United States.

At the same time, I have also formulated corporate strategic plans for a dozen enterprises, and become a famous expert in strategic management in China that closely combines theory with practice.

Chapter 5 Manage Your Strengths

Maxims for Success

After a failure and before a success, please find the general truth that is often neglected, operating your strength. —Napoleon Hill

Principles and Guidelines

The goal is the foundation for building the building of success. The goal usually consists of work goals, family goals and social goals. The three aspects are closely related to each other and every aspect is bound up with the other aspects. However, a work goal exerts the greatest influence, which is because the standard of a person's family life and his reputation in society, to a large extent, are determined by his performance at work. Thus, how can we select the correct job? Napoleon Hill told us that we must find out our real strengths when choosing a job and manage our strengths well, and then it will change our life.

Capturing your strength is the key to success

In daily life, many people have been eager to get out of their difficulties and achieve success, but they are struggling to find a way out. Therefore, they are exhausted physically and mentally, extremely disappointed, and even feel bored about their life. Why does this happen? Napoleon Hill once made it clear: "because our brain restricts the movement of our hands or feet, we can't master the way to achieve success with original ideas."

In a broad sense, such people make mistakes because they have no idea about what their strengths are, and they tend to overestimate or underestimate their own abilities. For what they could have been able to do. As a result, they were so hesitant that they missed the opportunity. For what they could have been unable to do. As a result, they took risks because they were eager to win. In real life, there are quite a few people like this. In view of this, it's useless to complain too much. The key is to face yourself soberly, find out your strength, and finally achieve success based on your strength.

It's clear that a person without any strength can only envy others in most cases, and a person who can't find his own strength can only act blindly. Both of the above two are pathetic. As long as you keep working on your strength, there will be a high chance that you will succeed. But if you compete with others on your own weakness, you can only hand over the fruits of success to others. If you fail in your strength, you will not have too many regrets in your life, because you have exerted your best in your work. On the contrary, you will leave more regrets. Of course, there is no life without regrets. But if you fail to find your strength throughout your life, it will be the biggest regret in your life. Therefore, we must find out our own strengths and manage it well. It is the key to changing our lives.

Proper ways to seek your strengths for victory

If a person has grown to eighteen years old, he or she may have to make the two most important decisions in life. The decisions will have a profound impact on life, as well as the income, well-being and health. Moreover, they may create or destroy a person. So what are the two decisions?

First, how will he make a living in the future? Be a worker, farmer, businessman, teacher, doctor, or a scientist, inventor, politician, writer, painter, engineer? Second, what will his life companion will be like in the future? For many people, these two major decisions, especially the first one, are usually like a gamble.

So, how can we reduce the gambling in the choice? Here are only several suggestions for the first decision as follows:

First, if possible, try to find a job you like.

Edison is a good example. He works hard in the laboratory for 18 hours every day, eating and sleeping there, but he doesn't think it's bitter at all. "I have never done a day's work in my life, as it is a great joy for me to spend every day." he declared. No wonder he can finally succeed!

Phil Johnson is also a good example. His father opened a laundry and asked him to work in it, hoping that he would take over the laundry in the future. But Phil hated the work in the laundry, so he was always lazy and listless, doing nothing except for what he had to do. At that time, sometimes, he didn't go to the laundry. His father was so sad that he had raised a son who had no ambition or desire to go further ahead, which made him very disgraceful in front of the employee. One day, Phil told his father that he wanted to be a machinist in a machinery factory and start from scratch, which surprised his father a lot. Phil put on his greasy working garments and worked harder than in the laundry for a longer time. But he was so happy that he whistled at work. He took engineering, studied the engine, and installed the machines. When he died in 1944, he was already the president of the Boeing Company and manufactured the Superfortress Bomber, which helped the troops of the Anti-fascist Alliance defeat the Axis powers in the Second World War. If he had stayed in the laundry, how would he and the laundry have been, especially after his father's death? It can be concluded that he would have destroyed the whole laundry.

Secondly, if your own interest conflicts with the needs of individual survival and the needs of the state, you should first obey the needs of individual survival and the needs of the state.

When the external environment can not provide you with a career, you like very much, and you have to engage in a career that you less prefer, for the time being , you should try to change yourself, enable you to gradually adapt to the needs of the environment and develop new interests and hobbies in the process of adaptation. In this way, after some efforts, you can still achieve some success. The father of Li Ka Shing is a principal. He had been dreaming of becoming a teacher like his father from early childhood and engaged in education. However, due to the early death of his father, he was forced to drop out of school at the age of 14 to work as an apprentice or shop assistant, so as to support his mother and his younger sisters and brothers. Until later, he went into business all his life and achieved great success.

For another example, Min Enze, a famous scientist and academician of the Chinese Academy of Sciences (CAS) and Chinese Academy of Engineering (CAE), said that the needs of the state had been the driving force of his life. He made a concise summary of his work throughout his life like that, "I have been only engaged in three careers in my life. The first is to meet the urgent need for national defense and petrochemical development. The second is to help enterprises make a profit instead of suffering a loss. The third is to engage in strategic, forward-looking and basic work." As He Mingyuan, academician of the Chinese Academy of Sciences who has cooperated with Min Enze since 1984, put it, "Mr. Min has a very distinctive feature, a strong sense of responsibility. People engaged in scientific research tend to attach great importance to interest since it is more likely to make some achievements in the fields that they are interested in. On the contrary, Mr. Min has laid more emphasis on social needs. He would study whatever had been urgently needed by the state, even if the field to be studied was far from his own profession."

Finally, learn to make multiple choices.

You need to make multiple choices in your life constantly. Thus, it is crucial to find out your strengths from a variety of choices. For example, you can't force yourself into an industry just because your family wants to do it unless you like it. However, we should still think twice about the advice from our parents, because they have accumulated a lot of experience and wisdom. But when it comes to the final decision, it's up to you. When you work in the future, it's you who feel happy or sad. Here, the following suggestions, some of which are warnings, are provided as a reference for selecting a job:

1. Read and study suggestions on how to choose a career

These suggestions are usually provided by the most authoritative experts or agencies for vocational guidance. However, these suggestions tend to be the most general views, while it has a huge gap from the situation of every person. Therefore, we should never act upon whatever they say but can only use them as a reference.

2. Avoid choosing jobs and careers that are already crowded

According to the survey, there are more than 20,000 types of jobs available for people to seek a livelihood in the United States, but in a school, more than two-thirds of boys and four-fifths of girls choose only five of them. It can also be seen everywhere in China. If you blindly choose the popular careers which have been overcrowded, you will be bound to encounter extremely fierce competition life the thousands of horses and soldiers rushing to cross the single-log bridge. Moreover, it is necessary for you to make great efforts before achieving success.

3. Conduct an overall investigation before you decide to enter a career

Before you decide to enter a career, you should first spend a few weeks conducting an overall investigation of the career in order to get a comprehensive understanding. How can you achieve this purpose? The simplest, feasible and reliable way is to interview people who have worked in this industry for 10, 20 or 30 years. These interviews are likely to have a profound impact and even become a turning point in your life.

Keep in mind that it is necessary to spend more time searching for the truth before making a decision. If you don't, you may be overcome with regret in the future.

4. Overcome the misconception that you are only suitable for one occupation

In general, every normal person can succeed in multiple occupations. Accordingly, every normal person may fail in varied occupations. Therefore, don't narrow your mind, stubbornly insist on your own ideas, or never take a turn.

Excavate your strength quickly

To find the strength is to find a way to success, but it does not mean success. To achieve the goal of success, you must also quickly tap your strength and manage it in a skillful way. Then, how can you tap your strength quickly?

Have vigorous passion, lofty ideals, and aspirations

It means that you are approaching your strength step by step when you feel an uncontrollable passion running in your heart, or find that you are so eager to do something, or your ideal and self-consciousness are making a silent cry. Therefore, do not let your passion cool down, or the flame of your ideal go out. Make up your mind and tell yourself that you can't spend your life in ignorance or vain, or succumb to the unsatisfactory state of life. Keep your spirits up and make strides toward the goal that is worth fighting for.

Have the courage to show your capabilities

There is a common failing among ordinary people that he doesn't want to work hard anymore and believes that it's useless to work hard anymore if he lacks special talents in a specific aspect. But many people, in the beginning, were no different from ordinary people and had no special talent, but they succeeded in the end. It is because their self-confidence is higher than that of ordinary people, and they can make arduous efforts with self-confidence as a pillar. If you don't go to the field, you will never know how much talent and strength you have in your body, and you will never be able to dig out your strength.

Excavate your strength from your shortcomings

If you can't find your weakness, you will be unable to find your strength. Many people tend to feel that they are not only talented but also defective in one or several aspects, so they worry that they can not develop their talents. The thinking is actually a stumbling block to success. It will destroy your self-confidence in making great achievements. In fact, you can overcome your shortcomings in some aspects.

Generally speaking, people's intelligence will change due to frequent utilization. The more you use it, the sharper your intelligence will be. If a person has defects and weaknesses in some aspects, he should make more efforts in those aspects and focus his thoughts on those aspects and think more. In this way, the brain cells in the parts where the mind is often concentrated will gradually become stronger and more developed and eventually turn into your strength.

Excavate your strength from confidence

If a person's confidence is extremely weak, his effort will be next to nothing, and it is impossible to excavate his strength. Confidence is the foundation of all achievements and contains great power. People who have great confidence in themselves will not doubt whether they are in the right position, and they will not doubt their abilities or worry about their future.

Confidence is a key link that connects subjectivity and objectivity or the human soul and body. It is with the help of confidence that you can tap into a great inner strength. Everything that can enhance your confidence can strengthen your power and thus enable you to excavate your strength.

Excavate your strength from nature

The experience of countless successful people has proved that we will never accomplish anything by completely imitating others. Only when we give full play to our own characteristics can we gradually position ourselves and turn our characteristics into the strength, thus becoming a means to change our destiny.

Charlie Chaplin is a model. When Charlie Chaplin started making films, the director asked him to imitate the famous movie stars at that time. Ultimately, he made nothing. It was not until he began to discover himself, to keep his true character and to become himself that he gradually managed to make films. Comedians in China, such as Zhao Benshan, Song Dandan, and Chen Peisi, have a similar experience. They used to sing and dance for many years, but they didn't succeed. They didn't really become in vogue until they developed their talents in performing skits.

So don't just imitate others, or your brain will get rusty. You should dare to discover yourself and keep your true character, so as to dig out your strength.

Excavate your strength from desire

It is because of so many human desires and pursuits that people's potential can be fully explored, and their abilities can be developed in an all-round way. Then, it is possible to evolve and develop to the present advanced stage. Therefore, in our life, we should take every driving force generated by desire as the driving force to excavate your strength. We should strive to associate with those who are better than us, have received better education, have higher quality, are more elegant and charming, and have profound knowledge and experience in the field we know little about. It will greatly stimulate our desire and do some help for us to excavate our strength.

Excavate your strength from the opportunity

There is no doubt that to play the strength, and we can't do without the ability to seize the opportunity. In our life, we may encounter an opportunity frequently, and then we should seize them, conquer them, and turn them into conditions for us to play the strength. The only thing that we need to do is to act right now.

Instead of waiting for opportunities to come, the talented people with strength seek and seize them, conquer them, and make them their servants. Don't wait for opportunities to appear, but create them. It's a law of mining the strength. Act right now! Like all great leaders in war or peace, you should create extraordinary opportunities to tap and play your strength until you finally achieve success.

Excavate your strength by concentrating your energy

To obtain the strength is to discard the dross and select the essential, which is known by the gardeners. The experienced gardener will cut off many branches that can blossom and bear fruit from the trees, which is often a pity for the common people. But the gardener knew that these side branches are cut to make the trees grow faster and better and the fruits grow better. Otherwise, the future harvest will definitely decrease. It's the same way to behave or start our own businesses. Instead of spending all your energy on many meaningless matters, it's better to focus on an important cause that suits you, concentrate all your energy and work hard. If you want to make great achievements in an important aspect, you should boldly lift up the scissors and cut off all the trivial, ordinary and uncertain wishes. In the face of an important thing, even those things that already have begun to take shape must be cut off. If you can cut off all the distractions in your mind, and concentrate all the nourishment in your vitality on one aspect, you will surely harvest beautiful and plentiful fruits in your career.

Manage your strength skillfully

Strength is a person's strongest ability and the ability to create the greatest value for himself and society. So, how can we manage our strengths well?

Become an expert in a specific field as soon as possible

Everyone wants to be eye-catching, have their own place in society, and play their own skills in one field. So, how can we do this? That is to become an expert in a specific field as soon as possible. Here we emphasize the idea of specializing in a field as soon as possible, but there is not a definite time limit. The earlier it is, the better it will be. In this regard, it means that when a person starts to work in an industry and the society, he or she should do his or her best to find out the industry he / she is in and become an outstanding person. If you can do this, you can soon surpass others.

Then, how can we become experts in an industry as soon as possible? The author gives the following suggestions for reference:

(1) Select the proper industry. In general, it is better to select an industry according to interest rather than according to major. However, no matter what you choose, you'd better not change your profession easily once you determine the industry. It is because changing the profession will make you stop learning and reduce the learning effect.

(2) Study hard. As the saying goes, diligence can make up for lack of intelligence. In fact, diligence is not only to make up for a lack of natural talent by hard work. Even a wise man is indispensable from the word diligence. When we read the stories of successful people, we can find that, in addition to the opportunities and talents, a person's success

is really inseparable from the word diligence. Diligence can not only make up for the lack of natural talent but can also give a helping hand.

(3) Set a goal. We can divide our study into several stages and accomplish the learning tasks within a specific time limit. It is a method of oppressive learning. It can not only force us to move forward, but also change our habits and train our will. Then, it will receive excellent results. When a person becomes an expert, his or her social status is bound to rise. However, when a person becomes an expert, he or she must pay attention to the trend of the development of the times, and constantly update and improve himself or herself, so as to live and learn. Otherwise, he or she will soon fall behind and even be eliminated.

Dare to pursue accuracy

Success is often related to precise action. Those crude actions can only lead to high error rates. The strong have the spirit of pursuing accuracy when they manage their own strength and give full play to their own strength.

George Graham was a famous watchmaker in London. At that time, when customers asked him about the accuracy of his clocks, he would reply: "you just need to use them at ease. Seven years later, you come to me. If the time error is more than five minutes, I will return the money to you." Seven years later, a customer came to him and said, "well, I've used it for seven years, and its time error is more than five minutes." He said, "Really? If so, I'll give you the money back." The customer said, "unless you pay me ten times the price, I will not return it." He replied, "no matter what you ask, I will not break my promise." He paid the customer in exchange for the watch for him to calibrate the time. As George Graham dared to pursue accuracy, the solar system instrument, steering wheel, mercury pendulum, and other instruments invented by him have been used by the later generations. There has been little improvement so far. He has made a big clock for Royal Greenwich Observatory in London, which has been running for more than 150 years now, but it is still in good condition.

Stephen Girard, an American financier, is the incarnation of accuracy. All orders issued by him must be strictly carried out without any violation. He would never break whatever he promised. He believed that if we couldn't pursue the greatest accuracy in everything, we would be ultimately unable to make great progress. He often said that he did not do well, but did not do anything wrong.

There are too many similar examples to list. Therefore, we should pursue precision just as we pursue wisdom and wealth. We should make up our minds and develop good habits of handling affairs, never procrastinate or deal with affairs in a perfunctory way. Precision is strength, personality, and power.

Organize your behavior in an orderly way

To succeed, you have to organize your activities in an orderly way. Otherwise, you can't have excellent strength. Those who make a mess of everything will ultimately fail one day. Some people can't find the reason for their failure. In fact, the desk in front of him has already explained the reason. The desk was full of paper and envelopes; the drawers were filled with all kinds of articles, completely in a mess. Newspapers, papers, stationery, manuscripts, and notes on the newspaper rack were in utter disorder.

If you want to overcome the confusion, the key to organizing your behavior in an orderly way is to understand time control. If you do a good job in time control, you can manage your strengths well. In order to manage time, we need to manage ourselves first, find out the reasons why we waste time and then find specific ways to solve the problems. The reasons for wasting time by ordinary people include lack of planning, low ability, improper authorization, poor communication, indecision, lack of willpower, etc.

It is a necessary step of time management to establish the goal first, then to arrange the sequence, and to work out the long-term and short-term goals. This principle should be abided by in the planning of life, and the schedule on an annual, monthly, and daily basis.

Keep energetic

If you want to manage your strength well, the most important thing is to maintain vigorous energy, which is the cost of achieving success. Once you are energetic, it will make it easy to do whatever it is difficult.

However, many people tend to spend their precious energy, their will, and devote their energy to what is meaningless and even brings trouble to themselves. But those things do no good for their success. If you can master the method of controlling your mind and spirit so that your energy can be accumulated and expanded, and you should never let a little energy be devoted to those meaningless things. Then, we will be bound to have a magnificent future.

In our life, we often see that some people are overworked and don't pay attention to striking a proper balance between work and rest, some rejoice with wild excitement for one night at the sacrifice of their rest and sleep time casually, or some have short tempers and lose their tempers quickly, or some are excessively indulged in disgusting orgies. All these bad habits will cause great damage to a person's energy in physical and mental capacities. In the long run, his health, wisdom, judgment, and creativity will be completely deprived of. In this way, he will lose his strength, and then there will be no hope for success.

All men are created equal. Anyone who is willing to work hard and make progress can achieve success. Once upon a time, a blind man in Britain became a great musician, mathematician, and philanthropist in the world. Many people came to visit him. His wife said to the visitors, "in fact, he is not smarter than anyone, but he is energetic and can constantly develop his talents and seize all opportunities at any time, so he can make the current achievements." We should understand the true meaning of success from the above sentences. Imagine that if the blind man had been derelict in duty and run irrelevant business and wasted his energy at will, he would be unable to develop his abilities and achieve success in his career and family, but also become a waste and burden in society.

Overcome the habit of procrastination

Everyone has all kinds of dreams, ideas, and plans in his life. These visions, ideals and plans are usually the embodiment of their strength. If you can give full play to your power and implement these visions, ideals and plans quickly, you can easily achieve success. However, if you have a well-designed plan but do not execute it quickly and simply delay it, you will treat what you used to be passionate about coldly, and then your strength will die away. Then, even the best plan is bound to come to nothing.

The habit of procrastination often blocks people from taking actions because procrastination destroys their creativity. There is a huge gap in the degree of difficulty and the bitter and sweets between when you are passionate about doing something and when you do it after your passion fades out. It's often fun and simple to do something while you are in high spirits. But it's often a pain to do it after the passion disappears, and it's not easy to accomplish it. In fact, if you put off today's work until tomorrow, the time and energy consumed in this delay will be sufficient for you to complete today's job well. So, procrastination is less economical.

If we want to manage our strength well, we must cure the bad habit of delay. The only way to cure procrastination is to complete your work that very day at once. You should know that the more delay, the harder the work will be. Therefore, we need to act immediately so as not to put off till tomorrow what should be done today.

Control your emotions

Everyone has mood swings, which are different from other animals. However, in real life, some people are adept at controlling their emotions and tend to have a poker face. But some people are given to capricious moods, and their tempers are constantly changing. If you can't control your emotions, it will not only leave a bad impression, affect your relationship with other people, but also make you lose your senses, and the ability to make correct judgments. What's more, it may damage your health. In particular, it may make you angry. There are numerous examples that people tremble with rage and even die of furor.

All those who have strengths are able to control their moods in their own way. In your life, there will always be a lot of frustrations in your interpersonal relations and businesses, which need to be resolved with your wisdom and patience instead of losing the temper. Therefore, whenever you feel unsatisfied with anything in your business or interpersonal relation, you should not say “anything I like is OK.”

Instead, you should restrain yourself, and then make a decision after thinking it twice.

Good at accumulating intangible assets

Human assets are divided into tangible assets and intangible assets. No matter what kind of asset, it needs to be accumulated before it can be increased and bring benefits to people. However, from the perspective of managing the strength, it is more important to accumulate intangible assets, because intangible assets will determine whether you can own tangible assets.

Intangible assets include the following items:

(1) Professional experiences. It is extremely easy to acquire professional knowledge, but the experience can only be accumulated in the long term. The difference between the master and the apprentice is that the master has experience that the apprentice does not have. So the more experienced a person is, the higher the position he or she will occupy in his or her professional field.

(2) Personal credit. As the old saying goes, a man cannot succeed without honesty. What is emphasized here is credit. If you have credit in your work and in your life, others will naturally believe you, dare to communicate with you, and dare to cooperate with you. For a person with strong credit but weaker professional ability, others will be willing to give him an opportunity. On the contrary, for a person with stronger professional ability but no credit, others will feel afraid of being cheated by him once. So there is a limit to what such people can achieve.

(3) Responsible and dutiful. No one likes a person who is derelict of duty. Therefore, if a person is responsible for significant or insignificant matters and does his or her duty, others will be bound to believe in him or her and then dare to entrust important things to him or her.

(4) Personal honor. Personal honor here refers to the honor given by a person's unit or other groups. Such honor may not involve money award, but represents the affirmation of the person. It may be a tiny honor in other people's eyes, but if you want to evaluate this person seriously, the honor will play its due role.

(5) Approachable and modest. No one likes those who are arrogant, haughty, and aggressive, because such an attitude may make the other side feel oppressed. But an approachable and modest attitude may make you feel so delighted just like bathing in the spring wind. As long as you relate well to others, you will make friends with different people and then be able to achieve success one way or another.

Examples of success

Be the fixed barrack, rather than the floating soldier

Sun Nan was once asked what he would have done if he didn't sing in this life. Sun Nan replied that he would have had a try in all trades and professions. That's true. In fact, if he didn't choose music, Sun Nan would probably try all these trades and professions. There is an example. Sun Nan was engaged in eleven industries in the two years when he was 16-17 years old, but in the end, he chose to engage in the music industry.

In 1985, Sun Nan graduated from junior high school and wanted to be independent, so he began to find a job. The first job he did was to be a construction worker. He was responsible for pushing the bricks while others were responsible for building the building. It was hard work. Sun Nan insisted on it for three days and earned 26 Yuan. He couldn't stand it. It was not physical work that he could bear at his age. Next, Sun Nan found a job for welding in a cadres' sanatorium by the sea. He learned the welding techniques from the master, but the master complained that he lacked the slightest knowledge of welding. Then, the master asked him to work in the woodworker room. Next, he worked as an electrician in the instrument factory and as an attendant in the urban and rural service association. In two years, Sun Nan changed 11 jobs. Among the jobs, Sun Nan's favorite job was a stoker in a boiler factory. In Dalian Electrical Machinery Plant, Sun Nan was the only one who obtained the stoker certificate among his classmates after three months of serious study. Sun Nan was very chatty after taking up his post. He would talk with others every day when he finished loading the coal, and they would chat for half a day every time. It dissatisfied the workshop director, as the workers in the workshop would chat with him whenever he was on duty. Sun Nan had no choice but to resign.

After doing so much work, Sun Nan felt that no job was particularly suitable for him. At that time, when pop music just came to China, Sun Nan thought the drummer looked quite handsome. Then, he practiced playing the drum while doing his work. At that time, he was a painter in the pencil factory, so he used a pencil as the drumstick and the oil barrel as the drum to act as an improvisational drummer. At that time, the pencil factory intended to set a band, but there was no drummer. Thus, Sun Nan could exercise his abilities. During the rehearsal of the band, Sun Nan suddenly felt that it was much easier to make music than to be a painter. He did not need to learn to play the drum but was able to do it. At that time, his father taught vocal music, so he practiced playing the piano since childhood. For the first time, Sun Nan came up with the idea that he would not need to be the floating soldier if he could turn music into his fixed barrack.

Soon after he became a drummer, Sun Nan was found to be highly talented in singing. His broad natural tone across the octave range was amazing. As easy as ABC, Sun Nan changed from drummer to a drummer and singer and was finally concentrated on singing. After that, Sun Nan was admitted to Dalian Baihua Art Troupe and began to perform with the troupe in various places in China.

In 1987, a city-wide karaoke Grand Prix was held in Dalian. Sun Nan itched to have a go, and he sang the song Shadow of Fencing Walls, winning rapturous applause from the audience. It was believed that he could have won first place. However, it was a pity that the organizing committee had another idea. The first place of the grand prix went to another contestant and Sun Nan won second place. The furious Sun Nan refused to accept the second place, and he didn't receive it on the stage, making the contest end on a sour note. As a result, Sun Nan was banned from performing on the stages in Da Lian for three years. Sun Nan was forced to stay away from his hometown, performing in Fujian, Hebei, Tianjin, Beijing and many other places, experiencing all the hardships of life.

1991 was undoubtedly a lucky year for Sun Nan. In this year, Guangdong Media Publishing House produced a record for Sun Nan, Curved Moon, which was fortunately heard by the famous composer Gu Jianfen. Gu Jianfen is also from Dalian. Sun Nan and Gu Jianfen's sister's son are classmates, so he got the chance to pay a formal visit to Gu Jianfen. After Sun Nan met Gu Jianfen, the song Rain of Petals sang better than its original singer Angus Tung. His tensile voice shocked Gu Jianfen. And then Sun Nan was admitted to the Gu Jianfen Vocal Training Center of China National Song & Dance Ensemble.

In 1992, Sun Nan, as one of Gu Jianfen's top ten disciples, participated in the performance of "Chinese style" in Hong Kong with Mao Amin, Na Ying, Xie Xiaodong, etc., and achieved great success. "92 Chinese style" won Sun Nan, an extensive market in Hong Kong. Shortly after that, the Hong Kong branch in Bertelsmann Music Group, where Andy Lau was, came to Sun Nan and discussed with him on contract signing. In this way, Sun Nan became the first singer in mainland China to sign a contract with an overseas record company.

After signing the contract, Sun Nan left Beijing for Hong Kong, China, and Southeast Asia for five years. During the five years, Sun Nan released three albums in BMG, and We're All Sad People, Life after Life and Understanding. At that time, he held more than ten solo concerts in Malaysia, Singapore and other places, and was the first time a pop singer in mainland China could hold a concert in another country.

In 1996, Li Jie, a close friend of Sun Nan, wrote a song "Keep the Red Flag Flying" to Sun Nan, and Sun Nan was too fond of it to let go of it. Humming the high-spirited lyrics, "Five-star red flag, you're making us so proud. Five-star red flag, so proud of you, " Sun Nan's eyes could not help but reflect the scenes of his wandering overseas in these years. A decision sprouted from his mind to return to mainland China to develop his career.

The most exciting thing for Sun Nan is that he found the key to develop his voice treasure when he returned to mainland China. His singing is implicit or passionate in proper situations. Following this direction, he released many songs, including Back to Your Heart, Blow

Up to North, and Just You Are Here, Young Justice Bao's ending theme song, all of which made remarkable achievements. His new albums, Go there and be Healed and Aurora, were all popular at home and abroad.

In the next few years, Sun Nan won a number of awards in the awards ceremony with his strength. But he is very modest, and he often said: "up to now, I can't say how good I am, but I believe that I have been working hard on the road of music. I have been holding the idea to move before moving others."

In 2003, Sun Nan released his new album, Heaven's Destiny, in which he composed many of the songs. In July, he was chosen by Disney as the only singer of the theme song of the Chinese version of the animated film Finding Nemo. In August, his seventh album was released, which is a collection of interlude songs of the hottest movies and TV plays at that time, including Jade Goddess of Mercy, Decade of Marriage, and The Legend of the Condor Heroes. In September, he held the Marvellous Nan Tour, his first solo concert in mainland China in his career, on the stadium of Changchun.

Sun Nan will put his whole heart and passion for singing. He said: "I always believe that the music that can move me can also move you. I hope my music can make your keen tentacles extend in all directions."

Data source: According to the report on the 19th issue of China Youth in 2003.

Selling pork is more technically difficult than selling computers

It is almost impossible for college students who just graduated from making a living by selling pork. Years ago, the news that Lu Buxuan, who graduated from Peking University, was a butcher once spread all over the country and triggered a large-scale debate on whether this behavior wastes talents. However, a few years later, Chen Sheng, who also graduated from Peking University, quietly entered the pig industry and opened nearly 100 pork chain stores in just one year. In an interview, Chen Sheng surprised the public, " Selling pork is more technical than selling computers ."

Arouse the idea of resigning due to a paper

Chen Sheng, born in Zhanjiang, Guangdong Province, is a Bachelor of Economics from Peking University and an EMBA from Tsinghua University. After graduating in 1984, he was assigned to a government office in Guangzhou. Three years later, he decided to turn to businesses. When it came to why he gave up such an enviable secure job, Chen Sheng said with a smile that, at that time, he was the only one who was admitted to the office with an economic background. One day, he had nothing to do and wrote a paper titled "China will enter the era of free economy sooner or later," which was published later. But somehow, his paper got known by his boss. After reading the paper, his boss called him to the office and believed that there was something wrong with his ideas.

"I was depressed at that time. I felt that I was out of tune with the colleagues and atmosphere of the office, and could not find any advantages in the work." Chen Sheng said that he likes to make decisions on specific things on his own. But in that working environment, he couldn't handle matters in accordance with his personality. It can be said that he made the decision to quit the office due to the paper.

Earn the first pot of gold by growing vegetables

In order to make a living after resigning, Chen Sheng became a haunting peddler and began to sell clothes on the stall. After selling clothes for months, he fetched a small fortune. One day, he went to a relative's house in a village in Zhanjiang. On the same day, his relative carried more than 50 kg of radish planted by him on the street for sales. However, due to the bad weather at that time, his relative only earned ten Yuan by selling 5 kg of radish. That day, other farmers in the village had similar experiences. All of them were so furious that they sat on the ground complaining that they would not grow vegetables the next year.

However, Chen Sheng, who was on the side at that time, was inspired by this sentence. According to economic principles, the price will rise when supply is less than demand. So he contracted 100 mu of vegetable land with his savings from selling clothes and led some vegetable farmers to cultivate the land. He found that in addition to supply and demand, the price of vegetables was most affected by the weather. Especially the day before the Siberian cold current approached Guangzhou, the weather was sultry and the vegetables were sold at an extremely low price. Then Chen Sheng took the opportunity to buy all the vegetables that were available on the market. On the day when it cooled down, it was the time for the festival. Most of the farmers did not sell vegetables in the market. "The purchase price is 0.1 Yuan, half a kilogram, and the selling price is 0.6 Yuan, half a kilogram." Chen Sheng said that the sale made him the first pot of gold in his life, amounting to more than 100,000 Yuan. After that, he began to engage in the business reselling vegetables. With regard to his understanding of the impact of the weather on vegetable prices, Chen Sheng said with a smile that he kept his mouth shut until he went back to chat with the vegetable farmers eight years later.

Two phone calls gave birth to vinegar drinks

In 1993, with the first bucket of gold, Chen Sheng began to devote himself to the real estate industry in Zhanjiang. In only three years, he became one of the top three real estate developers in Zhan Jiang. In consideration of some of the insecurity factors beyond the law involved in the real estate industry, Chen Sheng began to switch to manufacturing drinks. "I wanted to make a pure carbonated drink." Chen Sheng added that the phone calls from two of his friends changed his fate just as his research and development of pure carbonated drinks entered a final stage.

Chen Sheng said that, at that time, they called him to stop developing carbonated drinks, as vinegar drinks were in vague during that period. It turned out that a leader of the state chose sprite mixed with vinegar as a new way of drinking during their inspection in Zhanjiang, and then vinegar drinks became popular for a while. Chen Sheng carried out a market survey and found that everyone directly mixed vinegar with Sprite, but there was no ready-made vinegar drink. Immediately, he decided to make vinegar drinks.

Buy pork in the food market and engage in the pork industry

"I like to do something in an unknown field or in a more complex environment to satisfy some of my desires, including selling pork." Chen Sheng said he decided to engage in the pork industry when he bought pork in the food market. He found that this industry was misunderstood by others, and the profession was also misunderstood, as well as many other things. The annual output value of Guangzhou's pork market is several billion Yuan a year. Why didn't anyone further develop it? With such doubts and huge market temptation, Chen Sheng began to invest in the pork industry. He believes that the more neglected the industry is, the greater the chance it will be.

He explained that if he sold computers, he would have to compete with large enterprises, such as Lenovo, but he still had an advantage over his competitors when he chose to sell pork. He intended to make some great achievements in the pork industry. For example, others can sell a pig or half a pig, and he can sell more than a dozen pigs. It conforms to the capabilities of graduates from Peking University.

For the view that selling pork is more technical than selling computers, Chen Sheng explained that selling computers is to assemble all kinds of hardware and then sell them to consumers. Assembly is a technique, and he can do it as long as he learns it for some time. But for those who sell pork, how to divide and match fat meat, lean meat, ribs and other parts determines whether the dealers can make a profit or loss. It is extremely variable.

He gave an example that, if it is lean meat, it's not delicious if it's completely lean, while it does not taste good if it is too fat. In terms of taste, it may be best to add 3% of fat meat, but it can not be taught from the perspective of operation. It may be based on the hand of the dealer. It is the embodiment of techniques.

So in 2006, Chen Sheng built his pig farm near the boundary between Zhanjiang and Guangxi Province. Since 2007, he has opened a pork stall in Guangzhou to sell pork. In just one year, Chen Sheng's pork stall has developed into the largest pork chain store in Guangzhou City and even Guangdong Province.

Data source: Anonymous. A graduate from Peking University opened hundreds of pork chain stores. (http://www.jiameng.com/, 2009-01-10.)

Part III Hold the Steering Wheel of Success

With the right direction and goal, we need to follow the right path to achieve the goal, just like we have to hold the steering wheel if we want to drive to the destination smoothly. In order to hold the steering wheel on the road to success, we must resolutely implement two iron laws. One is to stay focused and control our attention, and the other is to enhance the self-discipline and control ourselves.

Chapter 6 Control Your Attention

Maxims for Success

Focus on the things that pay the most, and don't waste your time on things that do no good for success. Focus on one thing at a time and put yourself into it with a positive desire to succeed. Don't let your mind slide into other things, other needs, or other ideas. Focus on the important project you've decided to do and give up everything else. Successful people will focus on one thing at a time, and will not be distracted. As a result, they will know everything but are not proficient in any of them. —Napoleon Hill

Principles and Guidelines

When people have made clear the goal, they have already selected what they should concentrate on. At this time, we should forget the proverb of never putting the eggs in one basket. Instead, we should put the eggs in one basket and control our attention to protect the basket and successfully lead it to the market. To control our attention is to coordinate all thoughts and abilities and guide them to make joint efforts to achieve a set goal. On the one hand, attention control is the natural product of the interaction of other principles of success, while on the other hand, it is the most important auxiliary tool to ensure the implementation of these principles. It is like shooting a target. First, it needs to determine a bull's eye (established goal). You then aim precisely, hold your breath, pull the trigger and hit the bull's eye. The purpose of attention control is to make your mind aim at a clear goal and constantly think and act, and finally find a feasible way to achieve the established goal. Therefore, controlling attention is not only the concrete manifestation of controlling inner power but also the highest form of self-control. If you can subdue your mind, there will be nothing beyond your control.

A dedicated goal: "I do just one thing."

When Success Magazine celebrated its 100th anniversary in the United States, its editors excerpted some excellent articles from the earlier issues, one of which was impressive. Theodore Rosser, the author of the article, paid a visit to Thomas Alva Edison, the world-famous inventor, three weeks after setting up a tent outside his laboratory. The following is part of the interview:

Rosser: "What is the primary element of success?"

Edison: "It is the ability to apply the energy of your body and mind to the same problem and never feel bored. You work all day, don't you? Everyone does. If you get up at 7 a.m. and go to bed at 11 p.m., you've been handling affairs for 16 hours. For most people, they must have been doing something. The only difference is that they do a lot of things, and I do just one thing. If they spend their time in one direction and one purpose, they will be bound to succeed."

Edison's experience that "I do just one thing," is exactly the magic weapon that he obtained more than 1000 invention patents and became the king of invention. Whoever has mastered this magic weapon will be able to achieve success.

For instance, Andrew Carnegie has been focusing on steel and ultimately turned out to be a steel tycoon of the United States. John Davison Rockefeller has always been focused on oil and turned out to be the king of oil. Henry Ford has always been focused on automobiles and turned out to be the king of automobiles, and so forth.

It can be seen that concentration is a magic key to success, which can constitute an irresistible force. Furthermore, it is the key to the door to wealth, honor and health.

All the great talents of our human beings develop via the magic power of concentration. However, if we want to give full play to the power of this magic key, we must focus our mind on a specific desire, find out the way to achieve this desire, and successfully put it into practical action until the ultimate goal is achieved.

Gardeners know that after they cut most of the buds, nutrients can be concentrated on a few so that more beautiful flowers can bloom.

Being a man is like cultivating flowers and trees. Instead of devoting all their energy on many meaningless things, young men and women should focus on an important career that is suitable for them, concentrate all their energy and work hard, and then they will be bound to make remarkable achievements.

The reason why countless losers in the world fail is not that they are not talented enough, but that they are not focused and can not do their best to do what is proper. The greatest waste in the world is that a person unnecessarily distributes his precious energy to many different things. We have limited time, capacity, and resources. If we want to be able to know everything and do everything well, we will never be able to accomplish it. If you want to achieve anything in any area, you must keep this rule in mind.

In the current era, it is required to be refined and specialized instead of being extended and general. In this era, the division of labor is more and more detailed, and the specialized fields are more and more refined. If a person distracts his energy, he is doomed not to succeed. Wise people are the most aware of concentrating all their energy on one thing. Only in this way can they achieve their goals. In addition, the wise are also adept in striving to win in the fierce competition for survival with their unyielding will and persevering willpower.

Carlyle, master of science of success, said: "even the weakest life will achieve something once it focuses on one goal, and the most powerful life will ultimately achieve nothing if it distracts the energy. Water constantly dripping wears holes in the most solid stone; the turbulent river flows all the way, leaving no trace behind." The greatest people are those who go all out and chisel incessantly. Then they hammer and hammer at the same place until they realize their desires. The successful people in our era are those who are omniscient in their own fields, unswerving to their goal, and thoroughly engrossed in what they are doing, and always endeavoring to do still better. In a word, if you do something in an extensive and miscellaneous way, you will lose. But if you do something in a specialized and refined way, you will win.

Attention control and the law of harmonious attraction

When we can master the principle of attention control and apply it, we can find that we will benefit a lot from the principle. It can adjust our thoughts and help us get rid of all the negative moods from our thoughts so that we will be free from these moods. Therefore, the law of harmonious attraction, proposed by Napoleon Hill, can be achieved.

The law of harmonious attraction refers to the natural tendency of combining forces and things that can meet each other's needs. For example, the 18 principles of the science of success are not isolated from each other or irrelevant but are closely related to each other and supplementary to each other. The practice of other principles helps to control your attention. In the same way, the effective control of your attention also helps other principles to play a better role. It involves the following aspects:

Control your attention and make a clear goal

Determine what we want, make plans to get them, and act on them. All three tasks require us to concentrate most of our thoughts and efforts on a single goal. We need a specific object that enables us to focus on it. Once we select this object, it will get closer and closer to us, and we will see it more and more clearly.

Control your attention and establish a mastermind alliance

One of the preliminary effects of attention control is to establish a mastermind alliance. We must carefully organize this alliance and rely on their assistance to achieve our goal. At the same time, due to the collective operation of a mastermind alliance, it will increase our confidence, independence, imagination, creativity, personal enterprising spirit, enthusiasm, and will to win. So it reinforces our attention. If we can be aided and encouraged by others, we can always move forward to the road to success; otherwise, if we fight alone, we are likely to make slow progress, and may even feel depressed and retreat.

Control your attention and have the confidence to win

After defining the goal and organizing a mastermind alliance, we should show our confidence in achieving the goal with indomitable dedication. It's much easier to focus on what you think will succeed than on what is unlikely to succeed, so there will be some space available for your confidence by making efforts to control your attention so as to allow your confidence to grow sturdily. In a manner of speaking, the power of confidence is combined with the results of attention control, and they can give each other great power.

Control your attention and have a positive mental attitude

After completing the above steps, we will inevitably have a positive mental attitude. At this time, we have seen the evidence that we are approaching success and the self-limits that may cause our fear, doubt and depression will disappear completely. As we busy ourselves with achieving our definite goal, we will not hesitate or delay anymore, and we will not tolerate any other negative thoughts.

Control your attention and give a little more

To give a little more requires us to practice constantly. This principle should become an attitude and style we should adopt when we do anything. When we apply this principle, controlling our attention will enable us to be more energetic and stimulate our inner enthusiasm and enhance our confidence in the mastermind alliance. In the meantime, the process will strengthen a positive mental attitude, making it easier for us to control our attention.

Control your attention and have the personal enterprising spirit

Similar to the principle of giving a little more, attention control has a considerable impact on our enterprising spirit. Moreover, any positive things that arise from the enterprising spirit will enhance our will and then strengthen our ability to control our attention.

Control your attention and have the self-discipline

Self-discipline can allocate and control all the moods, including positive and negative moods, while our emotional strength can be used to help us control our attention. At this moment, our thoughts will function like perfect machines, while there is not any improper operation or friction that may lead to energy loss.

Control your attention and have the creativity

The above principles have already stimulated our imagination. The subconscious with a clear goal will enable us to put our imagination into action, and at the same time, it will produce ideas, plans, and intuitions that surprise us in terms of clarity and feasibility. We will find new opportunities to reach the goal, while others may also take the initiative to cooperate with us.

Control your attention and have correct thinking

Before we take the initiative to cultivate the ability to think in a correct way, we actually stopped guessing and began to make plans based on the known facts and correct assumptions. However, when our plan takes effect, correct thinking becomes an indispensable element. By controlling our attention, it enables us to think in a correct way, so that our attention will be focused only on what needs to be paid attention to.

Control your attention and learn from setbacks

A setback is merely a type of information that requires us to make greater, more, and more determined efforts. It is the fuel to ignite a person's will. We should study the setbacks that we have encountered and learn from the setbacks, so as to help us exercise better control over our attention and strive to achieve the goal.

Control your attention and have enthusiasm

Our enthusiasm will automatically direct our attention to the realization of the goal, and imprint the thoughts lingering in our mind on the subconscious. The process of controlling attention will also lead our enthusiasm to a clear goal. The closer we are to a clear goal, the higher the enthusiasm will be.

Control your attention and have an attractive personality

Controlling our attention is conducive for us to improving various elements that we need to cultivate in our personality, and endows us with the determination to change the bad habits. At the same time, if we can cultivate an attractive personality, we will have a stronger influence and more opportunities, so that there will be more space for us to control our attention.

If we can master the above principles of success, it means that we have taken an important step in terms of controlling our attention and mastering our thoughts. Therefore, we can have a better understanding of and a greater influence on ourselves, the greatest enemy and the best

Control your attention with self-suggestion

If you have been thinking about poverty, failure, and their tragic signs, self-suggestion can adjust your mind to accept that poverty and failure are inevitable. Finally, a sense of poverty and failure will come into being in your mind, which is the reason why many people live in poverty and suffer from repeated failures. On the contrary, if you always want to be rich, successful and brilliant, self-suggestion will also adjust your mind, so that it can accept that being rich and successful can be fully realized. Finally, a sense of wealth and success will come into being in your mind, which is the reason why those who are rich and successful finally achieve success.

If you can concentrate on a positive and clear goal and force it to become your central idea, you are adjusting your self-suggestion so as to make a contribution to the realization of the established goal. Here, we recommend a set of self-suggestion method, which can help us better focus the conscious and subconscious on the positive goal.

Motivate myself: you are the most diligent, and you will succeed!

Expectation for yourself: you want to be an excellent entrepreneur!

Demand yourself: you must work hard!

Praise yourself: You've done a good job!

Criticize yourself: you shouldn't have done that!

Care about yourself: you must take good care of yourself!

Enlighten yourself: you don't want to worry about trifles!

Order yourself: Do it right now!

Examples of success

Liang Boqiang, King of nail clippers

Liang Boqiang has made a big business with an annual sales volume of more than 200 million Yuan for nail clippers, which a big boss doesn't want to do and which a small boss cannot do. He has also become a real king of nail clippers. As the saying goes, in any profession, there is someone who excels all the rest, and it is the king, whether it is on a large or small scale.

A word from the premier moved Liang Boqiang

On October 27, 1997, when Zhu Rongji, then Vice Premier of the State Council of the People's Republic of China, met with representatives of enterprises and workers of the Sinolight Corporation, he especially showed three nail clippers presented to him by a merchant from Taiwan to encourage them to develop China's light industry by adjusting product structure and improving product quality and asked the representatives to pass them on to each other on the spot. Seeing the three beautiful, delicate and sharp nail clippers, Zhu Rongji said with emotion: "we should keep an eye on the market gap to find a way out, such as nail clippers. As for the nail clipper we made, I can't cut my nails after using it one or two times, and I can not cut my nails even with the greatest strength."

One day in May 1998, Liang Boqiang, the boss of Zhongshan Julong Metal Jewelry Co., Ltd., found the above report from an article titled On the Nail Clippers when scanning an old newspaper. Liang Boqiang, who has been in the hardware and accessories business for more than ten years, felt that the competition among his peers was becoming more and more fierce, so he had to find another way to make a breakthrough. This article made him realize that an opportunity to make a breakthrough has come. The prime minister, who was taking into account how to improve the national economy and the people's livelihood, even cared about the tiny nail clippers. It shows that the article is small but the matter is not small and that there must be a blank point and a business opportunity in the market.

Make a profound investigation and exploit the market

In the six months since then, Liang Boqiang almost traveled all over the nail clipper manufacturers who were well-known at home and abroad, collecting various first-hand information about nail clippers. It was found from the investigation that there are more than 160 nail clipper manufacturers in China and that the original top five nail clipper brands are all from state-owned enterprises. However, due to the mechanism and other reasons, these enterprises are all dying or bankrupt. However, the private enterprises or self-employed people who replace the state-owned enterprises, due to their consciousness, capital, technology and other reasons, produce relatively rough products, and they are largely identical with only minor differences. Therefore, the competition between them is almost concentrated on the price, and the nail clippers priced at the tenths of Yuan account for the vast majority, so these enterprises can only earn small profits. The growing high-end market is monopolized by world-famous brands, such as the brand 777 from South Korea and the brand Zhong from Japan, which has quietly had access to the Chinese market. And the unit price varies from a few Yuan to dozens of Yuan. In Europe, the highest unit price of the nail clippers of Zwilling from Germany is even hundreds of Yuan. Liang Boqiang saw that although the nail clippers are small, they are almost necessities in daily life. There are more than 6 billion people in the world, indicating that nail clippers have a large market.

Re-orientation and brand building

In a European survey, Liang Boqiang found that the nail clippers there were sold in pharmacies or personal care stores and were identified as beauty products or personal care tools. In China, nail clippers can only be sold with a kitchen knife, key chain and other products, and it is identified as daily hardware supplies. The difference in product orientation determines the high price of nail clippers in developed countries and regions and the low price in China. At that time, this discovery made Liang Boqiang have a clear idea of the way out for the nail clipper industry in China. As the living standard of citizens in China has been constantly improved, more and more people in China will accept the idea that nail clippers are personal care tools, just as vanishing cream has evolved into skin cream. Therefore, from the beginning of investing in nail clippers project, Liang Boqiang designed and produced nail clippers according to the standards of personal care tools, and selected the corresponding marketing channels.

In terms of design, he changed the approach of similar appearance of other enterprises' products, adopting different designs according to the needs of different users. For example, children's nail clippers are designed with lively cartoon images, and women's nail clippers are designed with fashionable romantic colors. In order to avoid splashing the clipped finger shell into the eyes, he added a cover to the nail clipper.

Since it is positioned as a high-end item, it is necessary to be in line with the international standard from the perspective of quality, and it is not allowed to let the inferior products in the Chinese market mix with his products. For this reason, Liang Boqiang invested 10 million Yuan in introducing equipment and high-quality raw materials, and invited professional talents such as Li Guoxiong, the former deputy technical director of Guangzhou Nail Clipper Plant, to improve the traditional technology on the basis of studying and drawing experience from foreign production technology. In particular, he carried out technological innovation on the cutting edge, changing the traditional extrusion type to shear type, so as to improve the sharpness. After 11 months of research, a new generation of nail clippers named St-allen came out. Through strict inspection by the National Quality Supervision and Inspection Center for Metal Products, all indicators of the new nail clippers reached or exceeded those of the Korean products that dominate the international nail clipper market, while the price of St-allen products is only 60% of that of South Korea.

Select new channels and avoid competition

Prior to the launch of St-allen, nail clippers had been basically excluded by large shopping malls or state-owned commercial enterprises because of their small profits. They could only flow to small and medium-sized stores or even local stalls through the wholesale market nationwide in China. Liang Boqiang chose the distribution channel of beauty products to sell " St-allen" nail clippers, avoiding the competition with other nail clipper products. In order to reduce the circulation link and facilitate the management, Liang Boqiang only set the first-level distributors, which directly exchange with the retailers or group customers. Liang Boqiang, a gifted ornament maker, attaches great importance to the gift market of nail clippers. And the nail clipper products made in China can be included in the list of gifts, which almost started from St-allen.

The benefits doubled with clever public relations activities

Because the profit of small nail clippers is not enough to support large-scale advertising investment, Liang Boqiang attracted the attention of the media and the public through clever public relations activities. On the evening of September 20, 1999, Zhu Rongji, then Premier of the State Council, visited the large achievement exhibition to celebrate the 50th anniversary of the founding of the People's Republic of China. When he came to the light industry exhibition area, Chen Shineng, then director of the State Light Industry Bureau, delivered the set of St-allen nail cutting products to Premier Zhu. On October 8, 2000, St-allen Company was authorized by the National Daily Hardware Standardization Center to draft the industry standard of nail clippers of the people's Republic of China.

Liang Boqiang's efforts in brand building have finally paid off. Since 2000, St-allen has occupied more than 70% of the medium and high-end market share of the nail clipper industry in China. At the beginning of 2001, St-allen was awarded "the first brand of nail clippers industry in China in 2000" by China National Hardware Association. The sales of St-allen basically doubled: 40 million Yuan in 1999, 70 million Yuan in 2000, 120 million Yuan in 2001, and 200 million Yuan in 2002.

Data source: Qiao Guodong, Liu Ruiting. Liang Boqiang, King of nail clippers in China. (China Economic Times, 2004-05-24.)

Concentration and paranoia of Zhang Yue

"Only paranoia can succeed," said Andrew S. Grove, former president of Intel Corporation. Zhang Yue probably belongs to the type of paranoia he talked about.

"At a certain stage, I have a strong interest in something, and even can forget myself. It is one of the necessary qualities for those successful people. Everyone who succeeds is stubborn to some extent." Zhang Yue said.

Zhang Yue appreciates his fanaticism and concentration. He believes that it is such a paranoid passion that drives him to success and gives him an impetus to surpass himself. “When I developed the first air conditioner, I lost more than 10 kg in more than half a month. From the first generation to the ninth generation now, I had become extremely feverish nine times,” He said, “I’ve got inspired from the fanatical passion and it also drives me to devote much more to my career.” In addition, he said, “maybe tomorrow, when I'm no longer crazy about air conditioning, I'll shift my attention and be interested in high-end articles. it is likely to be cooperation in solar technology, as long as it can produce some economic benefits. No matter what it is, I will devote myself to it and get crazy again.”

However, Zhang Yue said he had never been crazy about making money. “If entrepreneurship is a tennis competition, money is like a scoreboard when you play tennis,” he said, “and if you only focus on the scoreboard and don't pay attention to the ball, you will not receive the ball or play the ball with no strength, you will never succeed. For entrepreneurs, it is of great significance to take both into account.”

It can be seen that the concentration and paranoia of Zhang Yue are limited to specific objects, rather than his concentration and paranoia on everything. People's time and energy are limited. Focusing on everything will only lead to focusing on nothing. Zhang Yue has a good command in this aspect, as he only focuses on the knowledge and technology he is interested in, but not on money. In this way, he can make some achievements in his career.

Data source: Dang Ning. A Chinese billionaire talked about how he got rich. (Harbin: Harbin Publishing House, 2004.)

Chapter 7 Enhance Your Self-discipline

Maxims for Success

Self-discipline allows you to control yourself, starting with controlling your thoughts and actions. If you can't control your mind, you will be unable to control your behavior. People think before they act. The concrete expression of self-discipline is willpower. Will is the master of thought. It has the right to command all your spiritual activities. But this right comes from constant and ethical practice. Willpower trained by self-discipline is an irresistible force.—Napoleon Hill

Principles and Guidelines

Self-discipline allows you to control yourself. It is to control people's thinking and behavior as a starting point, gradually developing a habit, while people's success and failure are the product of habit. We all have certain habits, but because human beings are animals who are dynamic and can think, we also have the ability to change our current habits. Self-discipline is the most important function in cultivating and maintaining the habit of thinking in order to achieve a clear goal. If you can't control your thoughts, you will be unable to control your behavior. Self-discipline can help you develop a rational thinking mode, guide your thoughts, control your emotions, and guide your behaviors with a positive mental attitude and a clear goal, so as to make you achieve the ultimate success.

Control your emotions

Most people act first before thinking about the consequences of their actions, which is the root cause of why blind and spontaneous actions are so great in number and why there are always more losers than winners. In contrast, self-discipline requests you to plan before you act. To enhance your self-discipline, you should first control your emotions.

There are two main types of human emotions: one is a positive emotion, and the other is a negative emotion. No matter what kind of emotion, it is a kind of psychological state, and it is the object that you should control. You can imagine how dangerous it would be if you didn't control those negative emotions. For example, in daily life, people are often seen to have a sudden stroke, paralysis, or heart attack or even death under the fury. But you also need to understand that once a positive mental attitude and self-discipline eliminate the harmful elements of negative emotions, they can also make a contribution to realizing the goal.

For example, in some cases, fear and hatred can lead you to leave your life or death out of consideration, so that you can cut off all means of retreat to arouse bolder and more thorough actions. As a result, you tend to bring back to life and health and tide over the crisis. Also, if you can't consciously control those positive emotions, they may lead to devastating results. For example, although you won't succeed without enthusiasm, if enthusiasm gets out of control, you may monopolize the content of the conversation and finally have the final say alone. In this way, other people won't talk to you, let alone offer you advice and help. In short, if you can exercise proper control over the power of emotion, it may allow you to make achievements. But if you allow it to develop freely, it may throw you into the abyss of failure and lead you to run into bumps and bruises.

In addition, we need to understand that emotions can only be controlled, not destroyed. Emotion is like a river. You can build a dam to block it, control and channel it, but you can't restrain it forever. Otherwise, sooner or later, the dam will completely collapse and cause an even more serious disaster.

Emotions can give you impetus and make you turn decisions into concrete actions, but before you release your emotions, including both negative and positive emotions, make sure that you must test them with your rationality, because irrational emotions are bound to be terrible enemies. Self-discipline requires you to balance your emotions with your rationality. That is to say, before you make a decision, you should learn to balance rationality and sensibility. Sometimes, you should eliminate all sensitive ideas but only accept the rational ones. Sometimes you have to accept more sensitive ideas and use your rational ideas for modifications. It is what we often talk about the doctrine of the mean.

At all times and in all countries, the truly great people tend to be able to dominate their own emotions and mind. They are people with chemical minds, which means that they are good at managing their emotions. They can eliminate worry and relieve boredom, just as chemists neutralize acidity with alkalinity. Anyone will have worries in their mind, and he should guide himself with the power of reason and relieve all kinds of depressions in his mind with proper methods. When your heart is full of pessimism, extreme and hatred emotions, you will become optimistic, harmonious, and friendly as long as you immediately turn to the opposite emotions. It's like regulating the water temperature. When the water is too hot, turn on the tap of the cold water pipe, and the hot water will immediately cool down. A person with a chemical mind knows how to use happiness to alleviate his depressed mind and eliminate his depressed thoughts. Because such people know all kinds of ways to manage their emotions, their hearts will not suffer from all kinds of pain, and such people are more likely to succeed. Once a person has a healthy thought, his unhealthy thought will lose its living space, because healthy thought and unhealthy thought are irreconcilable with each other.

Orison Swett Marden once said, "emotion is the wind that blows the boat of our life forward, while reason is the rudder that drives the boat. If there is no wind, the ship will not advance; if there is no rudder, the ship will lose its way." You should skilfully combine emotion and reason, drive the boat of life, and run steadily to the other side of success.

Understand the structure of your thoughts

In order to enhance your self-discipline, it is also necessary to understand the structure of thoughts while controlling your emotions well. Human thought can be divided into six parts, each of which is controlled by human consciousness. Understanding these six parts will help you understand what is the self-discipline and enhance your self-discipline. The six parts are as follows:

Sense of self-respect

The sense of self-respect is the source of willpower and the most valuable thing you have. You must control and exercise your sense of self-respect, a treasure above price for you because it can help you accomplish anything you want. Among the six parts of the thought, the sense of self-respect plays a role as the supreme judicial court, which has the power to judge, overturn, amend, change and eliminate all other parts of the work. Therefore, be sure to regard your sense of self-respect as your most valuable asset and protect it as if it were life.

Emotion

Emotion is the engine to enable your thoughts, plans, and goals to be put into action. Self-discipline requires that emotion must be controlled. First, as mentioned before, your emotions should be balanced with your reason. Secondly, we should forget the unhealthy emotions caused by the negative memories hidden in our minds, such as the psychological emotions of fear, depression, inferiority, and despair arising from past setbacks and failures. Self-discipline doesn't allow you to have any negative memories in your mind. You shouldn't waste your time on things that have changed with the passage of time. In short, you should not look back, but forward. If you insist on looking back, it will only destroy your creativity, destroy your enterprising spirit, disturb your reason, and disrupt all six parts of your thought. As long as you can look forward, you can overcome the negative emotions in your heart and have the opportunity to open the door to hope, desire and confidence.

Reason

Reason is the tool you use to weigh, eliminate, and evaluate your imagination and emotion in a correct way. If the sense of self-respect is the Supreme Judicial Court, the function of reason is just like the trial work in the Supreme Judicial Court. Reason will evaluate what is created by imagination, revise the emotion, and approve the decision made by consciences. You should train your reason by observing, researching and analyzing the thinking activities of truth.

Imagination

Imagination is the source of wisdom for you to make plans and create methods so as to achieve the goal. All your creative efforts and new ideas arise from your imagination, and you must allow your reason to cautiously control the activities of your imagination, and focus on your imagination to serve your definite goal, instead of making blind and disorderly conjectures. Since imagination is the mother of all newly emerging things, it's a priceless treasure for you to go to the road to success.

Conscience

Conscience is the supervisor to test whether your plans and goals conform to ethical justice. Your consciences are constantly monitoring whether your thoughts and actions are morally just. If you can always accept the censorship of consciences and follow its advice, it can make you praised and respected by the public. If you don't follow the advice of consciences, you may be increasingly alienated from the member of your mastermind alliance and cut off from the power of infinite intelligence, and be full of fear at all times. You may even blaspheme against morality, violate the law, and fall into the hell of darkness.

Memory

Memory is the repository of all your knowledge, experience, and all the feelings and Inspirations from infinite intelligence. Memory allows you to remove all the memories that you feel dissatisfied with from the repository so that it has more space to accommodate positive memories. When you need the contents of these memories, you can call them out at any time.

The task of self-discipline is to coordinate these six parts of thought and exercise effective control over them. The direct goal it pursues is to focus and coordinate all personal efforts to achieve the spiritual harmony that is required to march towards the road of success.

Enhance your willpower

What makes emotion and reason come to a balance? The answer is willpower. Self-discipline will enable your willpower to be the backing of emotion and reason, and strengthen their performance.

The concrete expression of self -discipline is willpower. Willpower is the master of the whole thought. It has the power to command all your spiritual activities to achieve a balance between emotion and reason. Moreover, the power comes from your persistent and moral practice.

Willpower, which is trained via self-discipline, is a power that we can not resist. People's willpower has great power. It can overcome all difficulties, no matter how long it takes, how much it costs, and it will last until we ultimately achieve the goal of success. Willpower will approach when wisdom has failed, and genius can do nothing. Wit and skills think it impossible and other abilities are at a loss what to do, and it is declared to give up all hope. With willpower, we can overcome all kinds of difficulties and help us to win and succeed.

As the saying goes, if one works with constant effort, one can grind an iron rod into a needle. Edison also said, "once I make up my mind and know which direction to work hard towards, I will take my courage in both hands in the face of danger and try again and again until the final result is achieved." If a person changes his mind constantly, even a genius, he will eventually become tired and bored. Only with perseverance and willpower can we wait until the day of success by holding on what we are doing consistently and accumulating it little by little.

The experience of many successful people has proved that success depends more on people's perseverance and willpower than on people's talent or friends' support and other favorable conditions. Perseverance and willpower are the souls of conquerors. They are the most powerful supports for human beings to resist fate, for individuals to fight against the world and for the spirit to resist material. They are also the essence of the philosophy of success. Those who are not strong-willed tend to fail to achieve great things and can not be trusted and supported by others. Only those who have clear goals, firm confidence and determination, and tenacious willpower will be able to create everything, be trusted by others, play their own talents, and finally achieve success.

Examples of success

Aleksandr Isayevich Solzhenitsyn wrote Krasnoe koleso (The Red Wheel)

When talking about the principle of self-discipline, Napoleon Hill once mentioned a model of the people who made great achievements based on self-discipline. He was Aleksandr Isayevich Solzhenitsyn, a Russian novelist, and historian. Let's see how he disciplined himself.

Russian oppressors imprisoned Aleksandr Isayevich Solzhenitsyn in the Gulag prison camps (Gulag is an acronym formed from the official Soviet designation of its system of prisons and labor camps) for several years. During his imprisonment, he not only survived but also wrote about the situation at that time. At that time, he was writing on a strict schedule, even when he was exiled to the United States.

Before returning to Soviet Russia to participate in the national reform campaign, he got up at 6 o'clock every morning and began to write after having a simple breakfast. At noon, after a brief lunch, he continued to write until evening, and sometimes he may even write till the next dawn. At that time, he didn't allow the phone to interfere with his writing, or even rarely went out. Finally, through hard work, Aleksandr Isayevich Solzhenitsyn wrote a series of novels, Krasnoe koleso (The Red Wheel).

In order to complete this important series of novels, even after the downfall of the Russian oppressors, he refused to return to Russia immediately. At that time, he was very clear that once he returned to Russia, he would have interfered with a lot, which would affect his writing. He must spare no time and concentrate on finishing his work. He was not shaken by countless social activities and opportunities to appear on TV to be determined to accomplish his goal, although he could take advantage of these opportunities to promote his works. In the end, his self-discipline spirit helped him finish The Red Wheel.

From the story of Aleksandr Isayevich Solzhenitsyn, we can see that self-discipline is like a pipeline, through which people must show all their strength so as to achieve the goal of success so that they can ultimately achieve success. If your personal strength is compared to an automobile, the self-discipline is like driving the automobile. The automobile has a strong power, but it can not run without skilled driving. Only by a skilled driver's driving can it become a safe, fast, and comfortable means of transportation. On the contrary, it will become a creepy road killer like a wild horse running wild. Therefore, we can release the appropriate amount of power from the storage of potential power in a planned and controlled way and guide it in the right direction. It is the essence of self-discipline.

Data source: Napoleon Hill. Napoleon Hill's Road To Success (S. F. Zhang, Trans.). (Haikou: Hainan Publishing House, 1999.)

Qiu Bojun, " Bill Gates in China"

Born in 1964 in a remote and barren village in Zhejiang Province, Qiu Bojun used to go out to beg for food with his parents. He knew that it was not easy for him to go to school by his parents, so he redoubled his efforts to study. In 1980, he was admitted to the university with a full mark in mathematics. In 1988, he joined Hongkong Kingsoft Corporation.

In order to develop the WPS 1.0 system, he lived in a basement to program on a 386 PC almost to the gross neglect of his meals and sleep. During this period, he ate instant noodles when he was hungry, drank tap water when he was thirsty, and lay for a while when he was sleepy. And he stayed indoors, isolated from the world, working day and night like an overloaded machine. As a result, he had to be admitted to the hospital three times a year because of liver disease, but he still urged the hospital to allow him to move the computer to the ward to keep on programming. After 13 months of hard work, China's earliest word processor, WPS 1.0, finally came out. He was just 25 years old and was rated as Bill Gates of China.

In the face of strong competition from Microsoft, he embarked on a long journey to develop WPS 97. To raise funds, he sold his villa worth two million Yuan, and worked 14 hours a day for four years, and finally managed to develop WPS 97 in 1997. WPS 97 surpassed Microsoft Word in software sales because of its low price and high quality. Bill Gates admitted that WPS seems to be more suitable for the habits of the Chinese people.

Data source: Zhang Yanrui, Wei Xuefen, Qiu Bojun. Qiu Bojun's chivalrous complex. (China Enterprise News, 2007-04-13.)

How did I learn English?

I was born in a poor peasant family. I went to primary school in the countryside, and in the early 1950s, there was no condition for English classes in the school. Although I was admitted to the junior high school in the county town, there were no English classes offered in the high school at that time. After graduating from junior high school, I was recommended to study in a normal secondary school by the school committee, while there were still no English classes available. During my studies in normal secondary school, I was honored to join the Communist Party of China because I was politically motivated and had an excellent moral and academic performance. I was also approved by the school to graduate one year ahead of schedule. At that time, I was eighteen years old. Moreover, I was appointed to the faculty upon graduation as the secretary of the Communist Youth League and the teacher for politics classes. After working for four years, I was recommended by the school to release me from my work and take up advanced studies in the university as I had an outstanding performance at work and I was younger than other colleagues. After I was admitted to the university, it was just the time for the educational revolution in the university, and then I worked in the factory and in the countryside in a work-study model. Although there were English classes in the school, I only had two classes and then the Cultural Revolution broke out. For the above reasons, I had no chance to receive systematic English education from primary school to university.

After graduating from college, in response to Chairman Mao Zedong's call, I received three years of education for the poor and lower-middle peasants in the countryside and then took part in the education work for the second time through redistribution. I worked in a combined junior and senior high school under a super large military and industrial enterprise in China. I served as the deputy leader of the political and industrial group of the party branch of the school and taught political courses at the same time. During this period, I had no chance to learn English.

In the 1960s and 1970s, political movements continued in China and tended to expand due to the prevalence of the ultra-Left trend of thought. When I was in my 30s, I encountered a political movement. Due to the expansion of the movement, I was also quarantined, required to clean every day, write a self-criticism behind closed doors, and accept criticism. It took me from top to bottom and brought me political doom. During this period, I suffered the greatest shock and pressure in my life. But I have been firmly convinced that I do love the Communist Party of China, and I do love Chairman Mao and that I am never a counter-revolutionary. I believe that the Party will give me a fair conclusion.

Although the political movement deprived me of the right to work and increased my pressure, it also gave me a good exercise in my faith and will, and provided me with a large amount of spare time, which was a precious resource for me. I used my spare time to change "bad luck" into "opportunity" and started to learn English by myself from ABC with the help of the radio.

At that time, I insisted on English listening, scanning, writing, and reading every day. During this period, I was hospitalized for eye surgery. Even so, I insisted on studying on the hospital bed. Later, with the popularization of TV, I continued to study English by myself by watching TV until my forties. In this way, I passed the national professional and technical personnel of foreign language grade title examination for intermediary and senior titles. Moreover, I completed the translation of some chapters in the book Human Resource Management: The Canadian Dynamic.

When reviewing the experience of my English studies for more than ten years, I have a profound understanding of the important value of the belief, self-discipline, and willpower to our success. As Mao Zedong said, while the prospects are bright, the road has twists and turns, and where there is a will, there is a way.

Part IV Reinforce the Propeller of Success

In the journal to success, we tend to encounter a lot of difficulties, adversities, setbacks, and even temporary failures. In this case, if we want to succeed in the end, we must strengthen the three propellers of success, keep enthusiastic, give a little more, and do well in learning from setbacks and adversity.

Chapter 8 Keep Enthusiastic

Maxims for Success

Enthusiasm is the mainstream of human consciousness, which enables us to put the knowledge we have learned into action. There are many factors for a person's success, among which the primary one is enthusiasm. Without enthusiasm, you would be unable to give play to whatever ability you have. The relationship between enthusiasm and human beings is like that between steam and locomotive, while enthusiasm is the main driving force of action.—Napoleon Hill

Principles and Guidelines

The relationship between enthusiasm, a positive mental attitude, and successful action is the same as the relationship between gasoline, car engine, and car running. Without gasoline and automobile engine, it is difficult for a car to run; without enthusiasm and a positive mental attitude, it is difficult to take action for success. Therefore, enthusiasm is the primary driving force for success. Enthusiasm is the excitement that comes from the heart and spreads to and fills the human body. A person without enthusiasm is like a car without gasoline or a watch without clockwork. No matter what ability he has, he is unable to play it. In view of this, it's hard for anyone who lacks enthusiasm to win in any situation. Enthusiasm is a great power. When it works together with a positive mental attitude, goal, confidence, willpower and other elements of success, it can turn the shortcomings, disadvantages, adversity, setbacks and even temporary failures and other adverse factors into actions and ultimately achieve unexpected success.

Benefits from controlling your enthusiasm

You can control your mind with a positive mental attitude. In the same way, you can also control your enthusiasm with a positive mental attitude, so that it can continuously inject into the cylinder of your mind engine, and be ignited by the spark of a clear goal, and then push the piston of confidence and personal enterprising spirit to move continuously, so as to promote the mind engine to produce a strong and lasting driving force. However, the key to this change is your ability to control your enthusiasm. Enthusiasm is like gasoline. If you can make good use of it, it will do some meaningful work; if you don't use it properly, it may lead to terrible consequences. Therefore, only by controlling your enthusiasm, can you turn any negative performance and experience into positive performance and experience, and benefit you from the following aspects:

Increase the intensity of your thinking and imagination

To achieve the greatest success in life, you must have a passion for devoting yourself to turning your dreams into reality. Dale Carnegie, the master of science of success, once said, "You will look young if you have faith, but you will look old if you have a doubt. You look young with confidence and old with fear. You are young with hope but old with despair. Years wrinkle your skin, but if you lose enthusiasm, it hurts your soul." It is the best compliment to enthusiasm!

People who are full of enthusiasm in life, no matter what they do, will believe their work is a sacred vocation and have great interest in it. No matter how difficult the work is, it will always be carried out in an unhurried manner. As long as we hold this attitude, we will be bound to achieve success. Ralph Waldo Emerson said, "any great cause has ever been successful because of enthusiasm."

Infect others with your passion

Enthusiasm is a state of consciousness, which not only inspires and motivates you to take action on your goal but also has appeal and appeal to others. As is known to all, the greatest leaders of mankind are those who know how to inspire their followers to give full play to their enthusiasm.

Enable you not to feel the hardship in work and strengthen your physical and mental health

Enthusiasm is a state in which you think about something 24 hours a day, even in your sleep. In fact, it is impossible to think in a conscious state 24 hours a day. However, it is of great significance to be enthusiastic like this. If you do this, your desire will go into the subconscious, allowing you to focus your mind either when you wake up or when you sleep. If you can combine enthusiasm with work, your work will not be hard or monotonous. It has been proved from the deeds of many successful people that enthusiasm will make your whole body full of energy so that you can complete the work twice or three times as much as you normally do when you sleep less than half of the normal duration, and you will not get tired.

Enable you to have a more attractive personality

Enthusiasm is a great power, which can be used to supplement the energy in your body and develop a strong personality. Some people are born with enthusiasm, while others have to work hard to cultivate it. It is easy to develop your enthusiasm by engaging in your favorite job or providing your favorite service. If you can't do your favorite job at present, you can choose another very effective way, which is to regard your favorite job as a goal to strive for. No one can stop you from deciding on your goal for life, and no one can stop you from turning this goal into reality.

Enable you to gain confidence

Enthusiasm allows you to unleash the power of your subconscious mind. At the cognitive level, the average person can't compete with genius. However, most psychologists agree that the power of the subconscious is much greater than that of conscious. As long as you keep enthusiastic, you can greatly exert the power of the subconscious and enhance your self-confidence. If it can be achieved, even ordinary people can do wonder.

Enhance your personal enterprising spirit

If you don't have the ability, but you have enthusiasm, you can gather those who are talented around you with your passion. If you don't have money and equipment, but you have enthusiasm, you can use your enthusiasm to persuade and influence others, so as to get help from others and finally achieve your goal. Therefore, with your passion, you can enhance your personal enterprising spirit and win one victory after another.

How can we cultivate enthusiasm?

Napoleon Hill sums up the experience of successful people and his own personal experience, and puts forward some methods to cultivate enthusiasm, including the following:

Study and be familiar with relevant issues

The precondition of keeping enthusiastic about something is enthusiasm, and the key to being enthusiastic about something is familiarity. Therefore, if you want to be enthusiastic about anything, you must first study and familiarize yourself with those that you are not familiar with at present. After more research, you will be familiar with it. When you are familiar with it, you will easily be interested in it, and then you will be enthusiastic about it. Finally, you will burst out of enthusiasm.

Determine a clear goal

In view of the problems studied, a clear goal to be realized should be determined. Only when you know what you're working for, you'll chase closely without giving up like a hound chasing a rabbit. Then, you will develop great enthusiasm for your work.

Make a plan to achieve your goal

Write down clearly your goal, the plan to reach it, as well as the cost you are willing to pay to reach it.

Carry out your plan immediately and follow it firmly

Whether you are interested in something or enthusiastic about it, it will be reflected in your actions. You should force yourself to take enthusiastic actions. As Professor William James of Harvard University put it, "If you want emotion, you work as if you already have it. And if you pretend that you already have this emotion, it will make you really have such emotion. If you want to be happy, work happily. If you want pain, work in pain. If you want to be enthusiastic, work enthusiastically." Therefore, you need to dig deep into your goal, try to collect relevant information, study it, get familiar with it, and live with it. If you persist in doing so, you will unconsciously become more enthusiastic.

Regularly check the implementation of the plan

You should regularly check the implementation of the plan, discover the deviations, and find out the reasons for them, and take remedial measures immediately. If you fail, you should study the plan carefully and revise it if necessary. However, don't change the plan rashly just because of temporary failure.

Spread good news in time

When someone says, “I have good news,” all people there will stop their work and look at him, waiting for him to tell them. In addition to attracting people's attention, good news can also arouse other people's favorable impression and inspire their motivation and enthusiasm. To develop enthusiasm into a habit, you need to reinforce it with good news continuously.

Reflect on yourself and cheer yourself up every day

To reflect on yourself is to reflect on your own views and attitudes towards life, things, others, and yourself. If your mind is occupied by all kinds of harmful and morbid ideas, there will be a lack of soil for the survival and growth of your enthusiasm. If you want to change this situation, the key is to make your own efforts. You should constantly encourage yourself, cheer yourself up every day, arouse your enthusiasm for life, for others, for things related to yourself, and then let passion run through your whole life.

Make warm-hearted friends and form a mastermind alliance

Emerson said: “what I need most is that someone can instruct me to do what I can.” In other words, what a person needs most is someone to guide and encourage him. Although you can't control your work environment, you can make enthusiastic friends, hire experts with high perspicacity, form a mastermind alliance, and then live with the members. If you can share your enthusiasm with them, you can increase their enthusiasm, while they will also support your enthusiasm. In this way, you can stimulate your vitality by virtue of their enthusiasm and wisdom, and stimulate yourself to think and work in a more enthusiastic and creative way. But it should be noted that you should stay away from those who are spiritless, depressed in spirits, and less energetic and enthusiastic.

Strengthen your confidence and keep optimistic

Amand Sheffield, an evolutionary geneticist, once said, "No one else in the whole history of the world is exactly like you. In all the infinite time that is approaching, there will never be another person like you."

Believe that you are born to be a winner! You are a very special person. In order to protect the right to survive, you had fought against other cells in the survival of the fittest before you were born. When you come to the world and face all practical purposes, When you come into the world, it is all kinds of difficulties and misfortunes that hinder you when you are faced with all the practical purposes. But comparing these difficulties with those overcome in the war of childbirth, the former is less than one-tenth of the latter.

Remember that for living, victory is hidden. If you have such a concept and belief, you will certainly inspire an incomparably strong passion for your career.

Have the courage to cut off all means of retreat under extremely difficult conditions

Napoleon Hill once quoted a story about a general who, in order to win, took risks to carry his soldiers to the enemy's shore by ship, and ordered his subordinates to burn the ship after unloading the equipment. Before the dawn attack, he said to the soldiers, "As you all can see, the ship has been burnt down. Then, we must win this battle. Otherwise, none of us could leave here alive. Now we have only two roads, to win or to die, and no other choice." After the battle, they really won. It is a well-known historical story in ancient China, breaking the caldrons and sinking the boats after crossing.

Napoleon Hill wrote, "if we want to keep victories in the worst and most unfavorable situation, we must burn the ship automatically and cut off all possible means of retreat. Only in this way can we maintain the enthusiasm and mental attitude to win. It is a necessary prerequisite for success."

Break the spider web in the mind

A negative mental attitude weaves various spider webs in mind, and our thoughts tend to be entangled by the webs. Among the webs, inertia is the most powerful spider web. Inertia makes people apathetic, content with the status quo, fail to achieve anything or go on in the wrong direction all the time. For example, part of the reason why poor people are poor is that they are content with poverty, accustomed to poverty and that they have never thought of changing the situation of poverty and creating an abundant life. Therefore, the premise of changing from poor to rich is to break the spider web of inertia, stimulate the desire, enthusiasm, and motivation of becoming rich, and then create a prosperous life. It can be seen that to break the spider web in mind, and we must never be satisfied with the status quo, not only for ourselves but also for the world around us. In this way, we can be inspired from sin to holiness, from failure to success, from misery to happiness, and from disease to health. In a word, it can stimulate our desire, enthusiasm, and motivation to pursue success or wealth.

Dare to challenge yourself

"Challenge yourself," said Napoleon Hill, "Every time you do something, do what you can, do it better and faster than what you do last time, and you can refuse to yield to your peers." Therefore, you should dare to challenge timidity and turn it into courage. Dare to challenge misfortune and turn it into a fortune. Dare to challenge failure and turn it into success. Dare to challenge poverty and turn it into wealth. Dare to challenge all disturbing things and change your destiny and world. As long as a positive mental attitude can guide you, and you can always keep enthusiastic, dare to do what you want, and do not violate the objective laws, there will be nothing impossible for you in the world.

Examples of success

Liu Yonghao: An entrepreneur should be passionate first

Liu Yonghao, born in 1951 in Chengdu, Sichuan Province, is a senior engineer. He is one of the most active and concerned entrepreneurs in China, one of the founders of Hope Group and the chairman of New Hope Group. In 1982, Liu Yonghao and his three brothers resolutely resigned from the public office, which was rather popular at that time, saying goodbye to the comfortable urban life. Then, they went together to Gujia Village, Xinjin County, Sichuan Province, with the plan for getting rich, which had started long. They embarked on the hard journey to start their business with the 1,000 Yuan raised from the sales of four bicycles, four watches and some scrap iron in their home.

Liu Yonghao does not have an eminent family or receive an excellent education. He succeeds because he has grasped the opportunity offered by the times, and he has gone all out in his work with great enthusiasm. His enthusiasm is reflected in the following aspects:

First of all, he is passionate about life. Although he is busy with business every day and has to deal with the difficulties in business operation, he never lets the bad emotions caused by work pressure interfere with his daily life.

Secondly, he has a wide range of interests, especially sports and photography. In his spare time, he often plays around with his camera on his back. When he comes back, he often brings back dozens of films and thousands of photos. In the process of traveling, he is also fond of taking notes. Every year, he can write a dozen big notebooks, and others could not understand many of the things he wrote down. But he felt that it would not only help him remember some details but also exercise the brain.

Finally, his enthusiasm is mainly reflected in the process of entrepreneurship. At the beginning of his business, he resolutely resigned from the envied public office and sold his bicycle and watch as his only possessions. After the failure of his first business, he started work early and rode to sell eggs 40 kilometers away to repay the debt. At that time, when the market was saturated, he withdrew in time, killed all quails in pain, and actively sought new ways to gain wealth. In order to expand the scale and earn more profits, he invested millions or even tens of millions of Yuan in R & D. After that, he not only entered the financial industry and real estate industry but was also involved in the high-tech sector. All of these remarkable actions, again and again, reflect the spirit of Liu Yonghao as an excellent entrepreneur, full of passion.

When it comes to entrepreneurship, Liu Yonghao said: “entrepreneurs should first have passion, dare to imagine, try and explore, and take risks with a rational attitude. Entrepreneurship is involved in passion, dream, diligence, hard work, and exploration.”

Data source: Dang Ning. A Chinese billionaire talked about how he got rich. (Harbin: Harbin Publishing House, 2004.)

Jack Ma: Turn the ideal of a person into the ideal of all with passion

Jack Ma is a passionate person. No matter where he goes, people who have met him may say that he is so excited that these people will also be affected by Jack Ma's passion. It is the embodiment of Ma’s personality charm, and it is such a passion that enables Jack Ma to achieve success finally. When Alibaba was still at its infancy, Jack Ma swore to his entrepreneurial allies, “we're going to run a company for eighty years, and we're going to be in the top 10 among the global websites.” Isn't that passion? Jack Ma affected all people who had contact with him. One of those who had contact with him described Ma like this, “He is like a poison, making all impossibilities possible!”

Joseph Tsai, one of the founders of Alibaba, came to Alibaba because of Jack Ma's passion. It is a dramatic story. Joseph Tsai used to work for an international investment company. He went to Alibaba to discuss the possibility of investment. As a result, he was overwhelmed by Jack Ma's unique personality after several contacts with him. He immediately quit his job with an annual salary of $750,000 and switched to Alibaba, where he received only ¥500 a month. Ma was also surprised by his move. The joining of Joseph Tsai in Alibaba broadened its horizon and brought the connections with Goldman Sachs, a large-scale international investment company.

In May 2000, John Jiong Wu joined Alibaba. As the former chief designer of the Yahoo search engine and many application technologies, he has obtained the core technical patent of search engine granted by the United States Patent and Trademark Office. He was also drawn to Alibaba for Jack Ma's grand vision. The joining of Wu in Alibaba also mobilized a large number of elites of Chinese origin working in Silicon Valley to work for R & D of new products for Alibaba in the United States. These elites joined Alibaba because that Jack Ma has set up such a grand goal for Alibaba that they have been yearning for it.

The joining of these people also made Jack Ma realize that the new ideas and new thinking continuously injected into Alibaba could attract more and more industry elites, which is an important factor for Alibaba to develop into a large-scale corporation. However, the most crucial reason why Alibaba can attract so many talents is Jack Ma's entrepreneurial passion. Ma is not only passionate about his business, but he also affects the group with his passion, so that all the members in the group are sufficiently energetic to march forward courageously. Even in the blue period of Alibaba's development, he would encourage his team to aim high and work hard and strive to retain any of the talents for Alibaba. One ordinary worker in Alibaba used to have extremely negative emotions. After entering Alibaba, she had a monthly pay of 3,000 Yuan, but several months later, she told her friends who had a higher monthly salary than her with pride, "Please do not talk about such silly topics as suicide with me. I am making my contribution to China's e-commerce business." It means that she has said goodbye to the negative state before.

Jack Ma has brought his passion to both the employee and their family members. Jack Ma attaches importance to the feelings of the employee's family members, and he has frequently invited his employees' family members to visit Alibaba, which has made the employee and their family members perceive the power of enthusiasm. After returning home from the visit, the employee are all encouraged by their families to work hard in Alibaba. Jack Ma tends to go anywhere with his passion. Ma believes that young people are passionate, but their love is soon hot and soon cold. However, only when we have a passion for a long time, can we be motivated to make some achievements. For Jack Ma, he could give up his clients or projects, but he could never lose his pursuit, which is his passion. The failure does not mean anything, but it is vital to have the courage to make a comeback. Only with passion can we guarantee our success! Jack Ma declared in the program Win in China, "Entrepreneurs' passion is either on the surface or in mind, while their passion can not be damaged!"

An excellent leader can affect those around him with his passion so that the entire group will keep up with him spontaneously. It is because the people around Jack Ma have seen the bright future from Ma that Alibaba can come to where it is now. "Whenever you see Ma, you can see a confident Ma and the confidence to win from his eyes. You will always be energetic whenever you stay with him." Trudy Dai, vice president of Alibaba Corporation, said. Liu Wei evaluated Jack Ma that he would enable you to see a bright future when you are in despair, and then you would follow in his footsteps. We must be passionate about the ideal in our mind, because only in this way can we devote most of our life to the ideal. When your group is at its infancy, you can release your enthusiasm to its utmost so that other members of the group will be affected, and then they will put their heart and soul into work as you do. Only with the passionate support will your members and clients be more willing to believe in the future you depict for them, and then they will have the courage to have a try on the cake you make for them.

As a proverb goes, passion makes your dream come true. To realize your dream, you need to devote your passion to it. From another point of view, the dream is an essential factor to induce your passion. If an enterprise has any lofty goal, dream or ambition, the goal, dream, or ambition will become the entrepreneur spirit of its middle management and the driving force for an ordinary employee to forge ahead. It allows what is impossible to happen to become possible. A lofty dream is attractive enough for you to work hard throughout your life. If we have sincere love for what we are doing, we will gain an endless force and keep enthusiastic forever.

Data source: Qiu Dong Tong Hua. Jack Ma: Turn the ideal of a person into the ideal of all with passion. (Baidu, 2018-03-17.)

Chapter 9 Give a Little More

Maxims for Success

By giving a little more, you can be convinced that you are doing what is correct and beneficial. It enables you to be more responsible for your conscience and to be confident. Those who will take the initiative to do what they should do before being pressed by others and will not give up halfway are bound to achieve success. Such a person is made clear that he should give a little more and do more than others expect. —Napoleon Hill

Principles and Guidelines

Giving a little more is a mental attitude, a spirit, and an excellent habit that you must make efforts to develop. It is a necessary condition to achieve what you desire. If you are willing to make the efforts exceeding what you can gain, you will be repaid sooner or later. Every seed you sow is bound to take root, sprout, and bloom, and finally produce many times the fruit.

There is a fine line between success and failure

There is a fine line between success and failure. Sometimes, we may cross the boundary unconsciously and then achieve success. Occasionally, we may be unaware of standing on the boundary, cease to advance, and ultimately we might be just one step short of success. Many people will be able to cross the boundary as long as they can give a little more and be a little more patient, and then achieve success. However, at the critical moment, they stop trying and come to a failure.

Before Alexander Graham Bell, many people had claimed that they had invented the phone. The inventors, including Elisha Gray, Thomas Alva Edison, Dole Bair, McDonough, Van Daleway, and De Forest Lee, had a prior patent, among whom De Forest Lee was the only one approaching success. However, the Supreme Court of the United States judged that the invention of the phone should be attributed to Bell. Why? Let's check the conclusions drawn by the Supreme Court as follows:

"Lee had never thought of transforming the language through telecommunications. But Alexander Graham Bell did, so he finally succeeded. In this case, we could not argue that what Lee did was the prelude to Bell's invention. Supporting Lee, we fail, but if we support Bell, we succeed. The difference between the two is merely a gap between success and failure. If Lee had insisted on what he was doing, he might finally succeed, but he ceased to advance. Thus, he failed. On the contrary, Bell had been insisting on what he was doing until he finally achieved a successful result."

There are completely opposite outcomes between the two, as there is a slight difference in a separate screw. Lee did not know that if he had twisted the screw by one-fourth cycle, and converted the intermittent current into constant amplitude current, he had earlier succeeded. It is a pity that he did not do this.

There are some similar examples. From ancient times, people could see the dazzling lightning and heard the numbing thunder. The artillery fire from Heaven used to frighten the people, but no one noticed the ubiquitous and powerful electric energy. It wasn't until Benjamin Franklin conducted a simple experiment that he proved that lightning was just the manifestation of an irresistible and controllable force as abundant as atmosphere and water, which was electric energy.

Before the Wright brothers, many inventors had made great efforts to invent aircraft, but they did not succeed. In addition to applying the principles adopted by the previous inventors, the Wright brothers added something else. It is so simple that they attach a specially designed movable flap to the edge of the wing so that the pilot can control the wing, and then the aircraft can keep balanced. It's because of the addition of such tiny things that the Wright brothers could create a new airframe. Therefore, they succeeded where others failed and became the inventor of the aircraft.

Edison, the most significant inventor, conducted ten thousand experiments and did not invent the bulb until he turned the unknown part into the known. If he had ceased in the 9,999th experiment and did not move forward, he would fail to invent it. The 10,000th experiment is merely an experiment, but it is the key to determining the success of the bulb experiment. Edison persevered, adhered to conducting experiments, gave a little more, and finally achieved success.

Examples of giving a little more

Napoleon Hill, born in a poor family, made efforts all his life with a desire for success, and constantly sought for all kinds of possible opportunities and made efforts to improve and enrich himself. Especially after accepting the entrustment of Andrew Carnegie, steel tycoon of the United States, Napoleon Hill paid visits to more than 500 successful people from all walks of life in more than twenty years. During the period, he summarized the secrets of their success and then established the science of success that inspires millions of people to embark on the road to success. He has also become a great tutor for spiritual inspiration in the world. Moreover, he himself became a millionaire from a poor guy and a world-famous socialite from an unknown man. In the book My Own Journey, Napoleon Hill wrote,

When I was still a law student at Georgetown University, I was entrusted by Andrew Carnegie to publish a book on the philosophy of success. Apart from some travel subsidies obtained from Carnegie, I had to assume all the other expenses on my own.

My dedication to this job has borne me a lot of burdens. I have to make a living for my family, while many of my relatives have been laughing at me. However, in spite of these obstacles, I worked for the task for twenty years. During the period, I visited the presidents of well-known enterprises, inventors, founders, and renowned philanthropists. These figures usually had no idea about the principles of their success, since they are just engaged in all kinds of affairs. Therefore, I have to spend a lot of time observing them and determining whether the power that I initially assumed could work is working. In addition to earning the living expenses, I have to work for these people.

Sometimes, it is a tough task for me to maintain a positive mental attitude and indomitable spirit as I am working hard but teased by my relatives. One day when I stayed in a dull hotel room alone, I would even feel that my family members' words are right. The power that supports me to move forward has convinced me that I will not only be able to complete the book but will also take pride in my success at that moment.

Whenever there is a fire of hope burning in my mind, I must take advantage of the resources available to me to fan it up a little bit, so as not to extinguish it. What enables me to stick to my beliefs and ideas and then helps me get through the difficulties is the confidence that I have gained from infinite intelligence.

From the narratives of Napoleon Hill, we can get the following beneficial inspirations:

First of all, giving a little more is to achieve a clear goal, which is not only helpful to ourselves but also other people and society.

Second, to give a little more, we must be willing to dedicate and sacrifice. Otherwise, we can never do it.

Third, to give a little more, we must be supported by a positive mental attitude. Otherwise, we can't persist.

Fourth, to give a little more, we must have an infinite power source, which means the confidence we gain from infinite intelligence.

Fifth, giving a little more is an indomitable spirit and an excellent habit. Once we develop such a spirit and habit, we will not regard the act of giving a little more as a burden or loss, but we will feel delighted and enjoy it and will be proud of our success.

Sixth, giving a little more requires us not to be afraid of sacrifice regardless of pay, but such extra cost will not be lost in vain, and it will eventually bear abundant fruits.

Advantages of giving a little more

If you can develop the habit of giving a little more, consciously strive with a positive mental attitude, and continuously provide more services of higher quality for others and society, the seeds of each service you have sowed will bear many times the fruits. Napoleon Hill, after a lifetime of research, believes that there are the following advantages for giving a little more:

Cultivate compelling personality

If you are able to continue to give a little more and provide more services of higher quality if you cannot get immediate returns, you can cultivate your positive mental attitude. It is the basis for you to cultivate a compelling personality. When you have developed into a compelling personality, almost all people will be willing to cooperate with you, and work for you as you like, which is bound to be a useful helping hand to your success. The life journey of Napoleon Hill is a shred of typical evidence.

Enhance your personal enterprising spirit

Personal enterprising spirit refers to an excellent trait that we can take the initiative to do what we need to do before being reminded by others. Like our instinct of protecting ourselves, it exists in our lives. As a constant self-driving force, the personal enterprising spirit motivates us to advance towards our goals. By giving a little more, you will enhance your enterprising spirit, because you are not waiting for things to happen, but activity propelling them to happen. Once you have developed the habit of continually motivating yourself and moving towards higher and better goals, all the bad qualities and habits in us will die away, since there is no corresponding environment and soil for them to survive.

Strengthen your self-confidence

By giving a little more, it can strengthen your self-confidence, as giving a little more enables you to be convinced that you are doing what is correct and beneficial. It makes you more responsible for your conscience and strengthens your confidence. When you keep on giving a little more and strive to provide the best services, you are building your self-confidence. With the self-confidence, you can be encouraged to forge ahead courageously. Even if you encounter many setbacks, even temporary failures, you can have a clear idea about yourself and believe in yourself, which, in turn, will strengthen your self-confidence.

With such self-confidence, people will trust you more, and success will definitely favor you.

Make the best achievements

The meaning of giving a little more is to strengthen your ability to work and to make efforts to make the best achievements at work. You can carry out your tasks with the best mental attitude and based on the concept of offering the best services and inspire yourself with the spirit of giving a little more, and you will try your best to enrich your knowledge, improve your skills, strengthen your abilities and make the best achievements as you can. In this way, you will consciously develop a healthy habit of consistently surpassing the past, the rivals, and yourself, which will eventually lead you to the road to success.

Become an indispensable figure

As the saying goes, he who has art has a part everywhere. No matter what position you are in, you can become an indispensable figure in your organization by giving a little more, and provide the organization with the services that other people can not provide. Maybe other people can also provide general professional services, but if you can tolerate being woken up at two o'clock in the middle of the night and providing services with a positive attitude, the clients will keep you in mind. If you want to make your position so crucial that no one can replace you, you need to have the spirit of giving a little more in the service, so that you can decide on your own salary.

Create more opportunities

Giving a little more is an effective way to eliminate the fear of poverty, shortage, and failure, as well as to defeat numerous competitors. As long as you can give a little more, you will become a strong person and an indispensable figure. Then, when you become indispensable, you can not only retain your current position but also have many opportunities to choose another job. It might refer to the promotion or transfer of your position or selection of your clients. You can redouble your efforts, so it is possible that you will get many opportunities that are hard for others to seize. It confirms that the strong can create an opportunity while the weak have to wait for it.

Get a higher pay

If you can stick to giving a little more, and you always give more than others do for you, the others will repay more to you in the end. If you can provide more services of higher quality for those around you, the customers will definitely find you by name, and your boss will regard you as an indispensable figure. Nowadays, it is fiercely competitive in society, and the fittest can survive to the end. Then, you will be bound to stand out for the rendering of excellent services and get high rewards. It is the manifestation of the law of compensation increase revealed by Napoleon Hill.

To help the people better bear the principle of giving a little more in mind, Napoleon Hill specially designed a formula as follows:

$Q1+Q2+MA=C$

In the formula, Q1 represents service quality, Q2 represents service quantity, MA represents the mental attitude of the person rendering services, and C represents compensation.

The compensation here refers to all things that come into your life and that you believe are worth pursuing. It includes money, promotion, joy, harmonious interpersonal relations, spiritual inspiration, confidence, an open mind, patience, physical and mental health, honor, social status, and so forth.

Overcome the habit of procrastination

When you are eager and delighted to do something, you will not delay the time to do it. The reason why those well-known successful people can forget to eat and sleep at work is that they have a desire for their work. When you deem it necessary to take action, you should act immediately, and then you can overcome the habit of procrastination naturally. In fact, giving a little more, in essence, is to take action, and to do it immediately and continuously.

The essence of giving a little more is taking action

Giving a little more, in essence, is to take action, and to do it immediately and continuously. If there were no actions, there would be nothing. Only by taking unremitting actions can we achieve the goal step by step and finally succeed. When you study humanity, including successful people and ordinary people, you will find that successful people are proactive, and they are known as dynamic people, while those mediocre and ordinary people are in a passive position, and they are known as passive people. Proactive people keep doing something and do it immediately until they finally accomplish the task and achieve the goal. On the other hand, passive people tend to do nothing, and they will find an excuse to delay it until it is finally proved that they should not do it, or they are incapable of doing it, or it is late to do it.

It's evident that we should be proactive people, develop a good habit of taking immediate action. If you are always thinking of doing it right now, you will accomplish a lot of things. However, if you have been thinking of doing it one day or some time in the future, you will definitely achieve nothing.

In order to develop a habit of giving a little more and taking immediate action, we should keep in mind and practice the instructions by Napoleon Hill as follows:

(1) Be an active person, be brave in practice, and do something practical, instead of doing nothing.

(2) Do not wait until everything is ready, as there is nothing absolutely perfect in the world. We should anticipate that there will be definitely difficulties in the future and that we should solve any difficulty immediately once it occurs.

(3) Creativity itself can not lead to success. Creativity is valuable only when it is put into practice.

(4) Action enables you to overcome the fear and to strengthen your self-confidence. You can do whatever you fear, and then your fear will disappear right now. Have a try, and then you will know how it works.

(5) Push your spirit to do something, rather than wait for it to push you to something. Take an active part, and you will naturally become refreshed.

(6) Always keep in mind that the meaning of the sentence that I will do it tomorrow, next week or in the future is the same as

that of the conviction that it can never be achieved, and hold the idea of doing something right now.

(7) Get to work now. Don't waste your time on unnecessary preparations. Just start at once.

(8) Take the initiative and be a reformer. Volunteer to change the status quo, take the initiative to undertake the voluntary work and prove to everyone that you have the ambition and ability to win.

In a word, give a little more when you do everything and act now, and then you are bound to succeed.

Examples of success

Yuan Longping: from rural teacher to the "Father of Hybrid Rice"

Yuan Longping graduated from Southwest Agriculture College in 1953, was assigned to teach crop genetics and breeding in Anjiang Agriculture School, Hunan Province. He began to study hybrid rice in 1964. Then, he was transferred to the Hunan Academy of Agricultural Sciences in 1971, promoted to researcher in 1978, and elected as academician of the Chinese Academy of Engineering in 1995. Yuan Longping's research achievements of indica hybrid rice won the first special state award for inventions of China. Yuan Longping was awarded the title of "meritorious scientist" by Hunan provincial Party committee and provincial government. The asteroid No. 8117 discovered by China was named Yuan Longping Asteroid. Then, he won the UNESCO Science Prize by the United Nations Educational, Scientific, and Cultural Organization in 1987 and the UN FAO Medal of Honor for Food Security and other international awards. In 2001, he won the first State Preeminent Science and Technology Award.

In August 1953, after graduating from the Department of Agronomy of Southwest Agriculture College (now Southwest University), Yuan Longping obeyed the unified distribution of the state to teach crop genetics and breeding in Anjiang Agriculture School, Huaihua City, Hunan Province. In 1960, Yuan Longping, 30, learned from some reports that hybrid sorghum, hybrid corn, seedless watermelon, and other crops had been widely used in foreign production, so he began to carry out sexual hybridization experiments on rice. In July of that year, he found a mutant rice plant standing out from the rice in the early-rice field of the practice farm of Anjiang Agriculture School. In the spring of 1961, he sowed the seeds of this mutant rice plant in the field of pioneering experiments. The results showed that the plant was a natural hybrid rice plant. In the face of the severe famine at that time, he was determined to defeat the threat of hunger with agricultural science and technology and engage in the experiment of the sterile male line of rice.

From 1965 to 1973, Yuan Longping encountered great difficulties in improving the ratio of male-sterile plants, matching the three lines of rice, stabilizing the fertility of the seeds, finding hybrid vigor and production of hybrid seeds. Yuan Longping successfully produced the seeds in 1974 and organized the identification of seed superiority.

In 1975, with the support of the Hunan provincial Party committee and the provincial government, the hybrid seeds were planted in a large area in Hunan Province, which made preparations for the promotion in a large area in the next year.

In the winter of 1975, the State Council decided to rapidly expand the trial plant of hybrid rice and popularize the price. The state invested a lot of human resources, material resources, and financial resources in the production of three generations of hybrid seeds in one year. It popularized the hybrid rice at the fastest speed. In 1976, the designated demonstration area of hybrid rice was 2.08 million mu. By 1988, the planting area of hybrid rice in China was 194 million mu, accounting for 3.96% of the planting area of rice, and the output of hybrid rice accounted for 18.5% of the total rice output. Enormous economic and social benefits had been achieved. On June 6, 1981, Yuan Longping and his indica hybrid rice won the first special state award for inventions of China.

On August 26, 1982, Yuan Longping was employed as the technical consultant of the Ministry of Agriculture, Animal Husbandry and Fisheries, and the deputy leader of the National Hybrid Rice Expert

Advisory Group. In that year, Yuan Longping was hailed as the "father of hybrid rice" by his international counterparts.

With the trial planting of hybrid rice all over the world, hybrid rice has attracted worldwide attention. Yuan Longping has been invited to the Philippines, the United States, Japan, France, the United Kingdom, Italy, Egypt, Australia, and other countries to give lectures, impart the knowledge on hybrid rice production, attend academic conferences or conduct technical cooperation research. International counterparts praised the hybrid rice developed by Yuan Longping as the fifth invention of China to humankind after compass, gunpowder, paper making, and movable type printing.

At the award ceremony of CCTV's Touching China Person of the Year 2004, the citation for Yuan Longping was that "He is a real cultivator. When he was a rural teacher, he had the courage to subvert the authority of the world; when he was famous all over the world, he was still only focusing on the fields. He is indifferent to fame and wealth. As a farmer, he sows wisdom and reaps wealth. His lifelong dream is to keep all people far away from starvation. Looking at the rice plants waving with the wind with pleasure, Yuan Longping is the most distinguished."

Yuan Longping is over 80 years old, but he still has black hair, steady steps, and quick thinking. He joked that he was also a post-80s generation. He often said to others, "I am now in my 80s, my physical age is in the sixties, while my mental age is in the forties and my muscle elasticity in my thirties." Yuan Longping joked that there are three secrets to his youth. First, he has a good mental attitude, an optimistic and cheerful personality, and doesn't square accounts in every detail. Second, he has a regular life and insists on physical exercise. Yuan Longping loves work and fields and insists on going to the fields all year round. In addition, he insists on swimming in summer and playing ball games in winter. Third, he has a light diet. He mainly eats vegetables and not much meat. He said, "I can still work on the front line until I'm 90."

Yuan Longping is not afraid of hardship, is willing to dedicate, spares no pains, and tries hard to gain something. He has made great contributions to solving the problem of Chinese people's eating. “We call Mr. Yuan Longpin as the father of hybrid rice, as his achievements are not only the pride of China but also the pride of the world. His achievements have brought good news to mankind.” Dr. Swaminathan, director of the International Rice Research Institute and former Minister of the Ministry of Agriculture of India, spoke highly of him.

Data source: Chen Guohua, Yu Wei. The innovation marathon of the kidult in hybrid rice. (Beijing Youth Daily, 2009-09-04.)

Yang Yuanqing: From a salesperson to Chairman

Yang Yuanqing, born in Hefei, Anhui Province, graduated from Hefei No.1 Middle School in 1982 and Shanghai Jiaotong University in 1986. In 1989, he obtained a master's degree in computer science from the University of Science and Technology of China. In the same year, he joined Lenovo Group and worked as a computer salesperson first.

In 1988, Yang Yuanqing, 24, was writing his graduation thesis at the Institute of Automation, Chinese Academy of Sciences, while conceiving his future. His goal in life is to get a doctorate in the United States and then find a job in the famous Silicon Valley. Many of his classmates were rooted in Silicon Valley, which made him very envious. “In the late 1980s, a science student who graduated from a famous university but chose to work in China would be deemed as good for nothing.” Two-thirds of my classmates in Shanghai Jiaotong University have been abroad, and I have a lot more classmates in Silicon Valley than in Beijing. Not to mention my classmates at the University of Science and Technology of China. Before we graduated, most of my classmates had been abroad, and the classroom had been almost empty. He believed that the Institute of Automation was not far from Silicon Valley in the United States, as it would be only a dozen hours apart by air. However, the top priority was to find a job. On the one hand, he needs to exercise his ability in practical circumstances. On the other hand, he has to make money to support himself and prepare funds for studying abroad. And his professional ability and English proficiency still need to be further strengthened. All in all, he needs to find a springboard and Zhongguancun first comes to his mind. In 1988, Zhongguancun was identified as a high-tech park, known as China's Silicon Valley.

The company he came up with first was Lenovo because he had recently seen a want ad of the increasingly popular high-tech company. In accordance with the address posted on the ad, he came to the office building of Lenovo. In an office on the second floor, he had an interview with the examiner. He is not quick-tongued in argument, but his answers satisfied the examiner. After the initial interview for half an hour, there was a second-round interview. When he knew he had been accepted, he was happy, but not ecstatic, because he was using Lenovo as a springboard. He had dreamed of going to Silicon Valley in mind. He later learned that he was just one of the fifty-eight applicants Lenovo had publicly hired in 1988 out of 500 applicants from across the country.

It was an event for celebration for him, as he was one step closer to Silicon Valley. What's more, Lenovo is a well-known high-tech company in China, which is in line with his major, and he can apply what he has learned to practice. But when the company announced his position, he was stricken to the heart. He was given the position of a sales clerk and was responsible for selling the Sun Workstation products from other companies. The Sun Workstation, which used the Intel 80386 (i386), was something strange and impractical for the people at that time.

Many years later, he could still recall vividly the scenes that he promoted the Sun Workstation products at that time. He rode the broken bicycle bought from the second-hand bicycle market and ran through the streets and lanes to promote the Sun Workstation, which he had just known. He also remembers that his phone fell to the ground by the customer. He still remembers how it felt to wait for several hours at the customer's door. In addition, he remembers how he felt when he sold his first workstation. The first workstation was sold to the National

Administration of Traditional Chinese Medicine of the People's Republic of China. When the order was finally signed, he was in a complicated mood. He was also a little guilty in the excitement. He felt excited because he sold the first workstation while he felt guilty because he felt sorry for the customer. A PC was enough for the National Administration of Traditional Chinese Medicine , but he made every attempt to convince the employee of the Administration that the Sun Workstation was their only choice.

Later, Yang Yuanqing recalled, "you can imagine how delighted I was at that time, but I still think that, in fact, this customer should not have bought the Sun Workstation, but could solve its problems only by a PC." To make up for it, he did his best to meet the various service requirements put forward by the customer. Yang Yuanqing later admitted, "I'm ashamed to say that the Sun's workstations were not sold well at that time. The product that we represent is not a good one. It is the Sun's only workstation that uses the Intel 80386 (i386). Users make bad use of it, either not applicable, or not enough. Although the product is not ours, it is the product we sell as an agent, after all. Therefore, at that time, we were both excited and guilty about selling workstations."

It was the sale of the first workstation that made him understand and be confident about marketing. It was the experience of marketing that enabled him to face all difficulties in the future. It was his excellent service and good attitude to customers that attracted Liu Chuanzhi's attention. He used to make sales as a temporary job, but gradually he became interested in it. At that time, he was responsible for receiving customers, making out invoices and collections, welding network cable, debugging machines, and providing after-sale services. He felt the value of his work in the voice of thanks from his clients. Although he didn't use much of the computer expertise that he had learned for seven years, he learned something new from sales that the benefits come from the market, and the market comes from the service. Many years later, when he became a senior manager of Lenovo Group, one of his business ideas was to make Lenovo a serving Lenovo. Later, when Yang Yuanqing was asked about his life experience, he answered, "when we are in the age of twenty-four or twenty-five, we are already laying the foundation. It is perfect for finding a job that fits in with our vocational specialty, but it does not count much. Young people should not bear the burden of finding a job to fit in with their specialty."

In 1991, Yang Yuanqing served as general manager of Lenovo's CAD Department, mainly acting as an agent for the products of HP Inc. Since he took office, the business volume of the Department has grown at a rate of over 100% every year, and it won the Global Best Agent Award of HP Inc in the United States for many times. From 1991 to 1993, the sales of the CAD Department increased from 50 million Yuan to 110 million Yuan, and then from 110 million Yuan to 180 million Yuan. In 1992, Yang Yuanqing was appointed general manager of the Computer-aided Equipment Department. Liu Chuanzhi gradually found that Yang Yuanqing had a high professional ambition and was a rare talent as a field commander. Yang Yuanqing's dream of going abroad had never ceased. When he was invited by HP headquarters in the United States, Yang Yuanqing got ready to depart after picking up his luggage. At the end of 1993, due to the influx of foreign computer brands into the Chinese market, China's computer industry fell into a crisis, Lenovo failed to achieve its set goal for the first time, and Liu Chuanzhi admitted to losing the battle. He warmly and sincerely persuaded Yang Yuanqing, who came to bid him farewell, to stay in Lenovo, and entrusted him with the task of saving Lenovo's PC business. Yang was given a broad platform and a great opportunity to exert his talents and realize his ambitions.

In 1994, Yang Yuanqing served as the general manager of Lenovo Computer Co., Ltd. Under his leadership, Lenovo sold 42,000 computers of its independent brands, making Lenovo among the top three computer manufacturers in the Chinese market. Yang Yuanqing was also hailed as the marketing talent and the star of science and technology by people from all walks of life in China. At that time, Yang Yuanqing was only 29 years old. In 1995, Yang Yuanqing was appointed senior vice president of Lenovo Group and vice-chairman of the Executive Committee of Lenovo Group, becoming the core member of the decision-making team of Lenovo Group. In the same year, Lenovo's computer sales increased by more than 130%, ranking the top three in the domestic market with an annual sales volume of 105,000 units in China. Thus, it became the only Chinese computer brand among the top five best-selling computer brands in the Chinese computer market. In 1996, Lenovo, led by Yang Yuanqing, won first place in PC sales in China. Meanwhile, the company expanded the product lines for its independent brands and invested R & D, manufacturing and sales resources in the field of server products and notebook computer products. In 1997, Lenovo's computers continued to rank first in PC sales in the Chinese market, and for the first time, entered the top six brands in the Asian-Pacific region on behalf of Chinese brands. In 1998, Lenovo Computer jumped to fifth place in the Asia Pacific market (excluding Japan), which is the only computer manufacturer among the top ten manufacturers in the Asia-Pacific market with an increasing market share and a growing ranking for five consecutive quarters. In 2000, Yang Yuanqing was the president of Lenovo Computer Co., Ltd., and the sales volume of computers reached 2.62 million units, ranking the first in Asia (excluding Japan). At this time, the company's product lines are further enriched, and its independent brand products have developed into almost all information front-end equipment and components, including computer board cards, overall computer units, server products, notebook computer products, information home appliances products, digital assistant equipment, consumer electronics products, digital output products, and value-added information services.

From 1999 to 2001, Yang Yuanqing conducted in-depth and instructive analysis and research on the impact of the Internet on information products represented by computers, and the impact of e-commerce accompanying the Internet on all aspects of the traditional manufacturing industry. According to Yang Yuanqing, the Internet era has offered Chinese enterprises an excellent opportunity to keep up with the pace of the world. On this basis, at the Lenovo oath-taking rally on April 20, 2001, Yang Yuanqing solemnly announced Lenovo's development strategy in the next few years that the future Lenovo is positioned as a high-tech Lenovo, a serving Lenovo, and an international Lenovo.

Data source: Li Mingjun. Yang Yuanqing, the young marshal of Lenovo. (Beijing: China Commercial Publishing House, 2007.)

Legend of Xia Mingxian, godfather of the door industry

Xia Mingxian's life is a legend. Many years ago, he accidentally broke into the burglar-proof door industry and had been devoted to the industry since then. From him, we can see the spirit of persevering and giving a little more.

Start from iron-stick doors

In 1988, when the wave of national business swept across the land of China, Xia Mingxian, who worked as a sailor in Chongqing Shipping Company, also had an impulse to do business, and then he started a small business after resigning from the company.

Xia Mingxian started his small business in a hardware store. In the spring of 1989, Xia Mingxian found that there were suddenly more people purchasing the water pipe elbows in his store. He wondered why so many people bought the water pipe elbows. As soon as he inquired, he knew that they had bought them to make iron doors. With the improvement of living standards, many households bought expensive consumer goods. In order to guard against theft, people began to install an iron door like a fence outside the original wooden door. After the inquiry into more detail, he found that few families could actually make iron doors by themselves. After getting the materials prepared, they usually asked the people around them for help or paid others who knew it to complete the important process of welding. Xia Mingxian intuitively felt that his business would be much better than that of selling hardware if he manufactured finished iron doors for sales.

Xia Mingxian found five helpers and began to try making iron-stick doors in an air raid shelter left from the era of preparing for war and famine along the Chuqimen River in the downtown area of Chongqing City. "At that time, our tools were two welding guns, four hammers, several vises, and hand drills. All the materials were pulled back by a scooter." It took the six men a week to make more than 20 iron-stick doors. At that time, because there was no sample to learn from, Xia Mingxian's first work was really ugly. However, during that special era, there was an extreme shortage of goods. More than 20 doors they made were put in the hardware store and sold out in a few days. Xia Mingxian still clearly remembers that at that time, a door was sold for 158 Yuan and that he made a total of 1,500 Yuan as each door made a net profit of 60-70 Yuan after various costs were deducted. It is said that it was the first burglar-proof door sold as a commodity in China.

Xia Mingxian was encouraged by the victory of the first battle, and immediately put all the money he earned into reproduction. He made more than 50 doors in the second time and more than one hundred doors. In the same year, Xia Mingxian established the Mexin Burglar-proof door Plant, becoming the first plant specialized in the development and mass production of burglar-proof doors in China. By the mid-1990s, Mexin had reached the business scale of hundreds of millions. During that period, Hainan's real estate was becoming hot. "At that time, I was looking at the sky from the window and pulled myself up. I believed that there was nothing that could not be done. I was too arrogant to engage in the real estate industry in Hainan Province." But Xia Mingxian finally calmed down. "So far, I have been the most grateful for two incidents in my business experience. One is that I chose the burglar-proof door industry, and the other is that I didn't engage in the real estate industry in Hainan Province."

From iron-stick doors to luxury doors and then to security doors

As Xia Mingxian made a lot of money by making and selling iron-stick doors, followers in the market came one after another. In Chongqing alone, many door manufacturers came out in a few years. But even these followers had to admit, "Xia Mingxian is always one step ahead of us."

When the simple iron-stick doors became popular in the market, ordinary people generally thought that it was enough to make the door solid, but Xia Mingxian had the intention to manufacture luxury doors. He imitated the carved gate of the old-fashioned park, and designed some new images on the iron-stick doors, and made six flowers with a stiff iron stick. With these six flowers, Xia Mingxian's first batch of luxury doors were sold at 40 Yuan higher than the ordinary iron-stick doors. With the rise of home decoration, the simple iron-stick doors have become increasingly out of accord with the times, and the public has begun to favor the more beautiful and safer burglar-proof doors. Xia Mingxian was the first to launch the closed burger-proof doors.

The closed burglar-proof doors opened a larger market, and more followers swarmed in. Xia Mingxian began to think about a deeper problem on whether the burglar-proof door industry could still survive in the market after the problem of family anti-theft is solved. The six iron-stick flowers, which were originally crude and childish, began to flourish in Xia Mingxian's mind. "I don't want people to think of the door industry as just the industry with steel and welding guns, and Mexin will turn the cold steel into a vivid door art."

Xia Mingxian proposed the concept of security door and developed a series of products on this basis. From the second half of 2000, Mexin began to utilize the mature burglar-proof door technology to take the lead in launching the steel interior doors and fire-proof (anti-theft) doors in the Chinese market. Thus, one market was changed to three markets. And the prospect of market growth was suddenly doubled.

By the end of 2000, Mexin's sales volume exceeded 1 billion Yuan, and its market share was up to 20% in the door industry nationwide, far more than that of 3,000 similar enterprises of various scales in China.

Target: The largest door industry base in the world

Such achievements did not stop Xia Mingxian. He began to focus on the world door market. Xia Mingxian found that there is not a large-scale multinational company in the door industry like Coca Cola and McDonald's in the world, which made Xia develop greater ambition. In November 1997, Mexin's door supermarket opened in New York. Xia Mingxian raised his glass and swore to the dealers from all over the United States, "The present scale of Mexin will quickly become the past, and we have the ability to grow into the world's king in the door industry in three years."

Mexin also has a rarely known secret room, which is filled with thousands of burger-proof doors and decorative doors collected by Xia Mingxian from all over the world at the cost of ten million Yuan over the years. Mexin International Door Industry Exhibition Hall, in fact, is Mexin's design center. Designers achieve creation and transcendence through observation and study. In recent years, hundreds of types of burglar-proof doors of varied specifications and styles have been made here. The employee in Mexin said, "know the enemy and know yourself, and you can fight a hundred battles with no danger of defeat. It is also a magic weapon for Mexin's doors to enter the international market." Xia Mingxian said, "Mexin aims to become the largest door industry base in the world."

The way of overseas expansion for Mexin, a promising enterprise in the door industry

In November 2000, in the flash of more than 100 media, a door supermarket with an area of about 100 square meters opened in New York, and the news that Mexin Group advanced to New York spread all over the world.

At that time, a Tokyo newspaper warned the Japanese business community, "the global expansion of China's manufacturing industry has surpassed the competition level of the commodities of small scale, low level, and low price, and its goods have entered the world-class goods."

It is the beginning of Chongqing Mexin Group, an empire of the door industry, to make it heard by the world in a loud voice.

Why does it open a shop in Times Square, New York? Times Square is the center of world business and trade. If Mexin's door products can be recognized by the United States, they will also be recognized by other countries.

In Canton Fair (The China Import and Export Fair) 2002, Mexin Group met with a passionate partner, Dariush Yashar. Yashar came to the fair after he saw Mexin's door supermarket in Times Square. After communicating with the employee four times, Yashar opened DKS Co., Ltd., in Los Angeles to sell Mexin's commercial doors as an agent. DKS became the first enterprise in the United States to introduce the doors made in China to the United States.

In response to the different needs of American customers, Mexin Group launched nearly 20 kinds of commercial doors at one time. DKS establishes a base in Los Angeles but also sets up a warehouse and factory building in Texas and Pennsylvania.

"It is a tough task to sell the doors made in China in the United States. It took us three to four years to prove the high quality of Mexin's doors to the market. Many American customers think that the quality of Mexin's doors can be comparable to that of doors made in the USA." Yashar said.

A firm foothold in the United States marks the transformation of Mexin Group's production, logistics, and other links from the Chinese model to the world model. Next, it's natural for Mexin to copy its marketing tactics in the U.S. market to those outside China.

Data source: Du Gang. Xia Mingxian: From the Godfather of Door Industry to the Founder of An Empire in Door Industry. (Examples of Marketing, 2004(3)).

Chapter 10 Do Well in Learning from Setbacks and Adversity

Maxims for Success

When you encounter setbacks, don't waste time calculating how much you have suffered. Instead, you should figure out how much experience and asset you can get from these setbacks. You will find that what you get is much more than what you lose. Failure can be a stepping stone or a stumbling block. It depends on whether you hold a positive or negative attitude. For those with a positive mental attitude, each adversity contains the seeds of equal or greater benefits. Sometimes, what seems to be adversity is actually an excellent opportunity to disguise.

—Napoleon Hill

Principles and Guidelines

In the journey of life, no matter what achievements you have made, the life road may not go off smoothly, but you are bound to be confronted with difficulties, setbacks, adversity, and obstacles. Setbacks and adversity can overcome obstacles to your progress, steps, or springboards to your success, and the final result depends fully on your mental attitude and the relationship between you and them. In view of this, whether you can hold a correct attitude towards setbacks and adversity is a key factor for your success.

Setback does not equal failure

In daily life, people often mistake a temporary setback as a failure, which leads to many unnecessary sorrows and worries. Edison's practice of inventing the electric bulb is the best example to illustrate the difference between setbacks and failures. At that time, a young reporter asked him, "Mr. Edison, you failed ten thousand times before succeeding in what you invent now. How do you feel about this?" Edison replied, "young man, I will tell you a constructive tip for your future as your life journey just begins. I didn't fail ten thousand times, but I found ten thousand ways that didn't work."

Ordinary people think that they have failed after suffering a setback for the first time or more, so they may give up. As a result, they will fail completely. But Edison thought that more than 10000 setbacks did not equal failures, so he continued to do experiments and finally achieved success. It can be seen that because of the different views on setbacks, the consequences are totally different.

One of Napoleon Hill's friends is a very famous management consultant, but in the first six months of the start-up, he spent all his savings for six years. For several months, he stayed in the office as his home. He declined countless good jobs because he insists on realizing his ideal. He was also rejected hundreds of times by customers. There are almost as many customers who refuse him as welcome him. In this way, he struggled for more than seven years, but Hill had never heard a complaint from him.

Once, Napoleon Hill asked him, "is it exhausting you?" he said, "no, I'm still learning! It is an invisible and unpredictable business. The competition is so fierce that it is not easy to do. But anyway, I will continue to learn. I don't think it's hard, but I believe that I could benefit a lot from it." Later, he managed to do it and did it with vigor and vitality. Finally, he made remarkable achievements.

At all times and in all countries, those great men who have made great achievements were all subjected to a series of merciless attacks. It was because they were able to hold on to the last that they finally achieved great success.

In the dictionaries of numerous successful people, there are only words, setbacks, struggles, and success, but not the word failure. In their eyes, no matter how many setbacks there are, they do not equal failure, but they are the steps or springboard to the peak of success. In the face of setbacks, they never bow their heads and never feel blue. Instead, they have clear goals and persist in striving until they achieve ultimate success.

Setback is a sense of happiness

"This kind of temporary setback is actually a sense of happiness because it will cheer us up, adjust the direction for us to make efforts and then lead us to move in different but better directions." said Napoleon Hill.

Setback is a special language used by infinite intelligence to communicate with us and point out the mistakes we made. These languages are straightforward and ruthless, just like when we are advancing triumphantly in a certain direction with enthusiasm and ambition. We are hit on the head and punched on the back, which has forced us to pause, calm down, and reflect on ourselves profoundly.

Through reflection, you will gain the following benefits:

(1) Re-analyze the environment you are facing, and study whether the direction you choose is suitable for the opportunities existing in the environment. If you don't adapt to these opportunities, you will adjust the direction of your efforts to move in different but better directions.

(2) Reexamine your physical and mental assets and abilities and evaluate whether they are compatible with the goals you set. If not, you should adjust your goals accordingly based on your physical and mental assets and abilities.

(3) The setback will force you to lower your head when you disdain to investigate conditions at the lower levels and care for nobody, put down your arrogant attitude and hold a modest, prudent and kind attitude so that you can get a more harmonious interpersonal relationship and work together with more people to strive for the goal.

(4) Setback will force you to change your bad habits that have been manifested, cultivate good habits, and start a new struggle under the control and influence of good habits.

(5) Setback will sharpen your willpower, strengthen your courage and confidence, enable you to get back on your feet, accept greater challenges, and strive for greater success.

After recognizing the above, you don't have to think of setback as a failure, but as a temporary pause in the journey to success, so that you will move on. Setback is not a stumbling block, but a step, springboard, and the turning point for success. Moreover, it may make you feel happy.

There is no better school than adversity

About a century and a half ago, at a grand banquet in Lyon, France, the guests had a heated debate about whether a painting represented some scenes in ancient Greek mythology or the real historical picture of ancient Greece. When finding the guests flushed quarreling with each other, the host hit upon an idea. Then, he turned around and asked a waiter nearby to explain the artistic conception of the picture.

As a result, the waiter's explanation shocked all the guests present, because he gave a very detailed description of the theme of the whole picture. Moreover, he has a clear mind and a profound understanding of the picture, and his views are almost beyond all dispute. Therefore, the waiter's explanation immediately settled the dispute, and everyone present was completely convinced.

"Excuse me, which school have you been educated in, sir?" one of the guests asked the waiter with great respect. "I have been educated in many schools, sir." The young waiter replied, "but the school where I studied the most for the longest time is called adversity. " This waiter is Jean-Jacques Rousseau.

Rousseau had the opportunity to contact the bottom of society and was able to have a deep understanding of the whole life as he had lived a miserable life in poverty in his early years. Although he was just a humble waiter at that time, his works that sparked the wisdom of human beings made him the greatest genius of that era and in the whole of France. His name and thought lit up the whole of Europe like lightning in the night and spread all over the world.

There are many people like Rousseau who study and achieve success in the school called adversity. See the following examples:

Thomas Edison was a newspaper delivery boy on the railway. He had only received education in primary school for three months. At the age of 15, he began to dabble in the field of chemistry and secretly set up a mobile laboratory on the train. One day, while he was doing some secret experiments, the train suddenly took a big turn. As a result, the bottle containing sulfuric acid broke. An odd flavor drifted away, and it set off a series of complex chemical reactions. The head of the train crew, who had personally experienced the adverse effects of Edison's experiments and was driven beyond forbearance, slapped Edison in the face and drove him out immediately. From then on, Edison became deaf. However, he did not lose heart. Instead, he overcame difficulties, studied assiduously, and continued his experiments. Finally, he owned more than 1000 patents and became the most brilliant pearl in the global science circles and the king of the invention that has been highly praised.

Galileo Galilei is another typical example. Galileo's parents forced him to go to medical school in pursuit of money and status in the secular world. However, Galileo loved physics and astronomy. On many nights, while Venice was sleeping, he was standing alone on the tower of St. Mark's Cathedral, observing the phases of Jupiter and Venus through a telescope made by him. Later, he finally made a great discovery, but his heliocentric theory that the earth revolves around the sun was regarded as a heretical belief at that time. As a result, he was forced to bend his knees to accept criticism on a public occasion, and the inquisition inflicted heinous torture on him. Even under such cruel persecution, Galileo did not lower his noble head and still kept muttering to himself: "in any case, it does revolve around the sun." After being put in prison, he also used a wheat straw in a single cell to prove that a hollow tube is stronger than a solid stick. Even after he was blind in his later years, he still didn't give up his work.

In China, there are also many examples of miracles in adversity and heroes in misfortune. Here are just a few examples:

Sima Qian, although persecuted in the official arena and tortured by castration, still worked hard to write history, and finally wrote the Historical Records, an immortal historical book.

Cao Xueqin, whose family was stuck by financial difficulties and lived a poor life, wrote A Dream of the Red Mansions, one of the Four Great Classical Novels in China.

Li Ka Shing lost his father at the age of 14. He was forced to drop out of school to become an apprentice and a shop assistant, so as to make a living to support his family. Later, he ran an enterprise and became the richest Chinese.

Wu Shihong, with only a junior high school diploma, suffered from leukemia. Later, she was determined to succeed and worked hard teaching herself. As a result, she leaped from a nurse to a senior executive of IBM, Microsoft, and TCL. She was honored as a "Queen worker" in China.

Zong Qinghou started working on the farm for 15 years at the age of 16. At the age of 42, he also sold popsicles along the street with a handcart. 15 years later, he founded Hangzhou Wahaha Group Co., Ltd. Co., Ltd.

In conclusion, the reasons for the success of the above-mentioned successful people lie in their persistent efforts, and persevering will, disinterested mind, and honest and noble personality. It is these factors that impel them to rise tenaciously from adversity, from the trough of life, from the depression of psychology, and stand firmly in the world.

A British writer read a biography of the outstanding American people and said: "it seems that all the great American people were born in the small and simple hut." For example, Lincoln, Rockefeller, Edison, etc. were all born in poor rural areas, but they laid the foundation of wisdom, character and physical strength in their childhood, and later became eminent persons or leaders in society.

Another writer, Wingate, also said with emotion, "It's so strange that there are only a few celebrities from such a big city as New York! Among the celebrities who live in New York, more than 90% of them come from rural areas. This is not only the case in New York but also in big cities like London, Paris, and Berlin. It can be seen that people who grow up in the countryside are more outstanding than those who grow up in the city in many ways!"

So, why can adversity make people succeed? There is a mysterious power in our nature, which is difficult for us to describe, and explain. It seems that it is not in our ordinary senses, but hidden at the bottom of our hearts. Unless we are significantly hit and stimulated, the power will never be exposed. If a person doesn't stand the test of setback and adversity, he may only find out 25% of his talents. However, once he is stimulated like acupuncture by danger, hunger, ridicule, insult, fraud, etc., he will develop the other 75% of his talents and do what he could not do before. Thus, it can be seen that the struggle in a desperate situation can stimulate people's latent internal strength and promote them to make achievements that are difficult to do in ordinary circumstances. So, there is no better school than adversity.

How should we treat setbacks and adversity?

Two important facts are extremely evident in our life. First, everyone is likely to encounter a setback or adversity.Second, there are always opportunities for success in adversity, but you have to explore them yourself. Luck always wears the mask of disguise. Behind every setback and adversity lies the chance of success.

A wise man once said that it is impossible for you to meet someone who has never suffered a setback or adversity. At the same time, people's achievements are often in direct proportion to the setbacks and adversity they encounter.

In the face of setback and adversity, the most important thing is the mental attitude, which is the decisive factor whether setback and adversity can be turned into a change of success. If you regard setback as failure, adversity as hell, and both as great losses, you are doomed to fail. If you see the setback as a step or springboard to success, adversity as the best school and teacher, and both as the most valuable wealth, you are bound to achieve success. In a word, remember that a positive mental attitude will lead you from setbacks and adversity to success.

Examples of success

Wu Yijian: "Suffering is the best teacher."

On December 10, 1960, Wu Yijian was born in Xi'an Textile City Workers' Hospital. When he was just a month old, he was raised by his grandmother in Xitaiping Village, Yongji County (now Yongji City), Shanxi Province. There was a ewe tied under the pomegranate tree of his grandmother's house. When he saw the ewe, he cried "mother sheep" happily, because he grew up drinking the milk of the ewe. At the age of three, he was sent back to his parents in Xi'an. It was the summer vacation of 1967 when he returned his native place again. At that time, his grandfather was tortured to death for his class origin of the landlord. However, misfortunes do not come alone. Then his father, an ordinary cadre in Baqiao District of Xi'an City, was attacked again and arrested on a fabricated charge and locked up in a black room. There were guards at the door of the room, and the place looked like a temporary cell.

When he grew up, Wu Yijian served in the army and worked as an ordinary worker in a factory. In 1984, he firmly quit his job in a factory in Xi'an and went to Guangzhou alone to work with 600 Yuan. In 1985, he left Guangzhou for Hainan to develop his career, becoming the first group of trendsetters in Hainan.

After careful investigation, he began to set about establishing a company with an annual output of 200,000 TV sets. A 27-year-old man from Northern China was engaged in such a large-scale project, which was considered a liar or a psychopath at that time. However, it is exactly what makes Wu Yijian different from others. At that time, he had an idea that the TV sets were in short supply but in great demand in the Chinese market and that it just started in Hainan. He believes that we should be good at understanding everything around us, so as to mobilize all the favorable factors around us. It is to make a profit either by earning 1 Yuan with 100 Yuan or by earning 100 Yuan with 1 Yuan. But the two ways of making money are totally different.

To operate, we must strive for the fastest speed and the smallest investment in exchange for fast speed and high benefits. Through the contacts with a local real estate company in Hainan, he bought the land in the way that the plant and equipment will be handed over 25 years after operation, and contracted the construction project of the plan in the form of 3% quality guarantee deposit in advance, and made the company invest in his business with the promise that a company in Hong Kong would supply 80 % of the electronic components for production. In order to contact the electronic dealers nationwide, he negotiated every day, drinking a bottle of soda if he was thirsty, and eating a piece of bread if he was hungry. But the stores were closed when it came to the evening. Then, he had to be hungry. At that time, he was often so hungry that he had to drink as much water as he could. Several times, his leather shoes were cracked, but due to the hasty schedule, he tied them with shoelaces and ran around with them for another week. Moved by Wu Yijian's sincerity and insistence, all the major electronic distribution enterprises in China paid enough deposit to book the products ten months in advance. Thus, the matter to ask for help turns to a matter to be asked.

After the external environment was straightened out, Wu Yijian devoted his heart and soul to the construction site. As the wages were not paid in time, the workers slowed down, and then he explained to them one by one and gave all his money to the workers. At that time, he could not even afford a dinner as he had no money with him, so he had to steam some rice every day to allay his hunger. He did not have any vegetables or meat for more than ten days. When the workers knew it, many of them were moved to teachers. Due to Wu Yijian's sincerity, the workers were willing to share the rough and the smooth with Wu and finally built a large factory at an extraordinary speed.

Before the spring festival that year, the factory delivered 1.7 million Yuan of goods, but the purchasing company did not settle the accounts in a timely manner, and the company's employee was waiting to take the money home for the Spring Festival. To make the employee spend a happy Spring Festival, Wu Yijian borrowed money from all his friends and withdrew all his savings from the bank and distributed them to the employee in time. On the 27th day of the lunar December, all the employees returned home, but he could not go back home. At that time, he had only 50 Yuan left, which would support him for the next fifteen days and nights. However, he could not tell his family about his difficulties and was afraid to make them have unnecessary worries. To save money, he bought 100 steamed buns and ate them for fifteen days. When workers who came back from home saw him, they thought he went ill.

In this way, the first batch of TV sets was produced on this hot land in Hainan, which took only 10 months. After the TV set was put into production, the company's assets changed from 600 Yuan he held to 300 million Yuan, including the land price.

Wu Yijian often said, "I've realized from what I have experienced so far that suffering is the best teacher. Sufferings enable us to learn a lot of useful things and exercise our personality in practice. The more difficult a person is, the stronger will he will have, and the clearer his goal will be. In most cases, an entrepreneur needs to start from the simplest job, even as a porter. For instance, a person is like a pile of wet coal, and the suffering is like the cradle. Only by shaking the cradle can the coal be made into coal balls before they can burn. As the saying goes, what you suffer now may bring you glory tomorrow. As long as you are willing to work hard, you will inevitably make some achievements. The opportunity of life is won through our hard struggle." It may be the reason why Wu Yijian could stand out from tens of millions of people who engaged in business to follow the trend.

Data source: Dang Ning. A Chinese billionaire talked about how he got rich. (Harbin: Harbin Publishing House, 2004.)

Yu Minhong: Failure is the new starting point of my life

Before the rise of the Internet economy, especially before Jack Ma succeeded, no entrepreneurs in China had had such an inspiring experience as Yu Minhong in China.

Yu Minhong was titled as an expert in English teaching and management, chairman of New Oriental Education & Technology Group, co-founder of HONGTAI APLUS, vice president of the Chinese

Young Entrepreneurs' Association and member of All-China Youth Federation. In addition, he is often hailed as the godfather of international students or the mentor of teenagers in life.

But he is also different from the mentors who falsely exaggerate their life experience and sell chicken soup for their souls everywhere. He grew up in a village, and he had suffered from numerous setbacks and frustrations before he started his own business. However, Yu Minhong said with confidence that without those failures, he would not become what he is now.

Living in the countryside for eighteen years, he won the champion of rice transplanting in Jiangyin and the excellent walking tractor driver

Since Yu Minhong founded New Oriental, he has given lectures in many universities and middle schools all over the country. He told his story in a humorous and expressive way.

He has delivered so many speeches, but these speeches are not completely the same. His speeches are titled Believe in the Future, or Believe in the Power of Struggle, or Take Action with the Inner Desire. Sometimes, his speeches have longer titles, such as "I persist not because I am very strong, but because I have no choice." No matter what topic the speech is, he aims to deliver a kind of positive energy.

Before the age of eighteen, Yu Minhong spent all his time in a village in Jiangyin. He said that he had only been to two big cities, one in Shanghai and the other is Wuxi.

Yu Minhong said that two incidents made his mind fresh when he was very young. One was that the houses in their rural primary school were simple,e and the wind blew into the classroom on all sides. Then, he almost felt the same temperature in the classroom as outside the classroom. When he wrote, he could not even hold his pen. The other was that he would hesitate for several minutes before going to bed every night to make up his mind because it was too cold in the quilt.

"The hardships in our childhood will do a lot of good to our life, and now I can bear any hardship." Yu Minhong said.

In normal circumstances, he worked for sixteen hours every day and slept for six hours. For the last two hours, he spent one hour having dinner and one hour taking exercises. In his opinion, it does not depend on fortune to succeed.

By the age of eighteen, Yu Minhong had had no opportunity to be admitted to the university through an examination, so he could only strive to obtain an opportunity to be recommended to university via labor work. Since Yu was very young, his mother had told him children from rural areas must receive more education and that it is best for them to leave the villages and become a teacher.

He worked so hard that he won the honorary title of the champion of rice transplanting in Jiangyin at the age of fourteen and the title of excellent walking tractor driver at the age of sixteen. However, when he was yearning for his dream to study at university, the trace for his struggle changed due to the times. After the Cultural Revolution, Chinese society began to advance on the right track gradually, and the college entrance examination system was also formally recovered. However, it was a surprise for Yu Minhong at that time.

Three unforgettable failures: he suffered setbacks in the college entrance examination, the admission to Peking University and study abroad

Yu Minhong had to prepare the college entrance examination by reviewing the lessons. At that time, he intended to apply for the former Changshu Normal College (now Changshu Institute of Technology) in the college entrance examination. However, it was beyond his expectations that he even attended the college entrance examination three times in a row.

"I chose the English major at that time, and the main reason was that I did not need to take a mathematical examination." Yu Minhong joked that he only scored four points in the mathematical examination when he was admitted to Peking University in the third college entrance examination he took.

Yu Minhong could persist in taking the college entrance examination three times, which is closely related to the support from his family members and the encouragement of his English teacher as the headteacher.

At that time, Yu studied in a middle school, which was reconstructed from a ruined temple. He had more than thirty classmates, but no one intended to take the college entrance examination. His classmates did not believe that students from rural areas could be admitted to the university. At that time, their headteacher was their English teacher, who graduated from Nanjing University and used to work in Nanjing Translation Bureau. He was transferred to the village for teaching during the Cultural Revolution.

One day, their headteacher came to the classroom and asked all the students to take the college entrance examination. Yu's classmates all worried that they would fail in the examination. The English teacher said at that moment, "I asked all of you to take the college entrance examination, and I know none of you would be admitted to the university. But I still want you to take the examination. You will be able to remember that you have worked extremely hard to change your fate in spite of a failure, when you are busy with your farm work in the countryside after the examination, or when you are exhausted with your farm work when you sigh with the how, or when you watch the clouds floating in the sky."

The words greatly shocked Yu Minhong. Even dozens of years later, Yu could still recite his headteacher said without a single word mistaken. Because of what the teacher said, he made up his mind to work hard until he was admitted to the university, and he would let his teacher know that his prediction was wrong after he was admitted to the university.

In the first year, he scored 33 points in the English exam, while the minimum passing score for the former Changshu Normal College was 40 points. In the second year, he scored 55 points, but the minimum passing score rose to 60 points. In the third year, he scored 95 points, and he could not believe that his score was higher than the minimum passing score of the English major of Peking University. The setback in the college entrance examination was just the first failure that Yu Minhong suffered in the course of his struggle.

However, his study at Peking University did not go on so well as he imagined. The best students in the college entrance examination gathered at Peking University from all over the country. But Yu Minhong's scores had been ranking among the worst of the class. Growing up in the village, he did not perform as well as his classmates in literature and arts and sports except for academic performance. However, although he worked hard, his performance was not that ideal on campus before he graduated.

What's more painful for him is that in his junior year, he suffered from tuberculosis and had to be quarantined in the hospital for a year. "At that time, I felt that there was no hope."

However, after experiencing these failures, Yu Minhong completely got rid of the habit of comparing with others. From then on, he only compared with what he had been in the past and tried to surpass himself. So, in the year of being in the hospital, he read more than 200 books and memorized more than 10,000 words. His solid knowledge reserve has laid a foundation for him to make remarkable achievements in the future.

In addition, he had suffered another failure in his life, as he failed to go abroad. He showed a strong interest when seeing his classmates go abroad. He tried many ways to apply to American universities to get the chance to go abroad, but for various reasons, he gained nothing after struggling for it for three years.

"The failure to go to the United States has become the starting point of my life." Said Yu Minhong.

Be a good person. No matter success or ordinary life, we can't lose our true colors

Yu Minhong likes to be called Mr. Yu best. He often thinks about the nature of education. According to Yu Minhong's understanding, the inner spirit of education is to stimulate human's desire for truth, goodness, and beauty. The truth is to seek true knowledge and truly seek knowledge. Goodness is to have a strong personality, positive values, and tolerance for all living beings. What is beauty? It lies in the joy of the heart, in the ability to appreciate and create beauty.

Today's New Oriental Education & Technology Group has a market value of about $5 billion and about 35000 faculty members. In the pursuit of economic benefits, the Group has provided some funds and human resources to help the vulnerable groups in society and build schools in poor areas. According to Yu Minhong, these matters count a great deal, and it is a social responsibility of New Oriental Education & Technology Group.

For a long time, no matter how his career develops, Yu Minhong always keeps in mind his true colors to be a good man. In fact, this is one of the secrets of his success. Yu Minhong once said on other occasions that during his university years, he worked for his dormitory students on a voluntary basis all year round, such as fetching hot water and doing some cleaning. At that time, as long as he had some spare money, he would invite his classmates to dinner. The most important thing is that he has never cheated with his classmates. Yu Minhong said: "you may get a temporary profit by cheating, but people around you will never get close to you after they figure it out."

Yu Minhong said that when he went to the United States to invite Wang Qiang and Xu Xiaoping back to China, one of the important reasons why they were willing to come back was that Yu Minhong had never cheated them during their university life.

Yu Minhong often poked fun at his appearance, joking that he was not handsome or tall. With the joke, he repeatedly expressed his hope that the young could understand that a person's appearance is not the most important, and that many people who have achieved do not look handsome or beautiful in appearance, and that the accumulation of internal knowledge and the improvement of accomplishment are the most valuable.

He said that a person with a yearning for truth, goodness, and beauty would have the ability to pursue a better life and the courage to take a step backward in the intense competition.

Data source: Wen Yang. Yu Minhong: Failure is the new starting point of my life. (Wuxi Daily, 2016-01-15.)

Part V Start the Innovation Machine of Success

There are two ways to achieve success: one is the conventional way, the other is the innovative way, also known as shortcut. If you want to achieve success, it is slower to take a conventional path than to take an innovative path. If you want to succeed as soon as possible, you must have the courage to conduct innovations and do well in innovations. To take an innovative path, you must learn and use three skills, namely, learn to think correctly, cultivate imagination and creativity, and organize a mastermind alliance.

Chapter 11 Learn to Think Correctly

Maxims for Success

The power of thinking is the greatest power of human beings. It can build a great kingdom as well as lead a kingdom to perish. All ideas, plans, purposes, and desires originate from thoughts. Thought is the master of all energy and is the universal solution to all problems. If you don't learn to think correctly, you will never be able to make outstanding achievements.

—Napoleon Hill

Principles and Guidelines

All plans, goals, and achievements are the product of thinking. Your ability to think is the only thing you have complete control over. You can use your mind in a wise or foolish way. But no matter how you use it, it will show some strength. If you want to get a good harvest from your thoughts, you must make efforts and devote your heart and soul to preparations in all aspects. The arrangement and implementation of this work are the outcome of your correct thinking.

Utilize the power of correct thinking

As long as you are willing to think, there must be a certain power, which will vary according to the nature of thinking. Correct thinking creates positive forces. For example, the great leaders, scientists, inventors, entrepreneurs, model workers, and other elites, who have made outstanding contributions to scientific progress, social development and the continuous improvement of the living standards of human beings, can produce far more power than ordinary people. The reason for this lies in their ability to think in the correct way. On the contrary, wrong thinking may lead to negative or even destructive forces. For example, those reactionary leaders who are anti-science, anti-progress, and anti-humanity, as well as notorious figures such as war criminals and criminals of all kinds, can produce great destructive forces. The reason for this lies in their inability to think in the correct way.

Adolf Hitler was imprisoned in prison. Just when he was in the worst mood, he began to think about how to change his life. Shortly after, he wrote a book in prison, in which he faithfully wrote his goal of dominating Europe. Moreover, he made his goal known to all the people in prison. After reading this book, some people just laughed, while others thought it was completely written by a lunatic. Many years later, the lunatic really stepped on half of Europe, and the people in the other half of Europe used up all their resources to fight with Hitler to escape from his claws. Hitler's thinking is not the right thinking we are talking about, so it has produced a huge destructive force, getting millions of people into the abyss of death and pain.

Therefore, when you use your thinking ability, first of all, you should remember that you must think correctly and never think from a wrong perspective. It's not only beneficial for you to think correctly, but it also does well to the whole society. It's a moral obligation you should do to the people of the world. You can't accomplish anything great without correct thinking.

Methods and steps of correct thinking

Correct thinking is based on the following two reasoning methods:

(1) Inductive method. This method refers to a reasoning process from partial to whole, from the specific case to general case and from individual to universe. It is based on experience and empirical research, and then it comes to a conclusion.

(2) Deductive method. This method refers to a reasoning process from general principles to individual cases and from all to part. It is based on the general logical hypothesis, and then it comes to a specific conclusion.

There are great differences between the two methods of reasoning, but they can be used together. In our work and life, we are likely to make a wrong inference and come to a wrong conclusion. In view of this, we must put forward strict requirements for the correctness of reasoning, which means that we must strictly ask ourselves to think correctly and review the results of reasoning to find out the errors. In addition to reviewing our own thinking process, we can also use these two reasoning methods to check whether the results of other people's thinking are correct.

In order to be a correct thinker, we must take the following two essential steps:

(1) Separate facts from feelings, hypotheses, as well as hypotheses and rumors which have not been verified.

(2) Divide facts into two categories: important facts and unimportant facts. The right thinker will never listen to the gossip or listen to only one side, but will definitely understand the real facts and accept the opinions based on the facts or correct hypothesis.

Two obstacles to correct thinking

To think correctly, we tend to be confronted with the following two obstacles:

First, credulity, which means that a person believes in something without evidence or with little evidence.

It is a major drawback of human beings. The drawback gave Hitler the opportunity to develop his influence to a terrifying extent, not only in Germany but also in other countries and regions of the world, which made him occupy most of Europe in a short time. On the contrary, the right thinker always has a question mark in his mind. He will undoubtedly question everyone and everything, but this does not mean that he has no confidence, but it is the best manifestation of his respect for the facts. The reason why a few right thinkers have always been regarded as the hope of human beings is that they play the role of pioneers. If you are determined to be a correct thinker, you must be the master of your own emotion rather than a slave. You should not give anyone the opportunity to control your thoughts. You should not be influenced by your family, friends, or colleagues to accept the mistaken ideas that you have rejected.

Second, doubt, which means that a person does not believe in what he knows nothing about.

It is another major drawback of human beings. The drawback allows the people to take a skeptical and boycott attitude towards any newly emerging thing, so that they will follow the old routine and be content with staying where they are, always stand on the opposite side of the newly emerging things, hindering the development of science, technology, culture, and society. Due to the drawback of human beings, when the Wright Brothers announced that they had invented the flying machine (i.e., the airplane) and invited reporters to come to see it, none of the reporters accepted their invitation. When Guglielmo Marconi announced that he had invented an approach to transmit information without wires (i.e., the radio), his relatives even sent him to a mental hospital to check whether he had lost his normal sense. Such foolish and absurd cases are not rare in the history of science, technology, and human development.

The purpose of correct thinking is to help you understand any new ideas or new things, rather than to prevent you from investigating and researching them, or to make you blindly doubt and resist them. There is no doubt that it is incorrect to give credence to any idea or thing, but it is also wrong to doubt and deny everything. In particular, for those new ideas or new things, if you take the attitude of disdain or even resistance against them, you will only lose the possibility of success and limit your enthusiasm, confidence, imagination, and creativity.

Ways to eradicate the obstacles to correct thinking

There are the following two ways to eradicate the obstacles to correct thinking:

First, ask more "why" for each item of information.

To be a correct thinker, you must conduct a careful investigation on whether each piece of information you get is true, and you must learn about whether the information has been defaced, modified, or exaggerated. Therefore, you need to conduct some tests on the information. For example, when you read a book, you should ask the following questions:

(1) Does the author have recognized authority in the field covered by this book?

(2) In addition to conveying the correct information, does the author have any other motivation for writing? If any, what is it?

(3) Does the author have any stake in the topic of the book?

(4) Does the author have sound judgment, or is he just a fanatic?

(5) Is there any way to investigate whether the author's statements are true?

(6) Are the author's remarks consistent with common sense and experience?

To put it simply, before you accept anyone's remarks, you should first find out his motivation for delivering such remarks, and especially be alert to the Fanatic's statements. No matter who tries to influence you, you must give full play to your judgment and be discreet. If the statement seems unreasonable or inconsistent with your experience, you ought to make further investigation.

Second, ask what it is first and then why it is for every new idea or new thing.

For example, when you hear someone invent a flying machine, you should first ask what it is and then ask why it can fly, so that you will know that the reason why the machine can fly in the sky is because of the buoyancy of air and the power of the generator. In this way, you will not doubt or resist any newly emerging things or new ideas. On the contrary, you will become their advocates and promoters.

Development of the thinking habit

The thinking habit of human beings comes into being due to the following two aspects:

Physiological genetics

The nature and traits that are passed down for generations may affect your thinking habits. You may be a serious thinker as a left-brainer, or an unrestrained thinker as a right-brainer. The former lays stress on preciseness and detail, such as mathematicians and theorists as left-brainers. The latter lays stress on freedom and romance, such as writers and poets as right-brainers. Correct thinking can modify, strengthen, and guide these two ways of thinking because everyone has these two abilities, among which one may be stronger while the other may be weaker.

Social influence

Environment, education, and experience are all social stimulants, which have had the most significant influence on thinking. Many people start to think because they are stimulated by the outside world. For example, when most of the people choose to join the political party, believe in religion or even buy a house or a car, they make a decision not based on their correct thinking about their goals, but they tend to be influenced by others around them. However, the correct thinkers are totally different, as they will analyze the goals in a careful and discreet manner, make a choice freely, and gain more benefits from the process of choosing.

People's thinking habits are not only influenced by physiological heredity, but also by social environment. Once formed, it is difficult to change. However, people can give full play to their subjective initiative, exercise conscious control over their thinking habits, and lead them to develop in the right direction.

Examples of success

The secret of Wang Hai's success

Wang Hai is the former party secretary and president of Double Star Group. Under his leadership, Double Star has developed from a shoe factory that was on the verge of bankruptcy to a comprehensive super large enterprise group integrating the shoe industry, tire, clothing, machinery, and thermoelectricity industries. The products are exported to more than 100 countries and regions in the world. The number of employees has grown from more than 2000 to 60000. The fixed assets have increased from less than 10 million Yuan to 5.5 billion Yuan. The annual sales revenue has increased from 30 million Yuan to 10 billion Yuan, and the earnings of foreign exchange through export have increased from US $1.75 million to US $150 million. Double Star's professional sneakers, hiking shoes, leather shoes and tires have won the title of China Top Brand. Thus, Double Star Group has become the only enterprise that has four brands awarded the title of China Top Brand in China's rubber industry. Wang Hailong has won almost all the awards that a Chines entrepreneur can obtain, including the Outstanding Entrepreneur Award in China.

In 2008, China ushered in the 30th anniversary of reform and opening up. At that time, the national news and publicity department decided to conduct a comprehensive study and summary on the secrets of the success of an outstanding entrepreneur with 30 years of successful experience and then compile and publish a book in this respect. At that time, Wang Hai, President of Double Star Group, was the only outstanding entrepreneur in China with 30 years of successful experience. Therefore, Feng He, executive vice president of China Enterprise Confederation and China Enterprise Directors Association, and Zhang Laimin, editor in chief of China Enterprise News, organized an editorial committee on the secrets of Wang Hai's success, which was composed of 25 experts, including researchers, professors, editor in chief, writers, doctors and masters, and carried out corresponding investigation and research.

The experts of the editorial committee paid a visit to the Double Star Group for a three-day survey. They listened to President Wang Hai's comprehensive introduction to Double Star, visited the main products, main workshops and production lines of the Group and called for the main works published by the Group and relevant news reports and other materials for consultation. Finally, they concluded that the secret of Wang Hai's success is Wang Hai's thought and that the carrier for his thoughts is his theory, especially his writings.

Wang Hai often said, "if an enterprise had no theory or thought, it would stand no chance; if a backbone of the enterprise had no theory or thought, he would have no future; if a worker had no theory or thought, it would have no chance for promotion. If there were no good thoughts or theories, the career would lose its way ahead, and then it would be unable to succeed, and may even suffer a crushing defeat."

In the practice of building the Double Star Group and the Double Star brand, Wang Hai founded a number of new theories that reflect the objective laws of reform and opening up and market economy, such as ABW theory, market theory, law theory, cat theory, the theory of three nationals (national spirit, national brand, national entrepreneur), the contradiction theory, and the theory of emotion, passion and enthusiasm, the theory of three natures (Party character, human nature, and personality), and the theory of three wins that enterprises should always adhere to the triple-win principle of benefiting the country, the enterprise and the people), etc.

Data source: Zhang Xiuyu. Wang Hai: A famous great entrepreneur in China. (Chief Executive Officer Of China, 2014(1) .)

"Zong's Art of Strategies" and "Wahaha model"

As a result of the Cultural Revolution, Zong Qinghou spent 15 years on a farm in Zhejiang since he was 16 years old. After returning to the city in 1979, he worked in a school-run factory. At the age of 42, he also sold popsicles on the streets of Hangzhou. However, 15 years later, he founded the Hangzhou Wahaha Group Co., Ltd. In 2002, the sales revenue of Hangzhou Wahaha Group Co., Ltd. reached 8.8 billion Yuan, and the net profit reached 1.2 billion Yuan. Zong Qinghou's personal assets reached 1.64 billion Yuan due to his 29.4% stake in Hangzhou Wahaha Group Co., Ltd.

When talking about the secrets of his success, Zong said peacefully: "there is no myth in modern enterprises. Now we are far away from the era where we can succeed by only one idea or one operation. Nowadays, enterprises compete with each other in terms of comprehensive strength and full strategic advantage. To engage in business in the era where the legend goes downhill, we need to adopt an extraordinary way and a peaceful mind."

Based on differentiation strategy - from popsicle to Wahaha

In 1979, Zong returned to Hangzhou. In order to make a living, he took the rickshaw to sell textbooks and ice cream from school to school. In the process of delivery, Zong Qinghou learned that many parents were so worried that their children had poor appetite and malnutrition.

“At that time, I felt that there should be a large market for children's nutrition solutions.” At the age of 47, Zong Qinghou decided to seize this opportunity and fight hard. In the eyes of many people, he drove himself to a corner, as he gave up his stable life but made up his mind to develop new nutrient solution products by himself. When hearing the advice from his friends out of good intentions, Zong Qinghou seemed so stubborn: “can you understand how a middle-aged man, 47 years old, feel when faced with the last opportunity in his life?”

In 1988, Zong Qinghou borrowed 140,000 Yuan and organized experts and researchers to develop the first nutrition product for children, Wahaha’s nutrition solution product for children.

At that time, Wahaha was also a school-run factory, with only three workers and a business site with an area of 50 square meters.

At that time, there were more than 3,000 enterprises engaged in the production and sales of health care products in China and 38 kinds of nutrient solution products in the market. At that time, the competitive environment was quite brutal. The researchers concluded that the market was saturated and that they should withdraw from the nutrient solution market. However, Zong Qinghou decided to start with children's nutrition solutions and carry out the differentiated competition strategy. As a result, they succeeded instantly.

“According to our survey of 38 kinds of nutrient solutions on the market, it is found that they are suitable for all ages and that their functions cover a wide range but are not subdivided into specific functions. The central government's family planning policy of a single child inspired us to develop children's nutrition solution products. In a family, the parents, the grandmother, the grandfather, the maternal grandfather, and the maternal grandmother vie for the favor of a child. Six adults take care of one kid, and then the kid naturally becomes the core of the family and the baton of significant economic expenditure. But at the same time, children's anorexia and partial eclipse were becoming more and more serious, which had become the most troublesome problem for parents. Although there are 38 kinds of nutrient solutions on the market, none of them are designed for children to solve their poor appetite."

"Based on this discovery, I hired the head of Nutrition Department of Zhejiang University School of Medicine to study children's nutrition solution, so as to resolve the parents' worries about their children's diet. After Wahaha nutrient solution was launched, it was immediately welcomed by the market, and the advertising song that 'drink Wahaha and you will have a nice meal' was made known to every family. Many children can sing, recite, and even adapt this sentence into a jingle."

With the song that "drink Wahaha and you will have a nice meal" spreading all over China, Wahaha's children's nutrition liquid rocketed to fame. By the fourth year, Wahaha's sales revenue had reached 400 million Yuan, with a net profit of more than 70 million Yuan. Wahaha had reaped the first barrel of gold.

Develop based on the merger strategy — "eating the big fish"

In 1991, the sales volume of Wahaha's children's nutrition solution soared, and its products were in short supply on the market. In spite of this, Zong Qinghou still kept a sober mind, "At that time, I estimated that if Wahaha did not expand its production scale, it would lose the market opportunities. However, if we set up a new project, expropriate the land and conduct capital construction according to the traditional development ideas, it would take at least two or three years at that time, and we would probably fall into the dilemma that the factory building was built, but there was no market for our products."

At that moment, there were three roads for Zong Qinghou to choose. First, it is a joint venture. Second, it is the lease, and third, it is a paid merger. It is evident that the first two roads are secure for Wahaha, and it will take a considerable risk for him to conduct paid mergers. However, Zong Qinghou finally decided to take the third road with a huge sum of 80 million Yuan.

He aimed Wahaha's expansion at Hangzhou Cannery, the old state-owned factory in Hangzhou. At that time, there were more than 2,200 employees in Hangzhou Cannery, and its assets were insufficient to cover its debts. At this time, Wahaha had only 140 employees and a production site with an area of hundreds of square meters.

Wahaha's initiative of eating the big fish caused a sensation across the country. In the beginning, even the employee of the old Wahaha Factory was opposed to this initiative. Zong Qinghou finally managed to prevail over all dissenting views and quickly enliven the fixed assets of Hangzhou Cannery. He expanded the production utilizing the factory building and employee of the Cannery and made a profit instead of suffering a loss within three months. In the second year, the Cannery's sales revenue, profit payments, and tax turnover more than doubled.

The merger in 1991 laid the foundation for Wahaha's later development, and also made Zong Qinghou taste the benefits of the merger. After that, M & A has almost become the main means for Wahaha to expand in different places. By the end of 2002, Wahaha had established 30 production bases in 21 provinces and cities outside Zhejiang. In 2002, Wahaha produced a total of 3.23 million tons of beverages, accounting for 16% of the beverage output in China.

From brand building to diversification

Wahaha expanded its product range from the products designed for kids to the consumer goods suitable for all ages, such as mung-bean paste and eight-treasured rice porridge, which aroused a lot of criticism. Even some people think that Wahaha's practice destroys the purity and professionalism of children's products and that diversification is an erroneous zone in the development course of Wahaha. However, in the end, Wahaha managed to dispel such doubts with better sales indicators for each of its products.

“I think diversification is an inevitable step for an enterprise when it develops to a certain period.” With the passage of time and the deterioration of the competition environment, the background of the industry will change accordingly, and the average profit will reduce sooner or later. Therefore, it is the best way for an enterprise to seek a way out by making its capital flow to be able to change in different fields. Enterprises in China's beverage industry fall into a very serious homogenization of vicious competition. Wahaha now has been equipped with sufficient capital and technical strength to develop new products, instead of staying in the previous competitive strategy of innovation on the basis of keeping up with the market trend. In the future, Wahaha should focus on creating independent products with a new concept.

"I measure whether an enterprise can engage in diversified management, mainly with three criteria. First, according to the actual situation of the enterprise, we can see whether it is necessary to carry out diversified management. Second, taking into account, its own capital strengthens, we can see whether it is feasible. Third, after fully judging our comprehensive strength, we can see whether it is likely to continue the project."

With regard to Wahaha's future development, Zong Qinghou, 58, said: "We have more than one billion spare funds, which will be invested in two fields in the future. One is the food, health care products, and medicine, and the other is all the products designed for children."

Problems to be solved forever – Produce and sell cheap products with high quality

Many marketing masters who pay close attention to the growth of Wahaha point out that if they intend to support the network system of Wahaha, three problems must be solved forever. First, Wahaha must ensure that the products introduced to its dealers are in great demand among the public. Second, it must provide dealers with a reasonable profit for a long time. Third, Wahaha must have powerful capabilities of maintaining its market, and not shift the pressure of marketing management and advertising to its dealers.

But Zong Qinghou has his own view on this, "In the process of development, enterprises will constantly encounter new problems, while the strategies are effective for the time being, not permanent." As for the above three points of view, I have such an opinion that Wahaha's products are all close to the consumer pulse of the public, that our products may not be popular among the people of all ages and from all walks of life, but many consumers may hear about the enterprise titled Wahaha Group, which is widely known in China. We have been making unremitting efforts to provide a reasonable profit for dealers for a long time, and we will stick to it forever to ensure that our dealers can make a profit. In this regard, they will sell our products, and thus a marketing network can be built. The manufacturer and the dealers are as inseparable as fish and water, and they are dependent on each other. In practical management, Wahaha has provided its dealers with varied assistance in terms of warehouse management, public relations promotion, and other aspects. It has never shifted the pressure of market administration and advertising to its dealers.

"In my view, there is only one problem that Wahaha should always solve to always produce and sell cheap products with high quality. Only when the products are of good quality and low price can the manufacturer, its dealers and consumers achieve a triple-win result together. Only in this way can the ecological chain of food industry develop healthily."

Data source: Dang Ning. A Chinese billionaire talked about how he got rich. (Harbin: Harbin Publishing House, 2004.)

Chapter 12 Cultivate Imagination and Creativity

Maxims for Success

Imagination is the action of will, as well as a challenge and an adventure. Imagination is the workstation of the soul and nuclear power to make personal achievements.

—Napoleon Hill

Creativity is the most precious asset. If you have the ability, you can seize the best time of life and thus do a great miracle.

—Napoleon Hill

Principles and Guidelines

The greatest talent of human beings is thinking ability, which enables human beings to analyze, compare, choose, as well as imagine, foresee, create, and produce new concepts. Imagination is an activity, challenge, and adventure of the human spirit. It is the key to various achievements of human beings, and the main motive force for human beings to make efforts and the secret channel to the heart.

Infinite power of imagination

Since the beginning of mankind, especially in the past hundred years, mankind has been able to control many forces of nature with the aid of imagination. Here are several examples:

Birds can fly freely in the sky. People want to fly like birds. To achieve this vision, the Wright brothers invented the airplane.

Wild animals run like flying on the ground, and people want to run like flying animals. In order to realize this vision, human beings have created all kinds of means of transportation, such as automobiles, motorcycles, and trains.

Fish can swim freely in the water, and people want to swim freely in the water like fish. In order to achieve this vision, human beings have made ships, naval vessels, and submarines.

It can be said that all kinds of modern inventions and creations, such as telephone, telegraph, radio, receiving set, recorder, TV set, telescope, radar, camera, duplicator, film projector, computer, Internet and so forth, are all based on the premise of imagination. Up to now, human beings have not come to a climax of the utilization of imagination. As long as human society is still developing, the human imagination will never reach its peak.

There are two forms of imagination: comprehensive and creative imaginations. Both of them can improve your life and the environment where you live via your creativity.

Edison invented the light bulb: Comprehensive imagination

Comprehensive imagination refers to a new way to recombine some ideas, concepts, plans, or facts that have been recognized and then apply them to new purposes.

Edison invented the light bulb, which is a typical example of a comprehensive imagination. He starts with the fact that others have proved that a metal wire will heat up when it is connected to an electric shock, and will eventually glow, but the problem is that the strong heat will soon burn the metal wire, so the life of light lasts only a few minutes. Edison had tried more than 10000 times to control the heat, and the method he finally found was based on a universal fact that no one else had ever noticed. He found that carbon was the product of burning wood, which was covered by soil, and smoldered in the soil until the wood was burnt. As the wood is covered by the soil, the amount of oxygen flowing to the fire is only enough to smolder it, which will not be burnt. As a result, carbon is formed. When Edison came up with the fact, he immediately thought of heating the metal wire. He put the metal wire in a bottle and drew out most of the air in the bottle. In this way, he invented the first light bulb with a life span of eight hours and a half.

Wolowitz founded the ten-cent chain store: Creative imagination

Creative imaging is a medium, also known as the receiving set. All kinds of ideas, proposals, plans, and thoughts will flash in mind all of a sudden, which is called creativity, inspiration, or premonition. With the medium of creative imagination, we can receive all kinds of creativity, inspiration, or premonition in a timely manner so that our limited mind can communicate with infinite intelligence directly. Moreover, all new ideas and ideas can be passed on to human beings, and then it will take effect. Through this medium, you will know some new concepts and facts, act according to the changing circumstances, connect with other people in the subconscious mind, and then earn wealth and achieve success.

Wolowitz's founding of the ten-cent chain store can be regarded as an example of creative imagination. Wolowitz used to be a clerk in a hardware store. Once, his boss complained about a large number of old-fashioned goods that couldn't be sold. When hearing that, Wolowitz suddenly had a new idea in his mind.

"I can sell these goods." He promised. With the consent of the boss, he set up a counter in the store, and took out the things that could not be sold and then marked the price on every item at ten cents. To the boss's surprise, these things sold out immediately. After that, his boss tried to put the items that could be sold on the counter as much as possible. Any item that can be sold on the counter became the best-selling commodities in the store.

Wolowitz was confident that his new idea could be applied to all the commodities in the store, but his boss did not think so. Later, Wolowitz set up a sales chain across the country and made a lot of money for himself. His boss regretted, "every word I said when I rejected his proposal cost me an opportunity to earn about $1 million."

Gate's soundproof room: Creativity surpasses imagination

Comprehensive imagination originates from experience and reason, while creative imagination originates from the pursuit of a clear goal. Creativity depends highly on the creative imagination, but it goes beyond it. Based on infinite intelligence, creativity can lead to the door to the temple of wisdom with the help of the sixth sense, so that mankind can automatically and spontaneously communicate with infinite intelligence.

The best example of creativity is Gate's story. Gate was an inventor of the same era as Edison, but the methods the two used were quite different. Gate is a highly educated scientist with more than 2,000 patents, twice as many as Edison.

Gate takes advantage of his creativity in a simple process. He would first enter a soundproof room, sit at a table with paper and pen, and turn off the light. Then he would focus on a specific problem, and wait for his mind to come up with a solution to the problem with the help of the sixth sense.

At that time, sometimes he would come up with a solution to the problem quickly, but sometimes he had to wait for an hour before he was able to come up with a solution, or even he could not come up with any ideas once in a while. Several times he even thought of some solutions to the problem, which had never thought of before.

Gate's creativity has gone beyond his imagination because he has developed his creativity into an ability that can be used at any time. In other words, he can communicate with infinite intelligence automatically and spontaneously by virtue of the sixth sense. Although it has not been found in science where the organ producing the sixth sense is, human beings have been able to receive accurate information, generate all kinds of concepts, ideas, propositions, plans and ideas from the sources other than the body senses, and put them into practice so as to transform them into the material object or wealth that correspond to the items mentioned above.

In a word, imagination is to rearrange and combine the known concepts and facts, while creativity is to communicate freely with infinite intelligence with the aid of the sixth sense in order to generate new ideas or facts. Creativity aims to create a solution to the problem, rather than an excuse for not being able to solve it. As long as you are creative, you can solve any problem that you encounter and achieve any goal that you intend to achieve.

Ways to cultivate creativity

Although the strength of our creativity is bound up with our innate factors, our real creativity is formed in the course of nurture and practice. Then, how can we cultivate our creativity?

Have a personal enterprising spirit

Creativity bears the mission of creating human civilization. It inspires people to explore various fields, allows people to access advanced ideas, science, and machines, and provides people with a means to enjoy a higher standard of living. At the same time, creativity belongs to those who are aggressive. If a person does not have initiative, he will be unable to give full play to his creativity, and he will not gain anything new in his life.

Have the spirit of utter devotion irrespective of pay

The goal of creativity is to achieve what is impossible. It is not limited by normal working hours, but it also has nothing to do with pecuniary reward, and even we have to make make the necessary sacrifices. As a result, to cultivate creativity, we must have the spirit of utter devotion irrespective of pay.

Have the belief of winning, strong will and persistent willpower

The key to cultivating your creativity is to believe that you will be able to get things done. Only with this belief can your brain work actively to seek any way to manage to do it. At the same time, you should have a strong will and a lasting willpower like Edison to persist in what you are doing.

Capture your creative ideas or inspiration at any time

Creativity or inspiration is the fruit of thought. However, it will only be valuable if you grasp it in time, manage it properly and carry it out thoroughly, So, for creativity or inspiration, you need to record it in time, review it regularly and improve it constantly. The more creativity or inspiration you accumulate, the more creative you will become.

Master some skills

The concrete embodiment of creativity is to be good at conceiving new ideas and new things that have not yet arisen in reality. Therefore, the skill of conception is closely related to the cultivation of creativity.

James Webb, the great master of success, points out five basic steps of conception as follows in his book The Techniques of Conception:

(1) Collect information for reference.

(2) Digest and absorb the information in mind.

(3) New ideas gradually take shape in the subconscious.

(4) The conception is completed when a concept expressly emerges.

(5) Translate this concept into a practical and feasible scheme or plan.

The experience of countless successful people has proved that the technique is not only simple and feasible but also highly effective.

Examples of success

You can achieve whatever you can imagine!

Up to 1998, Jin Xukai, a male migrant worker, had made 58 inventions in extreme poverty and in the absence of any instrument and equipment, among which the state patented 23 of the inventions. At that time, eight ministries and commissions, including the Central Committee of the Communist Youth League of China, the Ministry of Public Security and the Ministry of Justice, awarded him the honorable title of top ten outstanding young migrant workers in China. At the end of 2002, he got the first intellectual property income of 300,000 Yuan, but he donated all, and once again, he became a pauper. When it came to the reasons for his inventions, he explained, "I should be grateful to poverty for my obtaining these inventions, and poverty forces me to have creative ideas burst out from my mind." Then he introduced how he made the inventions as follows:

" The wistful look in my younger brother's eyes stung me deeply."

When I was 6 years old, my father, who went to work in Xinjiang with the bedding on his back, left home while looking back again and again. From then on, he had never come back.

At that time, my mother was only 25 years old, and my mother, my younger brother and I lived together with my great grandmother and grandmother. The burden of the lives of the five persons of four generations in the family was all on her shoulders. In order to support my family, my mother worked harder than a man. When she had finished her work in the field, she would carry the honeycomb briquette for others in the town. Whether it is in summer with intense heat or in winter with drips forming into ice, she always stooped and pulled the cart loaded with honeycomb briquette across the streets and lanes in the town.

At that time, our family was poor and couldn't afford a toy. My younger brother was lost in thought when watching other kids playing with their toys. The wistful look in my brother's eyes stung me deeply. So I found wood, leather bands and other things to make windmills and birdcage by myself. Moreover, I also made the plane and train I imagined, as well as the sleeve arrows and back crossbows, which were depicted in the martial arts fiction. Those toys pleased my brother, and other kids also envied him. It was the first time I tasted the joy of creation. Every day, just before dawn, my mother would do the farmwork in the fields while I was waked up to keep an eye on the pot where the congee was being cooked. However, as the children at six or seven years old tend to fall asleep fast. I used to fall into sleep by the stove. As a result, the congee overflowed from the pot, extinguished the fire in the stove. My mother always blamed me for wasting every grain of rice when coming back from the fields. Then, I had an idea that it would be better if something could open the lid of the pot by itself when the congee was about to overflow. After many experiments, I managed to make a simple overflow prevention device by binding the two handles of the pot and the handle of the pot cover with a rubber band. From then on, I didn't need to keep an eye on the pot where the congee was being cooked, and my mother looked at me with quite different eyes.

Since then, I've been fascinated by inventions, and I was inspired frequently. I put a short pencil at one end of the bamboo tube and rubber in the other. It was quite convenient. Later, I found that several chickens in our house ran all over the village and that their eggs were seldom discovered. So I found some waste wood and made an efficient three-dimensional cage with the function of non-electric and automatic egg collection and feeding. That year, I was 13 years old. There are many similar inventions, and in most cases, I was inspired by the poor life.

In 1992, my mother was seriously ill and still had to struggle to get up and do some farm work. Sitting at her bed, I took a deep breath and told her, "Mom, I want to go out for work." My mother's eyes immediately turned red, and she said with a trembling voice, "your father went out to work and never came back. How can I live if something happens to you outside?"

I didn't retort anymore. The next day, I left a letter to my mother and left home quietly with only 100 Yuan. I said in my letter, "I swear I will give you a better life in the future. No matter where I go, I will never disgrace you."

"I can bear any hardship, but do I just come out to work for a meal?"

In the late autumn of 1992, I finally arrived at Hainan Province after many days of traveling. Standing in the crowd, I was nervous and at a loss. During that time, I ran around in the daytime, looking for a job and slept by the road at night. As I lost my ID card on the road, I got into trouble on all sides and couldn't find a job. At that time, I only dared to eat two steamed buns a day and drink tap water when I was thirsty. By the 15th day, there was only 0.5 Yuan left in mo pocket. In panic and despair, I came to the sea and walked involuntarily towards the waves. And the spray was as bitter and salty as tears, but I suddenly thought of my mother thousands of miles away, and then slowly retraced my steps.

I climbed up the bank hungry and went on seeking a job. The first job was to dig up the mud at a drain leading to the sea. The boss just provided shelter and food but did not pay wages. He threw a brick on the floor of the shed and said, "Go and sleep there." I dug the mud at the foul drain and then carried it to the nursery garden by cart one after another. It was a hard job, but anyway I could have something to eat. Twenty days later, I became unemployed again after the work was done.

At that time, my second job was as a security guard in a hotel. I could not go to sleep with my eyes wide open when others were snoring loudly. I was wondering if I went out to work just for a meal.

One day, one of my friends complained to me that he had just had to take a taxi for an urgent matter, but all the taxis had passengers when he waited for a taxi by the road for a long time. At that time, there was no sign on the taxi indicating whether there was a passenger on it. I was shocked to hear that, and the inspiration for creation which had been lost for a long time lit up the road under my feet like a fire. If I can design an indicator to show whether there are passengers in a taxi, there will be a huge market demand for it!

I was so excited that I wanted to start designing right away. However, that flash of inspiration is like a door that opens, while the world behind the door is too deep to be fathomable. At that time, I knew nothing about electronic circuits, remote control, and other knowledge, and could not take a step into that world. I had to learn from zero. Then, I worked under the master-worker in an electrical repair shop, where I spent more time watching how the master repaired, doing more chores, and asking the master and others in the shop whenever I did not understand. Several months later, I ultimately had a thorough grasp of the electronic circuit.

Finally, the design drawings came out. In order to devote myself to trial production, I rented a small nissen hut where fishermen kept their fishing gear at the seaside with the last 100 Yuan and locked myself in it for trial production over and over again. I had no money and no time to cook. Therefore, at that time, I cooked a pot of porridge without any salt or any vegetables or meat every day and drank a little when I was hungry.

One day, one of my friends inquired about where I was and came to the seaside. He asked the local fisherman whether he had seen me. The fisherman pointed to the small nissen hut and asked, "are you looking for the strange man who lives in it?" My friend opened the door with a doubt. When he saw me thinned to the bone with disheveled hair, a dirty face, and a stubble of untrimmed beard, he rushed to hold me tightly and cried out loud.

More than a month later, I walked out of the small nissen nut with the first taxi passenger indicator developed by myself. In November 1994, my taxi passenger indicator was patented by the state.

"During the six years, I lost a total of 17 jobs, and I was so poor that I couldn't find a coin in my pocket."

I no longer live to have a meal. The inspiration for creation keeps flashing in my mind. However, I have been excited by and tortured by those inspirations.

To facilitate my engagement in inventions, I gave up many good jobs but chose some jobs which required more flexible working hours but less income. Most of the time, I worked as a security guard at night. At that time, I went to work at night, and during the day, I either went to the market for a survey, to the library to look up materials, or to work on inventions in the hut. I didn't have the money to buy any books. Then, I read the books and copied what was useful in the bookstore. During that period, I was kicked out of the bookstore more than once.

One night, I worked as a security guard in the lobby of a hotel. Several guests from Hong Kong stood not far away from me talking about gonorrhea, syphilis, and AIDS, complaining that they could not easily sit on the stool as it is an important way to spread these diseases. I immediately realized that it would be a research topic with a broad market prospect. After work, I first went to the bathroom of the hotel room to observe the stool, and then found the old stools in the storeroom of the hotel. I observed, disassembled, and studied them over and over again. In those days, I was completely pondering the stools in my mind. With a preliminary idea, I began to do experiments after buying the necessary materials. Through continuous exploration and analysis, I succeeded in designing an electric device three months later. As soon as you press the button, it can automatically wrap a layer of paper washer on the toilet seat, and then it can also automatically recycle the washer after use.

However, when I conducted a market survey with my invention, I found that there are two serious disadvantages in this design, one is the high cost, and the other is that the electric device is not suitable for wet toilets. In view of this, I overturned all my designs and started from scratch again. I intended to work out a design scheme that involves highly concentrated functions, highly refined technology, and the lowest cost.

One year passed, two years passed, and three years passed. To simplify it to the point where it can no longer be simplified, I had overturned my design works repeatedly and then continued to start from scratch. However, every failure is a step closer to the ultimate goal.

In order to improve my invention, I went to more than 50 cities to conduct market research in those years. Apart from eating, I spent almost all the money I earned from working on the invention. I would eat the instant noodles if I was hungry and drink the tap water if I was thirsty. To earn the traveling expenses, I had to do some manual work while continuing my market research. I carried cement bags at the wharf by the Huangpu River and did some unskilled labor work at the construction site in Wuhan. At the end of that year, it was New Year's Eve when I came back to Haikou by doing manual work all the way. I lost my job and had no place to live and wandered on the street with the last three Yuan left in my pocket. At that moment, looking at the warm light from the window, my heart was filled with bitterness and sadness.

I missed my mother so much after leaving my hometown for six years. But I had been restraining my thought. Once I went to Chengdu for market research, it was more than an hour's drive from my hometown. I bought a bus ticket back home as soon as I got off the train, but holding that ticket, I didn't have the courage to get on the bus. I had nothing, and I was unable to make good on my promise to give my mother a better life. I felt extremely ashamed to meet her. With tears in my eyes, I saw the bus drive away to my hometown. Then, turning around, I tore up the ticket.

I spent that New Year's Eve on the concrete bench in the park pavilion. Sitting on the bench, I thought a lot for several hours, as I could not live up to my mother and my girlfriend, who was whole-heartedly waiting for me.

I met my girlfriend when I was working in a hotel. She comes from the town and has a stable job. Her family and friends were opposed to our love. No one could believe in the promise by a male migrant worker who had no fixed abode. But she believed me. "No one is optimistic about our future, but what does it matter? Only our attitudes and confidence do matter. You just concentrate on your work, and I will wait for you all the time." His girlfriend wrote in the letter.

Finally, I developed a kind of disposable toilet sanitary film pad, which is easy to operate and can be recycled automatically.

After that, with my efforts, many of my inspirations turned into a number of inventions that presented an entirely new world to the public, including the protective electric toothbrush, foldable portable bathtub, fully enclosed water storage device. In those eight years, I made a total of 58 inventions, of which 23 were patented by the state. The disposable toilet sanitary film pad and the protective electric toothbrush were also patented by the international community.

In 1998, eight ministries and commissions, including the Central Committee of the Communist Youth League of China, the Ministry of Public Security and the Ministry of Justice, awarded him the honorable title of top ten outstanding young migrant workers in China. When the news was conveyed to Haikou, I lost my 17th job and was looking for a job around the streets.

"With 58 gold mines on my back, I hit myself to the bottom again."

Some people say that my 58 inventions are 58 gold mines. Moreover, it is advised that if I sell any of them, I will be able to go from poor to rich.

When attending the commendation conference of "top ten outstanding young migrant workers in China" in Beijing, a leader of Tianjin invited me to Tianjin, promising to transfer the registered permanent residence of my family members and me to Tianjin and provide us with an apartment of three bedrooms and one living room. A group company in the United States said it would help my family and I immigrated to the United States and promised to create the best conditions for my invention to go to the global market. Some manufacturers in Shenzhen and Zhuhai also came to negotiate with me to buy out my patents.

I've been moved, but we can't just live for money. I have always had a dream in my mind, which is to transform my invention into a product by myself and launch my product in the market.

As the saying goes, the stage extends as far as the mind goes. But I know that the big stage is designed for the capable. There was so much I had to learn to turn an invention into a product and launch it in the market. I decided to spend two to three years learning knowledge, training my ability, and accumulating more experience.

In March 1999, I left Hainan for Shenzhen and served as an ordinary migrant worker, starting from the bottom. At that time, I chose those enterprises that needed to innovate and improve their products. There, I knew more details about their production equipment, technological process, business management, and capital operation. The manager of a company joked with me, "It seems that you are going to steal all the techniques of our company." In this way, I have worked in more than ten enterprises. I have benefited a lot from the fast-paced life and fierce competition in Shenzhen, especially its ability to accept new things and its open and active atmosphere of creation.

In October 2002, I declined all invitations and carried these "58 gold mines" back to my hometown Meishan City, Sichuan Province. Here, I founded Shuer Cleaning Enterprise (Sichuan) Co., Ltd. with the investor, and I acted as the general manager of the company. Our slogan is that if you can dream it, you can do it.

"Let them realize their dreams."

Over the years, I have been walking on a bumpy and difficult road. Without the help of those kind-hearted people, I would never have come to where I am now. I will never forget a worker named Gu Guobin, who lost his job, had no food or clothing but gave me the last 50 Yuan in his pocket. I will never forget that when I conducted a market survey in Shanghai, I had no money to have a meal, and a Jiangxi man who was on a business trip in Shanghai took me to have a full dinner in a restaurant and gave me 100 Yuan. He encouraged me a lot, "young man, you must stick to it and keep it up."

At the end of 2002, I got the first intellectual property income of 300,000 Yuan. I decided to use this sum as the initial fund to set up a foundation, which would be used to support and cultivate poor children who are interested in invention and creation. I want to do something to help those poor children, and let them realize their dreams.

I hope those children who have suffered many hardships will have less bumps on their way to life. I hope they are also told at the most difficult time, "You've got to hold on! After you walk through thorns and mud, you can see the blue sky and meet the spring of life. The stage extends as far as the mind goes. If you dream it, you can do it."

Data source: Wu Miwen. Thank you, poverty, for sparking in my mind. (China Youth, 2003(17))

A straight-A student from Tsinghua University started his own business for the third time

Two entrepreneurs in the Internet circles are named Ma Yun. In addition to Jack Ma (Ma Yun), the founder of Alibaba, few people in the industry know Ma Yun, CEO of M6go, who is also known as little Jack Ma. Ma Yun is a low-keyed person. As a straight-A student graduating from Tsinghua University, he started his own business when he was in college and got a venture capital of $1 million. After that, he founded the eFriendsNet, a platform for making friends, and achieved financial freedom at the age of less than 30. Later, he founded BabySpace, a communication platform for mothers, and M6go, a vertical e-commerce platform for maternal and child supplies.

First start-up: Sweet first and bitter later, it was forced to close

Fate will always favor some people. Ma Yun is one of the lucky ones. He was admitted to Tsinghua University in 1995 and then sent to the graduate school on recommendation. Ma Yun not only completed his undergraduate and graduate studies within four years but also earned the credits and got the first-class scholarship. He is a typical straight-A student.

In 1999, Ma Yun and his classmates, before they graduated, worked together to design FanSo.com, a web portal for college students. “At that time, the bandwidth of the internal network of the University and Sina was very narrow. It took us so long a time to access the Sina website that we copied the content of the external website to the internet website of the University. For this reason, we also raised $1 million, which was an astronomical figure for us at that time. My living expenses were only over 100 Yuan.” In 2000, FanSo.com ranked the 28th place among the top sites in China on Alexa (http://www.alexa.cn/).

But the good times did not last long. Due to the lack of the profit model, FanSo.com soon closed. The first start-up taught Ma Yun the most profound lesson in his life. “I’ve had a sober idea about my life that I must handle affairs in a down-to-earth manner.” Instead of starting a business, he found a job on a firm footing. In 2001, Ma Yun served as deputy general manager of NetEase Wireless Business. “During the two years when I worked in NetEase, I really buckled down on my work. However, most of my classmates chose to go abroad at that time.”

Second start-up: He achieved financial freedom when he was less than 30

It is difficult for people with entrepreneurial genes to position themselves as a migrant worker for a long time. In 2003, Ma Yun, who had only 1400 Yuan in his pocket, was ready to start something again. Together with two friends, he established eFriendsNet, a dating platform.

“At that time, my family put a lot of pressure on me. They said that when I went to university, I didn't study hard and ran out to blindly start my own business. This time, I wanted to start a business again.” But entrepreneurs tend to be stubborn in some aspect that others can't understand. Ma Yun didn't give up his second business plan because of his family's opposition. “We learn from the failure of our first venture. It is infeasible that a company does not make money. eFriendsNet is designed for casual dating, not completely for marriage. We have added the function of the wireless connection. You can check whether someone leaves a message for you on your web page with your mobile phone. You can get a message prompt by paying a monthly payment of five Yuan."

This time, Ma Yun succeeded. In 2005, eFriendsNet was selected as one of the "100 most potential non-listed companies in Asia" by Red Herring, a famous periodical of science, technology, and science in the United States, and won the title of top 500 innovative Internet enterprises in China.

This time, however, Ma Yun was calm in the face of success. In 2006, Ma Yun sold eFriendsNet to Meetic, the largest online dating company in Europe. Up to that day, Ma Yun had realized his financial freedom. This year, Ma Yun was less than 30 years old.

What made Ma Yun determined to sell eFriendsNet? Ma Yun confessed that there are two main reasons. First, at that time, the largest dating website in Europe was prepared to enter the Chinese market, which would result in potential competitive threats. Second, there was a problem in the business model of eFriendsNet that the operator collects the service fee of 5 Yuan per month as an agent.

"In 2005, we know that China Mobile and China Unicom will adjust the charging ratio by a large margin in 2006. Due to our dependence on operators in terms of revenue, we will suffer a loss rather than make a profit after adjustment."

"I believe that I made the right decision at the beginning. It is a praiseworthy quality to know where to stop and persist in what we are doing when we start our businesses." Ma Yun said.

Third start-up: He established M6go, not for listing

At that time, Ma Yun, who achieved financial freedom, did not cease to start his business. In 2006, Ma Yun established BabySpace Corp., an Internet high-tech enterprise established in the British Virgin Islands, to help Chinese families take care of their children in a proper way. It has two subsidiaries, one is BabySpace, and the other is M6go. BabySpace is a community for the mothers of the kids aged between 0 and 6 years old in China to exchange the views on upbringing, living, and consumption, while M6go is a vertical e-commerce platform specialized in the sales of maternal and infant products.

BabySpace only engages in three matters of storage, sharing, and shopping. "First of all, BabySpace provides users with unlimited online storage space to help mothers store the photos and diaries of their children. Now BabySpace and M6go have 20 million users, and each family stores 1,000 photos on the two platforms on an average basis.We have set up servers in Beijing, Shanghai, and Silicon Valley. The photos that describe the children's growth are of great significance. Even if one computer room is burned, the memory will never be lost. Second, we encourage mothers to share their experience and knowledge on taking care of their children via the Internet community. Third, we provide each user with a home page to display their profile. We have done it for two years, mainly relying on advertising for profit." Ma Yun said.

Later, Ma Yun found that there was a huge market potential for the maternal and infant industry in China. The marketing mode relying solely on advertising faces a very low ceiling, and many users have a rigid need to realize the healthy growth of their children. "Especially in terms of food safety, the melamine scandal took place in 2008. Since then, the parents have had great concerns about their children's food safety. So, we launched M6go."

Ma Yun didn't start his business on a large scale as fast as the previous two. This time, he deliberately slowed down his pace. "Our users are children and mothers, so we have very detailed requirements for the supply chain from the perspective of food safety. The company has raised five million dollars in seven or eight years since its inception, and we have managed to survive after numerous hardships. M6go is not intended to involve huge investments. We rarely run advertisements, but we just want to do a good job in service and make the company survive in a small-scale and beautiful way.

The biggest difference between M6go and other e-commerce platforms for maternal and infant products is that more than 80% of the products on M6go are infant food and that they are only imported food." Food safety is the most important thing for us, and our emphasis is not laid on the low price. " Ma Yun said. M6go will buy the goods to be sold on its platform in overseas supermarkets, only cooperate with merchants and general agents, so as to ensure that the products of a container are of the same batch number and ensure safety at the time of customs clearance and inspection.

Under the macro background of the development of the maternal and infant industry in China, M6go entered a fast-growing period from 2012 to 2014. Many investment banks came to M6go and intended to help the company with its listing. But Ma Yun, at this time, said, "it's more important that we do a good job in a down-to-earth way. There is a huge market for maternal and infant products, and we only account for a tiny market share. If the industry involves a market of more than one trillion dollars, our share is still very small, and there is still a lot to do."

Data source: Wu Linlin. Ma Yun, a straight-A student from Tsinghua University, started his business three times and established M6go, not for listing. (Beijing Youth Daily, 2015-05-18.)

It's never too old to invent something

The principal forces of invention and creation are naturally young people, but the elderly are also an important force. The old woman Luo Lijuan has made more than 100 inventions and participated in the personal scientific and technological achievements exhibition of China Beijing High -Tech Industries Week. It fully proves that it is possible to live, learn, invent, and create something till the end of life.

In May 2001, China Beijing High -Tech Industries Week launched the personal scientific and technological achievements exhibition for the first time. A total of 86 inventors attended the exhibition with their invention patents and scientific and technological achievements. Among them, the oldest inventor taking part in the exhibition is Luo Lijuan, who lives in Fangzhuang, Beijing. According to the organizers of the conference, they learned from the newspaper that old Luo Lijuan had many inventions, but could not transform her inventions into practical products due to the lack of an exhibition platform. So they especially found and invited the old lady to the exhibition.

Luo Lijuan intended to exhibit the multi-functional wheelchair in the personal scientific and technological achievements exhibition. The old lady had designed the product many years ago and applied for a patent for utility model in 1994.

At Mrs. Luo's house, she used a complicated model made of cardboard to demonstrate more than ten uses of the multi-functional wheelchair she invented years ago. It can not only be used as a wheelchair for the elderly and patients, but also as a dining table and walker for kids, and even as a sofa and bed for rest. In order to help the old lady take part in the personal scientific and technical achievements exhibition, the organizers of the conference specially funded to make the original cardboard model into a new plexiglass model, and made some innovations based on the original model. The old lady said that the current wheelchair is the second generation of products, and she is ready to continue to launch the third generation of multi-functional wheelchair.

In the old lady's home, there are some inventions which seem to be fresh but practical. For example, the old lady used to use the multi-functional tool table for many years. In the middle of the table is a box, in which many tools can be put, and the bed is opened from both sides, which can accommodate an adult more than 50 kg. Besides, it can also be combined into a large table of 2 square meters. The glass reflective lamp umbrella on the ceiling not only looks beautiful but also can increase the brightness of the lamp. Even in the street, there is a magic house designed by her. The house is 2 meters high and covers an area of 1 square meter. After being unfolded, it has a total of 4 square meters. It can be arranged in a straight-line type or a field type. There are partitions between each room, and each room is equipped with doors, windows, tables, and stools.

According to her family members, the old lady has a large cabinet with tools, raw materials, and samples. Besides, the old lady has the only key to this cabinet. Generally, she doesn't allow anyone to touch these items as her treasure. Most of these inventions were made by the old lady herself. As for some difficult inventions, she had to ask some masters for help. In addition, the old lady paid all the materials with the money from her own retirement pay.

It is understood that Mrs. Luo has been engaged in making inventions for many years. When she was young, she designed her own clothes and knitted some socks, which were sold well because of their novel style. After the old lady retired as a teacher for many years at school, her passion for invention came to her at one time. Mrs. Luo said that up to now, she has made more than 100 inventions on her own and that she was inspired by the daily life to make inventions. Moreover, there were more ideas of invention in her mind, which had not been realized one by one.

When asked if the old lady hopes that some manufacturers can buy her patents and put them on the market on a large scale after she made so many inventions, the old lady said that it was a good idea that the manufacturers could buy the techniques, but what she was more concerned about was that these inventions could be put into practice to contribute to society, rather than how much she could gain. In that case, the old lady felt that she could transfer the patents and technologies to them free of charge. According to the old lady's vision, it would be best if someone funded and organized the establishment of a factory by integrating the three parts of welfare, scientific research, and design so that the laid-off workers and disabled people could learn a technique and produce something useful.

Data source: It is based on the report of the China Business Journal on May 10, 2001.

Robin Li: Do it if you set your mind on it.

I was aware of the inequality of information and resource allocation when I was in middle school

I was very interested in computers at an early age. I remember it was in 1984 when I was in Yangquan City, Shanxi Province. The school where I studied bought only a few computers, but there were more than

400 students in our grade of school. As a result, only a few students could have a chance to learn how to use a computer. At that time, the school adopted an approach to take a test. Whoever had a higher score in mathematics would be chosen to learn how to use the computer. At that time, I worked on learning to use the computer with full confidence. After I studied for a year, our school took an exam and chose the top three to take part in the national youth program design competition. I remember that it was the teacher who took the three of us to Taiyuan by train. On the train, the teacher told us that as long as any of the three of us can make it to the top ten of Shanxi Province, his efforts that he had made finally paid off. I told the teacher to let him rest assured that we would undoubtedly win honor for him. The next day, we took the exam in Taiyuan. After the exam, I went to Xinhua Bookstore in Taiyuan and took a look at the books there. I was shocked as soon as I entered the bookstore, as the books on several bookshelves there were about computer programming. At that time, there was also a Xinhua Bookstore in Yangquan. I often looked for some books that I needed in the bookstore. However, all the books that I could find about computers at that time were the textbooks that we used in class.

Later, none of the three of us made it to the top 10, and I also know why we can't make it because the allocation of information and resources is extremely unequal between different regions. It is evident that the failure actually had a great influence on me later. At that time, I was in senior one. Later, when we went to the senior high school for college entrance examination, we had to fill in the applications for the college we expected to be admitted to. Although I like computers, I don't think I can apply for a computer major because I know that too many people in bigger cities, such as Taiyuan and even Beijing, have much more resource advantages than us. At that time, I wondered if there was any major that involved the application of computers but was not entirely about computers. Then, after looking over all the related majors of various colleges, I finally found one that fit me, the Department of Information Management of Peking University. Now I see it is why I was able to set up Baidu to make it so convenient for the people to find out what they wanted, because I have had such an idea in my mind since I was very young that I would enable all the people in China to have a convenient and equal access to information and find what they want, just like professors in Peking University, no matter how remote they are.

When I was asked "do you have computers in China" when I studied in the United States, I soon found that in such a major, there are fewer courses about computers and that the contents of the courses are superficial and simple. As is known to all, the United States has always been a leader in science and technology. Especially in our time, the United States was far ahead of China in this aspect. So if I want to learn better and more advanced science and technology, the best way at that time is to go to the United States. But when I found that there was no corresponding major of information management in the United States, I was at a loss. I needed to make a new decision. Then, what should I do next? At that time, I did two things. The first thing is to hope that I can know more about my field than others. As an undergraduate, I went to the library of Peking University every day to check the latest papers concerning my major. The second thing is that I applied for a computer major in the United States. Later, I was admitted to the computer department of University at Buffalo, the State University of New York.

When I first arrived in America, I was not suited to the life there. On the one hand, it's cold in that place. It snows for six months a year. On the other hand, we had a tight timetable, and there were some courses that I had never learned during my undergraduate studies. I couldn't understand the postgraduate courses. I was completely confused after attending a class. Once I asked the classmate next to me what flip-flop is. He told me, "you don't know that? It is a trigger." I asked him what the trigger was because I didn't learn any knowledge about hardware in my undergraduate courses.

I suffered many difficulties in the first year there. Moreover, I had the pressure to support myself and wanted to earn money as soon as possible. Once, I saw a professor other than our department studying computer graphics. He intended to recruit an assistant graduate student with some pay. I wanted to have a try and sent my resume to him. Later, he had an interview with me and asked me several questions about computers and computer graphics. I don't think I answered well. Finally, he asked me a question, which impressed me so much. He said, “do you have computers in China?” What does this mean? Does he imply that “do you have a computer in China”? At that moment, none of the Chinese people could afford a computer. He asked me whether there were any computers in China. How could I answer him? I wanted to say that I would build the largest search engine in the world in the future, and that I wanted to make it convenient for hundreds of millions of people to find whatever they intend to discover, and that I wanted to buy a large number of computers to achieve the goals mentioned above. But I didn't say that. Instead, I just answered, “Yes, there are.” and left his office in silence.

More than 20 years later, neither the professor nor I thought that in today's China, the ownership of smartphones is twice the total population of the United States. The CEOs of those chip manufacturers met me and said, “what kind of chip do you want? I will customize it for you. What do you want from the computer? Tell me, and I will tailor it for you.” When they say that, I really call the question by the professor at that time to my mind. Sometimes I also think about what happened in the past two decades, what led to these changes and how I have become a person that attracts the public interest step by step.

“Do not follow the trend or waver until you succeed.”

Now that I think about it. In fact, it is nothing more than a choice you make every time on the road of life. If you make the right choice, the future will be as boundless as the sea and sky; if you make a wrong choice, the future will be thickly sown with thorns. How can we make the right choice? In my view, there are actually three conditions. First, people can't be too stupid. Most people can meet this condition. Second, you need to have a strong interest. If you want to make a correct judgment on a matter, you must first show an interest in it. On this basis, you will be willing to spend some time thinking deeply about it. Last but not least, you must have an abundance of information sources.

After talking with the Professor, I was aware that I am not good at computer graphics, but I have my strengths as I am interested in information retrieval. I first went to Wall Street to develop a real-time financial news retrieval system. The retrieval system used by the Wall Street Journal may still be the version I programmed at that time. Later, I realized that Wall Street is not my real home because the most valuable people on Wall Street are not programmers, but traders who are engaged in stock trading. As a result, I made up my mind to turn to Silicon Valley.

I joined a search engine company at that time and began to make up my mind that as long as I worked in this company for one day, I must ensure that this search engine would be the best one in the world. During that period, I did apply the most advanced technology to that search engine, but I had no say on many matters. As my words did not count, these suggestions were not adopted. When the suggestions failed to be adopted one after another, I realized that I needed to do something that I was my own boss. Therefore, at the end of 1999, I decided to leave the United States and start a business back in China, which was an opportunity for the birth of Baidu.

On August 5, 2015, it was the 10th anniversary of Baidu's listing, and the CEO of NASDAQ sent me two pictures, which showed the characters “Happy 10th Listing Anniversary Baidu” were playing in Chinese and English on the large screen of the Times Square in the United States. When seeing these pictures, I recalled the professor's words, “do you have computers in China?” In the face of one opportunity after another, you have to make various choices. If you make the right choice and set your mind on it, you won't be afraid of any failure or setback, and you will not fear of being turned down. Instead, you will stick to it, and you will not follow the trend or waver until you succeed.

Data source: Anonymous. Robin Li: Do it if you set your mind on it. (Beijing Broadcasting and Television Weekly, 2015-10-22)

Chapter 13 Organize A Mastermind Alliance

Maxims for Success

A mastermind alliance is a group of two or more members who work together for a common goal with a harmonious attitude and an active spirit. The principle of a mastermind alliance enables you to turn the power arising from other people's experience, training, and knowledge into your own power and utilize it. If you can make effective use of a mastermind alliance, you can overcome almost all obstacles regardless of the varying degrees of your own education or intelligence.

—Napoleon Hill

Principles and Guidelines

In the introductory remarks of the biography of Napoleon Hill, W.Clement Stone wrote, "As I read the book Think and Grow Rich, I realized that Napoleon Hill's view was exactly the same as mine. What I'm particularly interested in is the concept of a mastermind alliance proposed by Napoleon Hill. It is defined as two or more people working together for a common goal. I believe that by applying this principle, I can keep my interests in line with those of other people, so as to improve myself. They can share my work so that I can free up my hands to do other work." So, what is a mastermind alliance? How does it work for our success? How should we organize a mastermind alliance? How can we maintain the mastermind alliance? Here is a brief introduction.

You can acquire all the knowledge you need

If you want to achieve a certain goal, you can't do without relevant professional knowledge. However, you can't possess all the professional knowledge alone, which requires you to learn to organize and use a mastermind alliance to get all the knowledge you need. Those who are able to plan and dominate the mastermind alliance plays a decisive role as any of them who are educated and have professional knowledge.

In terms of knowledge acquisition, the following two aspects need to be paid special attention to:

First of all, you need to determine what kind of professional knowledge you need, and what is the purpose of it. The main goal of your life and the direction of your future efforts are the first premise to help you determine what kind of knowledge you need.

Second, you need to figure out which of the knowledge sources are reliable. Generally speaking, reliable knowledge sources include a mastermind alliance, colleges, and universities, libraries, specific training courses, etc. What we need to emphasize here is that knowledge only has potential power and that it will not lead to wealth. Only after reorganizing, can knowledge become an exact plan of action, and then it will be directed at a specific goal, ultimately enabling you to gain wealth and achieve success.

How can we organize a mastermind alliance?

No one in the world can succeed without any help because the power of the individual is limited. All the great figures depend on the help of others to succeed in the end. Organizing a mastermind alliance is the best way to strive for success with the aid of the power of others.

In order for your mastermind alliance to function properly, you must give clear and correct instructions to the members of your mastermind alliance, and the members must be willing to cooperate with you fully. Here are four simple steps to make sure your mastermind alliance can work.

Step 1: Define your goal

The first step to make a mastermind alliance work is to set a clear goal. At the same time, you must define your clear goal as the common goal of your mastermind alliance, or at least make it very close to your goal.

Step 2: Select members

It's a matter of caution to choose proper members to help you achieve your goals. If you can always grasp the following two traits, you can quickly select the right talents.

The first trait is the ability to work. Don't choose someone as a member just because you like or know them. Your best friend may not be the professional talent that you need. Members of your mastermind alliance must be equipped with related professional capabilities.

The second trait is the ability to work in harmony with others. The disharmonious atmosphere at work will offset the efficiency of a mastermind alliance. This situation may not happen immediately, but it may break out at the critical moment when it is decided to win or lose. You must eliminate any disharmony in your mastermind alliance so that the members will devote themselves unreservedly to the alliance with their wisdom. Moreover, you should ensure that the ambition of the members themselves, including your ambition, is subordinate to the common goal of your mastermind alliance.

Step 3: Determine the remuneration

It is an important factor for maintaining a harmonious atmosphere in the alliance by determining the remuneration of the members. In the beginning, you should determine how much remuneration the members are likely to get, which will significantly lower the possibility of disputes in the future. The remuneration of the members is determined based on the basic behavior motive of the members. Wealth has the most considerable appeal to its members, but we cannot ignore the importance of other motives. For many people, identity and a sense of achievement are just as important as money. You should distribute among your members the most influential motivator, wealth, in a joyful, impartial, and generous manner. The more generous you are, the more help you can get from your members.

Step 4: Determine the time and place of the gathering

By determining the time and place of the gathering, we can ensure that the members can make continuous progress and take this opportunity to solve the problems faced by the mastermind alliance. As the mastermind alliance constantly matures and the members get along with each other in an increasingly harmonious atmosphere, you will find that these gatherings can generate a series of ideas in the minds of the members.

In addition, do not replace the free and frequent contact between members with regular gatherings, such as making phone calls, texting, emailing, leaving messages, or talking in the aisle. Through these ways, members can get the information they need at the time of gathering so that they can cope with various emergency circumstances in a short time during the gathering.

How can we maintain the mastermind alliance?

The leader of the mastermind alliance must undertake the task of maintaining the harmony in the mastermind alliance. Here you should pay attention to the following four aspects:

Confidence

As a leader of a mastermind alliance, you should make contributions to achieving your clear goal, so as to arouse the confidence of your members in you.

Communication

All members should have a comprehensive understanding of the situation they are facing, so they should often communicate with each other. All members should have the ability to deal with the core problems in each decision. After making a decision, each member of the mastermind alliance must be convinced that it is a good decision and that each member is willing to spare no effort to support the decision.

Fairness and justice

When you organize a mastermind alliance, each member of the alliance should be willing to contribute to the common goal. And all the members should reach a consensus on the distribution of profits, as well as get along with each other in an ethical manner. The members are now allowed to sacrifice the interests of others in exchange for their own interests. If the members fail to comply with the above requirements, there will inevitably be differences of opinion among them, which may even destroy the alliance as a whole.

Courage

Every member should face all dangers and difficulties with firm faith, indomitable spirit, and courage. The spirit of taking the bull by the horns stems from self-confidence and a well-developed sense of success. The courage of one person cannot be compared with the courage of a group, just as the power of a battery is far less than that of a group of batteries. The more minds you gather, the higher power you will generate.

In a word, the key to the success or failure of a mastermind alliance lies in harmony among its members. You have to make sustained efforts to strengthen the harmonious relationship.

Examples of success

Why could the "ignorant" Henry Ford succeed?

Henry Ford was born in poverty and didn't even graduate from elementary school. But he started from scratch and became king of cars in the United States within 25 years. By analyzing the reasons for his success, we find that in addition to his own traits of success, his mastermind alliance has made great contributions.

During the First World War, an editorial published in a Chicago newspaper called Henry Ford, the king of cars, as an ignorant opponent of the war. They call Ford the ignorant opponent of the war because he didn't even graduate from primary school. Ford protested against the statement and sued the newspaper for defamation. When the court heard the case, the lawyer of the newspaper office asked the court to invite Ford to the witness stand in order to testify the innocence of the newspaper office. Therefore, it can prove to the jury that Ford was ignorant. The lawyer of the newspaper office asked Ford many questions, the purpose of which is to testify that Ford knows a large amount of professional knowledge about automobile manufacturing, but he remains ignorant on the whole.

Ford was bombarded with questions, such as "who is Benedet Arnault?" " how many soldiers did Britain send to the United States to suppress the rebellion of 1776?" and so forth. At last, when asked a particularly hostile question, Ford leaned over wearily and pointed out his finger to the lawyer who asked, "if I really have to answer the silly questions you just asked, and the questions you have been asking since just now, I can remind you that there is a row of buttons on my desk. As long as I press the button, someone will come to help me. These people around me can give me the knowledge I want at any time. Then, why should I fill my mind with general knowledge in order to be able to answer these questions?"

The answer made sense, so Ford beat the lawyer. Everyone in the court knows that this answer is not an answer to the ignorant but that of an educated person. An educated person does not necessarily have a great deal of professional or general knowledge, but he knows where to get it when he needs it, and how to organize it into a definite plan of action. Henry Ford has his own mastermind alliance. With the help of his mastermind alliance, he can acquire the required professional knowledge and general knowledge at any time, instead of having such expertise by himself.

Data source: Napoleon Hill, Michelle Ritter. A Lifetime of Riches (Z. Q. Zhong & S. Li, Trans.) . (Haikou: Hainan Publishing House, 1999.)

Is it worth spending 12 million Yuan on consulting?

There is a theory in the western management circles that if an enterprise does not have a mastermind alliance after its assets exceed 10 million US dollars, its life cycle will be no more than five years. As long as the enterprise makes a severe error in decision-making, it will come to an end.

In the development course of Kingya International Holding Group Co.Ltd, the macro environment, has undergone tremendous changes. When you face and control the dramatical change, it is far from enough to rely solely on the wisdom of several decision-makers of Kingya International Holding Group Co.Ltd. It must use the outside brainpower as the decision-making employee, try to reduce the blindness of the decision as much as possible, and seek the long-term development of the enterprise. To this end, Kingya International Holding Group Co.Ltd invested 12 million Yuan in asking McKinsey & Company of the United States to give a consulting report.

They had contacts with the employee of McKinsey & Company for the first time at a seminar in late 1997. Researchers in McKinsey &

Company attracted them with their speeches delivered at the seminar. After the seminar, the group leaders had a preliminary conversation with McKinsey & Company. During the conversation, they feel that McKinsey & Company has a leading concept of management consulting and that it is highly operatable. Moreover, McKinsey & Company has a global vision, and its research institutions are all over the world. Furthermore, it is ready to deploy experts from the global network to serve its customers at any time. Most important of all, McKinsey & Company has decades of experience in management consulting and has grasped the information on the operation experience and lessons of the failure of the leading enterprises in various fields. If these experiences and lessons can be used and absorbed by Kingya International Holding Group Co.Ltd, through consultation, it is bound to increase the connotation of the Group and improve its competitiveness.

After communication, several decision-makers of the company finally reached a consensus that the development strategy of Kingya International Holding Group Co.Ltd is to strive to be the first in the industry. Therefore, when hiring a management consulting company, it should also hire a world-class company. The Group should serve as an altar lamp burning day and night, rather than a trotting horse lamp or a flashing lamp. They have found that a great many emerging enterprises in China prosper rapidly and advance irresistibly, but they die out unexpectedly in a short time. The root cause of this phenomenon lies in the fact that the decision-makers are at a loss after the enterprises grow bigger. Therefore, they either blindly implement the diversification strategy and finally die in the greedy for grandiose and rapid growth, or they will have internal strife, and finally die in the bottlenecks of management. If the Group intends to bypass the crisis period of business management, it is necessary to ask McKinsey & Company as a consultant.

They have another concern about the pursuit of improving the core competence of the enterprise. Today, the market economy is more and more developed, the social division of labor is more and more detailed, and any enterprise should pursue the development goal as a going concern, by relying on its core competence, which means the unique advantages of the enterprise in some aspects, rather than its comprehensive capabilities. Therefore, enterprises should focus on their efforts to improve their core capabilities and obtain other relevant capabilities with the aid of external service consulting agencies.

After the newspaper disclosed the practice of Kingya International Holding Group Co.Ltd, some people questioned whether it was worth spending 12 million Yuan asking a foreign company to issue a consulting report. Based on the practice, the Group uses the following two facts to prove that it is worth doing so:

First, McKinsey & Company sent researchers to communicate, exchange, and discuss the company's future development strategy with the special committee of the Group within three months. From the perspective of the communication process, it can be seen that the participants of the company in the communication have gained a lot. They have had an idea about the operation ideas and practices of the world's top enterprises of the same industry, and have learned to view the issues from a strategic and integrated perspective.

Second, the managers of the company have acquired skills in dealing with interpersonal relationships and working pressure and other skills after they receive specialized training. They are more engaged in their work and on friendlier terms with each other. These gains are all assets of the Group, which seem to be intangible but actually have too much value.

Data source: Yang Jieqiang. Is it worth spending 12 million Yuan on consulting? (China Enterprise News, 1998-07-31)

Part VI Lay a Solid Foundation for Success

To grow up healthily and achieve success, we should have five basic conditions, to keep healthy, to cultivate an attractive personality, to develop a good habit, to make a budget for time and money and to encourage teamwork, so as to lay a foundation for success.

Chapter 14 Stay Healthy

Maxims for Success

All achievements and all wealth begin with a healthy body and mind. As the maxim goes, a sound mind lives in a healthy body. It can be traced back to the ancient Roman times, and it is still applicable up to now. Only when you are energetic can you persevere in what you are doing now. Here I might tell you that a healthy body is the capital to make money. Because of poor health, you may lose hope for yourself and even the world.

—Napoleon Hill

Principles and Guidelines

It is above criticism that we all aspire after wealth, success, happiness, and joy and that we set a goal for our life and encourage ourselves to work towards the goal. However, if you neglect or even sacrifice your health as the most valuable asset when pursuing what you want, how can you acquire wealth and achieve success? Even if you have achieved wealth and success, but you are seriously ill, how can you enjoy a happy life? The direct manifestation of a healthy body is life, which is just one time for each of us. A person who does not know how to keep healthy and cherish life is doomed to have nothing at all. A wise man said: "wealth is for children; power is, for the time being, reputation is for the future, and only health belongs to us now." In view of this, we must pay attention to keeping healthy in the journey when we work hard and perseveringly for success.

Connotation of health

Human health consists of physical and mental health. At the same time, physical health is inseparable from mental health. Any factors that affect mental health will also affect physical health. On the contrary, any factors that affect physical health will also affect mental health.

Human body and mind are integrated with nature, so you must first understand how nature goes in order to understand the methods of maintaining physical and mental health. Man must live in harmony with nature, not against it. In addition, just as you have to understand the whole nature and move with its regularity, you also have to understand your whole body and move with its rhythm.

The human body and mind are a whole, which influence each other. However, the human mind has a higher level of function than the body. The human body is a functional machine that bears the thoughts and carries out the instructions of the thoughts. To have a healthy body, you must have a well-functioning mind. Mental health has a direct impact on physical health.

Although some people are restricted in their physical functions, the power of thinking allows them to live a creative life. In this regard, Helen Keller, Zhang Haidi, Thomas Alva Edison, and Ludwig van Beethoven are the best examples.

Good health is priceless

Some rich Americans say they are willing to spend $10 million if they can extend their lives by 10 years. You may want to be the best scientist, inventor, Professor, doctor, lawyer, general manager, salesperson, or employee, but you may never want to lie under the decorated tombstone early. Thus, it can be seen that life is extremely precious to us.

In the journey of human life, one side is growth and health, and the other is aging and death. If you can grow up in a healthy way, you will feel full of vitality and hope, and you will be able to clearly realize that you have the power to deal with all crises and know that you are the master of the world. What could be more important, more precious, more proud, and happier than such a healthy state? In the final analysis, a person's happiness and glory lies in his health and strength.

The most important reward in life is health, firmness, and strength. We do not need to have a big figure or a mighty appearance, but we should have a healthy body, strong vitality, and great spiritual strength. The strength is reflected in the arduous journey of the Long March covering 12,500 kilometers of land by the heroic Red Army, in

Napoleon's indomitable spirit of staying on the saddle for 24 hours day and night, and in Franklin's dedication to camping in the wild at the age of 70. All of these above are the most important things in life.

In a word, wealth is priced, power is priced, and reputation is priced, but good health is priceless. Therefore, it should be the sacred mission of each of us to keep healthy and cherish life. At the same time, being able to enjoy life with a healthy body and a long life is also the main reward for a person in the course of life.

Health is the guarantee of success

Your body is the most significant capital for a great cause. Health is the main source of vitality. If you are in bad health, you will live a dull life, and your efficiency will be declined drastically. And your life is bound to be gloomy. For a person, physical strength and intelligence are the most important things because physical strength and intelligence, his mental state, vitality, and ability to handle affairs. The intensity of physical strength and intelligence depends on whether you have a sound body and mind. Therefore, if you can have a healthy body and a sound mind, it is a sense of well-being.

A healthy body is the carrier of physical strength and intelligence and the foundation to make any achievements. As a result, those who intend to achieve great things must cherish their bodies, strengthen their physical strength, develop their intelligence, and concentrate on what they are doing, and make the most economical and effective use of their physical strength and intelligence.

A person's success or failure depends on whether he can take care of his body and makes himself always in an energetic state. A person who is in weak health tends to feel afraid of difficulties and become melancholic in some cases, and he will not have any creative spirit. If a person does not have enough strength in his body, blood, and brain, he is often unable to cope with any impending major event. Moreover, he will inevitably become exhausted, listless, feeble and spiritless. Therefore, he will never make great achievements and eventually fall down. And it is why so many people fail.

If you have a strong body, you will never fall into a passive position but will completely take the initiative no matter what you do. In this way, you will become strong and forceful, and devote your heart and soul to what you are doing, and eventually, you will undoubtedly make unique and pioneering achievements. A strong body contains great creativity. A strong body can increase the strength of a person in every functional part. So compared with those who are physically weak, they are naturally more efficient and successful in handling affairs.

Those who have made great achievements in history tend to attach great importance to their health. In the call to keep fit, study well, and work well issued by Mao Zedong to the young people in China, the priority is especially given to keeping fit, which is because it emphasizes that only when we keep fit can we study well and work well. Keeping fit is the premise, foundation, and guarantee of studying well and working well. In his youth, Mao Zedong loved to swim and climb mountains, and insisted on taking cold baths all the year round. At that time, he intended to exercise his body and will, improve his health and get well prepared for the great cause in the future. Theodore Roosevelt, the US President, was able to save the critical situation and carry out the New Deal and achieve success because he is in good health, which is the capital of success. He once said, "I had been feeble and sick since I was young. If I can take more exercise, I will become much healthier and more energetic. So every time when I do something, I am sure to achieve the predetermined goal." It can be seen that the first thing we need to do in our life is to protect and maintain our health, develop our strength, enhance our energy, and get fully prepared for the career that we are likely to engage in in the future. It is everyone's sacred duty. Our bodies are priceless, so we must cherish them.

Duration of health: How long can a person live?

Only when we are healthy can we live long. So, how long can a person live? According to the research results of cytology, there is a sea turtle in the Pacific Ocean. Its cells divide 72-114 times in a lifetime, and its life span can reach 250 years. Chicken cells divide 15-35 times in a lifetime, and the life span of chicken can reach 30 years. Human cells can divide about 50 times in a lifetime, and the human life span can reach at least 120 years. Recently, according to the research results of cytology, embryology, genetic engineering, neurology, genetics, and other disciplines, put forward the view that mankind can live to 150 years old. Based on the fact that there are many long-lived people in the news reports, it shows that it is possible for people to live to 150 years old. According to the Gerontological Society of China, in the first census in 1953, there were only 3,384 centenarians in China. By 2014, there had been 58,789 centenarians in China. Although the centenarians still account for a tiny proportion of the total population, the census data of the countries in the world shows that people's life expectancy is longer and longer and that the number of long-lived people is on the rise.

How can we live a long and healthy life?

There are divergent opinions on the reasons for people's longevity. Some say it's heredity, and some say it's a living environment, while others say it's occupation and medical condition. In fact, all statements make sense to some extent. According to the World Health Organization, among the factors that affect the health and longevity of human beings, genetic factors account for 15%, social factors account for 10%, medical conditions account for 8%, climate conditions account for 7%, and human factor accounts for 60%. In other words, people's health and longevity mainly depend on themselves. To live a long life, we should take good care of our health and protect our bodies. If we are congenitally deficient, we can acquire health by making up for the deficiencies. Otherwise, even when we are congenitally perfect, I'm afraid that it is impossible that we fulfill our wishes if we do not keep in good condition. "If you don't live to be 100 years old, it's all your fault," Ribala Aliyev, a centenarian from Azerbaijan, said to the guests with a smile as he celebrated his 100th birthday! It makes sense.

It is a long-cherished wish of people to live a long life. Everyone is willing to explore the way to live long. There are no immortals in heaven, but there are methods of longevity in the world. There are rules and ways to live a long life.

Have a positive mental attitude

Your body is controlled by your brain. Thus, if you want to be in good health, you must have a positive mental attitude, which means that you should have a sound consciousness. Whether you are young or old, your psychological concept can determine the quality of your life. If you always think that your body is going bad and aging, your energy will gradually disappear with the growth of age, and you will not have sufficient energy and vitality any longer, not to mention a healthy and long life. On the contrary, if you have a young mental state, every cell in your body will continue to regenerate and renew itself, and you will not show any signs of aging. If you believe that you can live a long and healthy life, you will indeed live a long and healthy life!

To cultivate a positive mental attitude, you need to absorb mental nutrition frequently. The main way to absorb mental nutrition is to persist in learning. When someone asked a long-lived man the secret of retaining his youthful vitality, he answered, "my secret is to insist on learning something new every day." The ancient Greeks had the same view that the secret to remaining young forever is to learn something new till the end of life. All kinds of inspirational books and biographies of celebrities contain a wealth of mental nutrition, so you should read the books frequently, like doing some reading for an hour every day, and constantly absorb the mental nutrition, in order to strengthen the cultivation of a positive mental attitude.

The simplest and effective way to cultivate a positive mental attitude is self-suggestion. Every day, you should tell yourself, "I'm healthy! I am very happy! I'm sure I'll be better today than I was yesterday." If you can live with a positive mental attitude, you can get a sound mind and a healthy body. With a positive mental attitude, you can enjoy a healthy and long life.

However, keep in mind that the key to the success of this method lies in your belief in this sentence. The more you believe in it, the better the effect will be.

Have a scientific dietary habit

The function of food is to provide the energy we need for our activities, and that should be the sole goal of your dietary habit.

If we think of the digestive system as a factory, we must supply different raw materials to make the system function well. If the ingredients are not appropriate, the factory may not be able to complete the manufacturing task or manufacture some defective products, or even some raw materials may pile up in all corners. As a result, the factory will be overwhelmed.

According to the knowledge of diet and nutrition science, the following can help you achieve a balanced diet:

(1) Fresh fruits and vegetables should account for the largest proportion of the food eaten. They are rich in vitamins and efficient substances, which are most easily absorbed by the human body.

(2) The second food you should eat more is carbohydrates, such as wheaten food, grains, and potatoes.

(3) Protein, such as lean meat, eggs, fish, milk of cattle and sheep, is an extremely important food. But you shouldn't eat too much. Just take the right amount every day.

(4) Avoid oily food, control the consumption of animal oil and other edible oil, and refuse to eat fried food. At the same time, you should also avoid eating more sugar, such as candy, coke, and so on.

(5) You should also eat a variety of foods, such as all kinds of coarse cereals, to meet different needs of the body. You should not have a partiality for a particular kind of food and should refuse to overeat and refuse other improper eating methods.

In addition, do not eat anything when you are angry, frightened or worried, because when you are in a state of tension, your body will not be able to fully absorb the nutrition of the food you eat, which will only make you fatter and fatter.

In addition to paying attention to the scientific composition of food, it is also of great significance to develop a good dietary habit. There are three important points to note here. First, have a meal at a fixed time and by a definite quantity. In general, you should not change the time of eating at will, and the amount of food you eat for each meal should not be too much or too little. Second, chew carefully and swallow slowly. Don't bolt and overeat while eating, but chew your food well before swallowing it. Third, eat neither too much nor too little. It is the best way to leave off with an appetite. It is reported that more than 50% of the diseases suffered by modern people are caused by over-nutrition. So, remember never to overeat. In addition, some people, especially young women, will go on a diet blindly to lose weight in order to keep a slim figure, so that they may be undernourished, physically weak, mentally depressed and suffering from various diseases. It will not only affect normal life and work but also make it impossible to live a long and healthy life.

Keep working and exercising

As the saying goes, life moves in movement, actions do not fade, but uses do not fade. The movement consists of two aspects. On the one hand, the human body should exercise. Otherwise, the function will decline and eventually die out. On the other hand, the mind, especially the brain, should also move. Otherwise, the function of people will also decline, and finally will be completely lost, and even lead to disease - Alzheimer's disease. The human body is composed of cells, and cell life is continued by the continual division and proliferation of cells. Once the cell stops dividing and proliferating, it will head for its doom, and the man will also die. The driving force of cell division is action. There are two forms of action, one is labor, including both physical and mental labor, and the other is exercise. Labor and exercise are the panacea to cure many chronic diseases, and they enable the people to have bright eyes, rosy cheeks, strong muscles and a sharp mind. Moreover, it reduces dyspepsia, circulates blood throughout the body, makes the feet light and vigorous, and allows the people to live a much healthier and longer life. In view of this, labor and exercise are the main driving forces of a long and healthy life.

There is something in common among a lot of centenarians that they all stick to working and exercising all their lives. For example, a pair of centenarians in Beijing is a good example. The husband, Wu Tunan, died at the age of 105 years old. He is a descendant of Wu's Taijiquan. In his early years, he studied traditional Chinese medicine and dabbled in many subjects. He is a professor of archaeology and psychology. The learned professor can speak English, French, and Russian and is an expert in many musical instruments, such as Qin, wind musical instrument, and bamboo flute. His wife, Liu Guizhen, died at the age of 103 years old. The couple lived a regular life with a regular diet in the eighty or ninety years. They play taijiquan every morning and every night. After retirement, both of them received the offer of the Beijing Institute of Culture and History, to continue their work and make some contributions in their remaining life.

Labor and exercise are both movements, but they are not the same. Due to the limitation of occupation, labor can only make the local function and system of the human body move, which has both positive and negative effects on the health of the human body. For instance, it can be testified by the occurrence of various occupational diseases. Therefore, labor work is beneficial to human health, but it can not replace physical exercise.

There are many forms of sports, such as boxing, playing ball, swimming, mountain climbing, running, walking, martial arts, and so on. These forms do not need to be used in all kinds. You can choose one or two according to your physical condition and objective conditions. The key to the ability to receive good results by physical exercise lies in two aspects. First, exercise should be moderate. It doesn't mean that the more you exercise, the better you will be. Especially for the middle-aged and the elderly, they should pay more attention to the right amount of exercise. Second, you should exercise in a persistent way. Do not work hard for one day but do nothing for the next ten days. You must persevere and stick to it all your life so that you will receive good results.

Pay attention to a proper balance between work and rest

As the saying goes, all work and no play makes Jack a dull boy. Tension refers to work, and relaxation refers to rest. The main ways to take a rest are to relax and sleep.

1. Relax

When you choose a goal as the object of your attention in your mind, such as working out a work plan, writing an academic paper, and solving a technical problem, it means that you have excluded all other things in your mind, just focusing on the established goal. However, after a long time, people will feel tired. If you consciously shift your focus from the established goal to other goals, such as playing the piano, singing, reading novels, or doing anything else that can distract you, you will overcome fatigue and recover your physical strength and energy in a short time. Relaxation is not a sign of laziness, but a magic pill to keep your mind at its best all the time. It is a positive way to rest.

In order to really achieve the goal of relaxation, we need to pay attention to ways and methods. You will be unable to relax when you do something, such as watching TV for a long time, watching a film, singing karaoke and so on. Instead, they will make you become exhausted. The key to relaxation is to cultivate a variety of interests so that your mind can have a change in the environment. For example, the manual workers should cultivate some interests that are involved in the brain, such as doing some reading, listening to lectures, taking up advanced studies, and so forth. Mental workers should take more physical exercises and take part in some physical work in an alternative and proper way. In addition to mastering your major, you should also become an expert in his profession while possessing all-round knowledge and ability and try to develop as many interests as possible, such as music, dance, art, calligraphy, gardening, etc.

2. Sleep

Sleeping is the most thorough way to rest. A person spends about one-third of his life sleeping. Thus, it is the most unwise way to increase working hours by reducing sleep, because you need to recharge yourself for the activities the next day, while the way to recharge is to sleep. If you refuse to sleep, you cut off the power source of the activities the next day.

The enemy of sleep is insomnia. Insomnia is usually caused by your inability to relax before you go to bed. Remember to stop working before you are tired out. Don't do anything that may highly stimulate your nerve before going to bed, such as physical exercise and emotional fluctuations, and so forth. You can do some preparations before going to bed, such as brushing your teeth, washing your feet, making the bed, etc. All of these actions will deliver a message to your brain that now it is time to go to bed.

Give play to the driving force of sex and love

Sex is the most valuable and constructive driving force for human beings, the pillar of all creativity, and an important force for human beings to become in good condition and make progress. Once sex is combined with love, it will produce the most powerful and dynamic impetus. It not only enables you to build a family and clan but can also serve as a strong impetus to your physical and mental health.

In scientific experiments and the history of human life, it has been proved that sexual desire and sexual function are important standards to test whether a person is healthy and strong or not. Those who have strong sexual desire and vigorous sexual function are bound to have a strong physique and more likely to live a long life. On the contrary, those who have lost their sexual desire and function will inevitably suffer from physical weakness, and they are less likely to live long. If sexual desire can be closely bound up with love, it will generate a greater driving force for people to live a healthy and long life.

Develop a good character and living habits

All those who live a long life tend to have a good character and living habits, which is also an important reason for their good health and longevity. Good character and living habits are manifested in many aspects. The main characters closely related to good health and longevity are an open mind, a calm mood, a lively and cheerful attitude, and excellent control over the temper in any case. Related habits include quitting smoking and drinking, eating less meat and more vegetables, having meals at a fixed time and by a definite quantity, leaving off the table with an appetite, chewing carefully and swallowing slowly, keeping clean, paying attention to safety, taking more exercises, making a proper balance between work and rest, speaking and conducting in moderation, going to bed early and getting up early, taking a moderate nap after lunch, adhering to exercise, and persevering in what you are doing, and so forth.

Character and living habit is the force of inertia. Once it is formed, it will work for a long time. Good character and habits will play a positive role in promoting your efforts to live a long and healthy life and achieve success in your career. On the contrary, bad character and habits will play a negative or even destructive role, as it may not only spell an end to your career but also destroy your health. Therefore, in order to achieve a long and healthy life and a successful career, you must develop good character and living habits.

Prevent a disease when you are healthy and treat the disease if any

It is inevitable that we will be infected with various diseases in our life, due to various external reasons, such as environmental change, seasonal change, alternation between day and night, temperature rise and fall, pathogen and virus infection, or different personal factors, such as family heredity, excessive fatigue, aging, aging of the body, functional decline, weakened resistance, etc.. When we are in good health, we should take all kinds of measures to prevent any possible disease and strive to eliminate the disease in its infancy. Once we get sick, we should treat it as soon as possible, prevent it from aggravating and try to be restored to health as soon as possible.

Examples of success

The secret of Zhou Youguang's longevity

Zhou Youguang lived a legendary life. He dabbled in various fields of academic studies and made great achievements when he changed his profession at the age of 49. He married Zhang Yunhe, the second daughter of the well-known Zhang clan in Jiuru Lane, Suzhou. He has never stopped writing and published the new book titled Zhao Wen Dao Ji, at the age of 106.

On Zhou Youguang's 100th birthday, the younger generation made a beautiful autograph album for him and sketched out the track of his study and life with a large number of precious photos. It properly annotated Zhang Yunhe's good wishes to Zhou that "Zhou Youguang lives an honorable life."

When it comes to his old age, Zhou Youguang joked: "God is so busy that forgets to take me to heaven." A new version of An Eulogium on a Humble Cell adapted by Zhou Youguang tells the secret of his longevity, "Mountains need not always be high, as long as there are lush woods. Waters need not always be deep, as long as there are migratory fish. It is a humble cell, as long as I can find where my joy lies in a materialistic way. The room is dark, making the windows brighter. My desk is uneven while I have bent over my desk, working for long hours. The threshold is broken, but there are more casual visitors. We dance on the floor to welcome old friends. The bedroom also serves as the kitchen, making it convenient to have a meal. The bookcase can also be used as the kitchen cabinet, making the dishes cooked with the fragrance of books. I like listening to music from my neighbor's radio and reading the articles sent by some strangers. I make every effort to squeeze on the tram to exercise my muscles and bones. To make a public phone call, I go out for half a kilometer while taking a walk. When I look at the clouds and the sky, the universe is my roof. When I go on a tour of the countryside, the field is my garden house."

Zhou Youguang had tuberculosis and depression when he was young. When they got married, their nanny secretly took the Eight Characters (in four pairs, including the year, month, day and hour of a person's birth, each pair consisting of one Heavenly Stem and one Earthly Branch, formerly used in fortune-telling) of the two for fortune telling. The fortune-teller told the nanny that Zhou couldn't live to be 35. He didn't believe it and said with a smile, "I believe that the end of the old will be the beginning of a new one."

At the age of 80, he decided to start his life again. He took 80 years as 0 years old and calculated the age progressively. At the age of 92, he received a greeting card, which said: "Congratulations to the 12-year-old Grandpa for a happy New Year! " Up to now, the old man is overjoyed when speaking of that.

He added: "I went to the physical examination at the age of 97, but the doctor didn't believe it. He thought I had written the wrong age and changed it to 79. The doctor asked me why I was in such a good condition, and I wondered why he asked me this since he was a doctor." Meanwhile, he said, "a lot of people have asked me this question. I had never thought about it before, but later I thought about something that makes sense. First of all, a positive mental attitude is essential to health. When you encounter something bad, don't be disappointed, and don't punish yourself for the mistakes of another person. Second, I live a regular life and not eat without caution. I used to have a consultant doctor in Shanghai, and he told me that most people didn't starve to death but ate to death. Eating at random is adverse to your health. If you eat a lot at a party, you should throw it up. Another interesting thing is that I used to suffer insomnia for many years, and it was so difficult for me to fall asleep. During the cultural revolution, I was transferred to the countryside, but my insomnia was cured. Up to now, I have no longer suffered insomnia but have had a sweet sleep. So, my wife and I both believe in the saying that misfortune might be a blessing in disguise. Don't be disappointed when you encounter something bad. There are two lines that I often encouraged myself during the Cultural Revolution that 'Don't panic in an emergency situation, and don't be furious when being insulted by others for no reason.' It is a true saying of the ancients, which makes sense. Ji Xianlin wrote the Random Recollections of the Cow Shed, and he told us not to be angry or panic even if we were convicted of various crimes. It tests our ability to control ourselves. In my view, first of all, we should live in a regular and scientific way. Second, we should be able to control ourselves and not punish ourselves for the mistakes of another person. We should not panic in an emergency situation and not be furious when being insulted by others for no reason."

Later, Zhou Youguang summed up several experiences:

(1) Don't smoke or drink too much, and just drink a little beer.

(2) Don't eat casually at the party. Eating at random is not good for your health. Eat more homemade dishes.

(3) Pay attention to hygiene in your daily life, and take a bath and wash your hair every day.

(4) Hold an optimistic attitude, and see the good in the bad.

(5) Go to bed at about 10 p.m., get up at 7 or 8 a.m., and get a good sleep. You need to take a nap at noon. Thus, you can live a regular life.

At the age of 108, he also specially warned people, "God endows us with a brain, not for eating, but for thinking. By thinking about different problems, we will become young in body and mind."

He added, "If you have nothing to do all day long or do not use your brain, or you are interested in nothing or think about nothing, your brain will age fast. If so, what's the point of having a healthy body?"

Data source: Cao Kefan. The secret of Zhou Youguang's longevity. (Shanghai Observer, 2016-01-13.)

Professor Zheng Ji, 109 years old: He completed the book on maintaining good health at the age over 100

Zheng Ji, also known as Zheng Libin, was born in 1900 in Liujia Town, Nanxi County, Sichuan Province. He is not only a famous biochemist in China, but also the founder of the subject of aging biochemistry, and one of the forerunners of biochemistry and nutrition science in China. At the age of 109, he published a book titled The Secrets of Anti-aging: The Regimen of the Most Aged Professor.

Zheng Ji has been eager to learn since he was a child, but he has been ill and had bad luck all his life. He has gone through countless tests of life and death, and has been fighting against disease all his life:

In 1916, he had tuberculosis.

From 1961 to 1963, he underwent three laparotomy operation and was hospitalized for nearly a year and a half.

In 1997, he lost more than 1,000 ml of blood and was hospitalized for 80 days.

In 2001, he broke his hip.

In 2004, he was hospitalized for more than four months due to stomach disease, and he was at death's door many times.

However, illness and dangerous circumstances were not enough to bring Zheng Ji to his knees Zheng was steeled in repeated struggles and lived over a hundred years. Professor Zheng Ji is very fond of learning and never stops writing. He taught himself Japanese at the age of 74 and completed the book titled Assurance of Longevity: The Regimen of the Most Aged Professor. He went to work every day before he was 100 and didn't rest during the summer vacation. It is because of his habit of learning and thinking that he lived to 109 years old. According to Professor Zheng, an important factor that affects longevity is to keep an open mind and an optimistic attitude. Zheng spends his daily life in a strictly scheduled way. He was able to keep exercising, his diet was completely in line with nutrition, and he had been continuously taking vitamins for decades.

Professor Zheng Ji not only made great contributions to the development of nutrition and biochemistry science in China but also verified his own longevity theory with his vigorous energy, incredible sharp thinking, and positive mental attitude.

In 1961, when Zheng was seriously ill, he wrote a poem to cheer himself up and warn himself, "Where there is life, there must be death. There is a natural law of life and death. Pengzu (Jian Keng) lived to eight hundred years old, while a mayfly only lives for a short time. Although the life span of the livings varies, they all finally come to death. It is arranged by nature, while mankind can do anything about it. Do not ask for sempervivum, and there is no elixir of eternal life in the world. Pay attention to protecting your health and do not go to extremes. When you worry less, you will naturally feel comfortable. Laugh and grow fat. You should balance your work and rest in a moderate way, and be concerned about your diet. If you have a minor illness, seek medical advice early. If you have a serious illness, don't worry. Take the disease as it comes. You should never stop improving yourself. Conform to the natural law and you will be bound to live a long life."

"People who live a healthy life should care about the rejuvenation of the country and make more contributions to it," he said, "We should keep in mind that the value of life lies in dedication, not in acquisition."

In his whole life, he adhered to the "Ten Secrets of Health" created by himself and lived an optimistic life. The ten secrets of health are as follows:

(1) Have an open mind, an optimistic and positive attitude, and a stable mood.
(2) Live a regular life.
(3) Adhere to manual labor and physical exercise.
(4) Have a good rest and sleep.
(5) Pay attention to food hygiene, and do not overeat.
(6) Quit smoking strictly and drink less.
(7) Control of sexual desire and bad habits.
(8) Don't neglect minor illnesses.
(9) Pay attention to environmental sanitation and have more contact with sunshine and fresh air.
(10) Pay attention to labor protection to prevent accidental injury.

Zheng Ji said an optimistic mind is the priority of the ten secrets. If you want to live a long and healthy life, first of all, you should be in a calm mood, and grin all the time. In fact, the secrets of Zheng Ji's longevity can be summarized as that you will be able to live a long life, as long as you are not frightened by the disease, believe that you have the ability to be restored, and then keep working in the field that you love.

Data source: Li Ping. Professor Zheng Ji completed the book on maintaining good health at the age of over 100 . (Beijing Broadcasting and Television Weekly, 2009-02-26)

Liao Jingwen's psychotherapy

In 1953, Xu Beihong died of a sudden cerebral hemorrhage, leaving Liu Jingwen, 30, and his two young children behind. Under such a huge blow, Liao Jingwen was trapped in the abyss of grief and was unable to extricate herself. Those days, her life was filled with tears. From then on, her strong physique has collapsed, while coronary heart disease, hypertension, neurosis, and so on came to her. For a time, she was utterly fatigued, both mentally and physically, due to various diseases. In the daytime, she often sat alone for hours without saying a word. At night, she lay in bed with her eyes open all night, feeling that she was on the brink, and maybe she would go to her husband sometime. But she was not hospitalized or recuperated at home, and she even declined the plan for her to travel abroad arranged by the party organization. She thought that she should immediately start to write the life of Xu Beihong who is excellent in arts and moral honesty so that the readers who love Xu Beihong and his works can have a more distinct and detailed understanding of the paintings and personality of the master of painting.

It's so strange that, once people have spiritual sustenance and ideal pursuit, they will go out of grief. After the idea came into being, she felt refreshed and greatly relieved. "When the idea of writing a book arises, it is deeply rooted in my mind. From then on, I felt that I was supported by a cornerstone and a pillar in my life, and I was cheered up." She said. In order to write the biography of Xu Beihong, Liao Jingwen took up advanced studies with her weak body at the Department of Chinese Language and Literature, Peking University. After graduation, she began her hard work as director of the Xu Beihong Museum. At night, she spread out the paper and wrote with passion. One night, she even wrote 36,000 words in one breath! Because of heart disease, she always worried that she would sleep on the writing desk at any time and never wake up again. But the power of spirit is so strong that it makes death step back, and Liao Jingwen did not fall. After ten years' hard work in bad health, the literary biography, The Life of Xu Beihong, was finally completed.

However, misfortune came to Liao Jingwen again. During the Cultural Revolution, Liao Jingwen was devastated, and her manuscript was confiscated. And her hard work in ten years was gone with the wind. However, in the long and miserable nights, the spiritual pillar of Liao Jingwen did not collapse, and she had kept thinking about the manuscript with all her love. After the Cultural Revolution, her manuscript was not returned to her, and she had to conceive and write a new book again. In August 1982, The Life of Xu Beihong, a newly compiled biography, was finally published. By this time, Liao Jingwen was already sixty years old. To the surprise, when Liao was sixty-two years old, she went to the hospital for a physical examination, and the doctor told her that her coronary disease had been cured. It fully demonstrates the old saying that "Seek yourself where you get your sore." Spiritual power can create a miracle. (Editor's note: psychotherapy can help to cure the disease, but we should not give up the right medical treatment).

Data source: Wei Derui. Liao Jingwen's psychotherapy. (Science and Health, 2004 (1) .)

Zhang Xiuyu's motto of health: The pithy formula of health

(1) Have a sunny mental attitude and a good state of mind
(2) Care for major events and have a far sight
(3) Don't fly into a rage when angry and don't be arrogant when happy
(4) Have a scientific diet and eat coarse cereals
(5) Eat less meat and more vegetables with a balanced portion
(6) Chew carefully and swallow slowly, and have meals at a fixed time and by a small quantity
(7) Quit smoking, limit alcohol and exercise regularly
(8) Practice your physical and mental strength
(9) Live a regular life and balance your work and rest
(10) Keep clean and change clothes frequently
(11) Maintain good health properly and prevent injury

(12) Treat the disease immediately if any and prevent any disease if you are healthy

Chapter 15 Cultivate An Attractive Personality

Maxims for Success

Your personality is the most valuable asset but also the heaviest burden because it accepts everything you can control, including your mind, body, and soul. Personality shapes your thoughts, behaviors and relationships with others, and it also encloses the spatial borders between you and the world.

— Napoleon Hill

Principles and Guidelines

To achieve sustainable success, we must have an attractive personality. The attractive personality is charming. Then, what is personality? What is an attractive personality? What is the relationship between all kinds of personalities? What is the highest pursuit of personality? Let's discuss these questions.

What is personality?

Dr. Orison Swett Marden, the founder of Success Magazine in the United States and the great inspirational mentor of success, quoted the words of Henry Drummond's biography in his essay "Personality is the greatest power" in order to explain what personality is, as follows:

"When you meet him, you will find that he is a gentleman with elegant manners and proper clothes. He has a long stature and a graceful posture. He walks with a light and rhythmic pace. He has a bright smile on his face. He doesn't look a bit sad, and he doesn't know what arrogance and shyness are. When you talk to him, you will find that he is full of interest in what you are talking about. He can fish, shoot as well as skate. Few people are as proficient in so many sports as he is. He often plays cricket. In order to watch a fireworks show or a football game, he will come over regardless of the long distance. Every time you meet him, he will tell you new stories, new riddles, or new jokes. In the street, he takes you to watch two children delivering letters play a prank on others. On the train, he reads his favorite new story to you. In a rural farmhouse on a rainy day, he tells the people a new game. In no more than five minutes, the people there rush to play the game. At the children's party, the children will applaud his clever magic tricks. When he was a child, he had a manly temperament. But when he became a man, he had a childlike mind. The young people who know him call him the prince. He has an extraordinary ability to make friends with others. ”

In addition, a man called Mark Laren said, “Drummond has more influence on people than anyone else I know. It's a magic power. To be exact, other people influence the people around them via their words and deeds, but he attracts people around him by his living personality at once. ”

After quoting the above two paragraphs, Orison Swett Marden asked, “What is personality?” He answered, “Personality is a unique combination of all the excellent qualities of a person which are different from those of another person.” In other words, personality is a combination of the qualities where one person is distinct from another person, such as appearance, expression, tone, dress, knowledge and wisdom, interest and hobbies, mental attitude, behavior, character, habit, style, quality, etc. So, Napoleon Hill said, “personality is a combination of one's psychological, spiritual, and physical traits and habits, and it is a valuable asset that has a great impact on the people around. It determines whether a person is different from others and whether a person is loved or disliked (Hill, 1999: 250).” It can be seen that there are two kinds of personalities, among which one is the charming personality, also known as an attractive personality, and the other is the disgusting personality, also known as the personality that repels people. Henry Drummond's personality belongs to a pleasant and charming personality, also known as an attractive personality. There is no doubt that we should cultivate a charming personality, and resolutely abandon the disgusting personality. So, what is a charming personality?

Charming personality

After a lot of research, Napoleon Hill made it clear, "The third step to achieve sustainable success is to cultivate an attractive personality, also known as the charming personality, which is well developed. In order to achieve the goal, you must perfect the 25 kinds of personalities listed as follow (Hill, 1999: 32)."

1. A positive mental attitude

A positive mental attitude is a primary trait to attract others, and it is a correct mental attitude that anyone should be possessed under any circumstance.

The mental attitude is composed of positive personality factors, such as honesty, confidence, honesty, hope, optimism, courage, initiative, generosity, willpower, wit, etc. In fact, among the eighteen principles of success, many principles take a positive mental attitude as a critical element. A positive mental attitude will affect the mood, posture, and facial expression when you are talking with another person. It will modify every word you say, determine your emotional feeling and have an impact on your thoughts. At the same time, a positive mental attribute is also a component of other personalities. By understanding and applying other personalities, you will enhance your positive mental attitude.

2. Be flexible and adjust to changing circumstances

On the way to success, we will never go off smoothly, and we may be confronted with all kinds of sudden changes, difficulties, setbacks, and even temporary failures. When confronted with such a rapidly changing environment and an emergency situation, whether we panic or meet the danger calmly will affect the final result of the incident. The personality of being feasible and adjusting to changing circumstances requires you to adapt to the environment where you are as quickly as a chameleon. However, it doesn't mean that you can give up the principle or change the goal, but you should change the color of your body as quickly as a chameleon so that you can adapt to the situation you are facing, adhere to the correct principle and achieve the established goal.

3. Sincere attitude towards the goal

Nothing can take the place of your sincere attitude toward achieving a clear goal. You should show your sincere attitude towards the goal in your words and deeds so that everyone can catch sight of your attitude. If you are not sincere enough, it will be immediately reflected in your speech and behavior. Any disguise skill is unable to cover the dishonesty in your heart. If you can hold a sincere attitude towards the goal, this attitude will strengthen all other personalities.

4. Make quick decisions

People who are sluggish tend to be less popular. Today's world is rapidly changing, and those who are irritatingly slow in doing everything are unable to keep up with the pace of the times. It is a habit to make a quick decision. However, the habit needs to rely on the support of a positive mental attitude because it will make you more confident. Your sincere attitude towards your goals will also help you make decisions in a short time. The more clear you are about the value of your goals, the more quickly you will be able to the confusing remarks but choose those that will help you achieve the goals.

Nowadays, although there are opportunities everywhere, they are fleeting. If you fail to a quick decision, the opportunity will ultimately leave you even if you have found it.

5. Mind your manners

Etiquette is one of the cheapest and most profitable traits in the world. Although it is a kind of spontaneous behavior of human beings, its performance adds more value to the person. Etiquette is a good habit that you can respect others' feelings under any circumstances, have an intention to help the weak and the unfortunate, and consciously control various forms of individualism and departmentalism.

6. Wit

There is an appropriate or inappropriate moment when you do anything. Wit is to do the right thing and say the right words at the right time. Wit has a lot to do with etiquette, and it is impossible that you only have either of them but do not have the other. Wit is an invaluable skill for you to conduct yourself in society. Only the witted will be favored by others.

7. Tone of voice

Tone is the most common way to express our personality. When we use different tones to express the same sentence, the meaning we convey also varies from each other. When you speak with a confident tone, your positive mental attitude, and sincere attitude towards the goal will also show up. On the contrary, if you speak with a depressed and wavering tone, your negative mental attitude and skeptical attitude towards the goal will inevitably emerge.

8. The habit of smiling

Keeping a smile can make you beat a cold opponent because it's not easy to get angry with someone who smiles at you. You should always smile. This simple action can calm you down and remind you not to forget to keep a positive mental attitude.

9. Facial expressions

We can usually detect what's going on in other people's hearts through their facial expressions, and we tend to make judgments on this basis. For example, experienced salespersons have unique skills in this aspect. The more you can understand and control your facial expressions, the better you can analyze other people's facial expressions. Then you can judge other people's moods, control your facial expression according to other people's moods, and cultivate a charming personality.

10. Tolerance

Tolerance is a kind of temperament that you show patience and aboveboard attitude towards people who are different from you in terms of opinions, habits, and beliefs. Tolerance requires you to open your mind to accept all kinds of new ideas and information, grasp new things that are beneficial to you, and take the initiative to understand, study, and accept them. The less tolerant you are, the more enclosed you will be so that you will not be able to come into contact with a variety of social phenomena. Moreover, it will hinder the development of mind and imagination, hinder your correct thinking and reasoning, and even make those who are willing to be friends with you become your enemies.

11. Sense of humor

A proper sense of humor will help you to keep flexible and adapt to the changing living environment. In this way, you will relax under pressure, and your life will not be too serious, and you can keep your human feelings all the time, instead of becoming cold, alienated, angry, or distressed. In addition, it will make it easier to smile, thus enhancing your positive mental attitude.

12. Confidence in infinite intelligence

All the principles of success are involved in the component of confidence. Those who have confidence in infinite intelligence, in themselves and others, will inspire others to have confidence in them. Confidence gives us a vision for ourselves and for the people who inhabit this planet, a vision that enables us to have a better understanding of all the interpersonal relationships. Confidence can also endow us with the power to overcome secular obstacles and create new solutions and new methods for success. Confidence contains inexhaustible power. It is one of the resources that can be recycled endlessly. Everyone is free to access and utilize it.

13. Sense of justice

A sense of justice is intentional honesty. It is not only a tool to obtain substantial benefits, but can also strengthen various interpersonal relationships. It can drive away greed and selfishness, and allow you to be more aware of your rights, interests, and responsibilities. Then, all other personalities will become more powerful due to the sense of justice.

14. Appropriate wording

It is of great significance to make correct use of the words because ordinary people usually judge a person based on the quality of what he speaks of. If you can speak or write in a way that is direct, distinct, and easy to understand, all of your other personalities will be faster manifested with better results.

Successful people always get what they want with care and concentration. Therefore, your wording must accurately reflect this trait, just like a well-designed sales plan. Remember not to get into the habit of making fabricated, superficial, or obscene remarks. You should use the words accurately so that they can expressly convey what you want to say.

15. Vivid speech

Vivid speech is more important than appropriate wording. Combining the candid and appropriate wording and other personalities, you will become a communicator and agitator with firm belief and persuasion. A vivid and inspiring speech has a considerable impact on the development direction of civilization.

The speech should be delivered in a way that the audience is willing to accept. Otherwise, it will lead to failure. The tone of your speech should be full of enthusiasm, confidence, and strength, especially sincere enthusiasm, which is the core element of all kinds of speeches and can endow your speech with great appeal. You should make full use of your gestures in your speech. The shorter the speech is, the better it will be. Stop as soon as you have said what you want to say.

16. Emotional control

We may often be affected by our emotions when we are doing something. A positive emotion will help us achieve our goals, while a negative emotion may hinder us from advancing. For example, when you lose control of your emotions, you may suddenly say or do something that causes great harm to yourself and others. Therefore, in order to achieve the goal of success, you should guide your thoughts and pay attention to controlling your emotions.

17. Interest in people

It is a common failing of mankind to pay no attention to the details of the behavior, as well as the trivial things that take place around. It is extremely important to maintain a high level of interest in the people you work with, while you can explore their ways to succeed and the reasons for their failures. Therefore, you must be able to maintain interest in any person, matter, place, or article, and keep this interest and habit as long as it is necessary. If you can't do that, your other personalities will be of no use.

18. Versatile talents

No matter how well you know your major, others do not think you have any charm if you don't have a wide range of interests in the world. Therefore, you should ask yourself to be familiar with the new issues arising in the contemporary era, and cultivate some hobbies in the spare time, and make great efforts to become an expert in one field while possessing all-round knowledge and ability. Thus, it will greatly expand your personality and create a greater attraction for others.

19. Strong social skills

People are born to repel those who do not like them but will be attracted by those who show sincerity and enthusiasm to them. Therefore, if you are not interested or enthusiastic about others, or care about, love, respect or tolerate them, they will reject you out of instinct.

20. Courtesy

Among the attractive personalities, there is absolutely no sign of arrogance, megalomania, or departmentalism. But don't confuse courtesy with cowardice. A truly courteous person knows the truth that even the greatest man is but a small part of the whole. Those who are courteous understand that what they have achieved should be used for the benefit of all, rather than as a topic among the public. People with strong confidence hold a courteous attitude towards everything, and the trait is always worthy of praise. It is an eternal truth that modesty helps a person to make progress, whereas conceit makes a person lag behind.

21. Vivid performance skills

It is the outcome of the mixture of all the personalities mentioned above, including facial expression, speech tone, appropriate wording, vivid speech, emotional control, etiquette, versatile talent, sense of humor, and wit.

By combining these personalities, you can attract people's attention whenever necessary.

The performance here is not to show off your skills, play the clown, and make witty remarks. Although these traits will attract people's attention, they will make people tired of you. It refers to the effective and moderate use of the aforementioned personality traits. If you own these traits, you will get along well with one person or thousands of people with high proficiency.

22. The spirit of not being dizzy with success and not being discouraged by failure

If you are not made dizzy with success and not being discouraged by failure, you will soon be respected by other people. This kind of spirit is a habit, which can only be developed through long-term struggle and practice. It is an excellent opportunity for you to develop a trait by developing different interests in your spare time. Flexibility, wit, and courtesy also help you develop this spirit. At the same time, you should ask yourself to be friendly with others in many instances, so that others will be delighted to work with you.

23. A firm handshake

A weak handshake signals that you despise the other person, or that you are weak. When you shake hands with others, you may as well say some greeting words, and talk with others in a direct and affirmative tone, and hold the hand of the other when emphasizing some keywords. In this way, the other party will associate the trait with your personality as a whole, and enhance their impression on you.

24. Personal charm

In real life, a young man often falls in love with a young woman at first sight. The main reason why two people fall in love, at first sight, is that their natural conditions have a strong attraction to each other, which is a personal charm. If you can make the correct use of your personal charm, it will be of great help to you. You should integrate your personal charm into the practical actions so that your actions will become the force to attract others. And you should use your personal charm to cultivate your enthusiasm, show your traits that you like to contact with people, strengthen your style of treating others and handling affairs, and improve your tone when you speak. At the same time, you can show and strengthen the trait with your eyes, gestures, and postures, so that it will become your unique capital to attract others.

25. Honesty

A man with a sound personality must have the noble character of honesty and trustworthiness. And even if it is not good for him, he will still keep his word. Honesty is a kind of spiritual trait, a kind of virtue, and the root of conducting ourselves. It says more about a person's heart than any other quality. Whether a person is honest or not will be naturally reflected in his words and deeds and even in his facial expressions, which can be perceived immediately.

Honesty, as a moral character, has a great attraction to people. No one likes people who are deceitful, cunning, devious, and dishonest. Moreover, people who are cunning and who talk in a roundabout way are absolutely unreliable. If you think you can use the various personalities listed above to cheat, you are absolutely wrong. If you are dishonest and break your promise, none of your other personalities will take effect.

The above 25 personalities are not isolated from each other, or on an equal footing. On the one hand, they are closely related to each other. In other words, improving a personality will help to improve other personalities. On the other hand, there is a difference in the relationship between the principal and the subordinate among the personalities. Honesty is the master, the commander, and the soul; the other personalities are the subordinates, soldiers, and bodies. Therefore, when cultivating an attractive personality, you must give priority to honesty. If you have had the virtue of honesty and developed other personalities, you will grow like a tiger with wings added to ensure your success.

Honesty is the supreme pursuit of personality

Among China's Economic Persons of the Year 2002 selected by China Central Television (CCTV), one of the most striking women is Liu Shuwei, a researcher at the Central University of Finance and Economics. When Liu Shuwei studied the data of the listed companies in China in December 2001, she found that Lantian Co., Ltd. was already an empty company and had been unable to generate cash flow and that it operated entirely on the bank loans. After finding out this situation, she wrote an essay on Financial News, proposing to cease to lend to Lantian Co., Ltd. immediately, because she knew that the loans that had been made could be no longer recovered. After the essay was published, she immediately attracted pressure from all sides, and even she was threatened with death. Later, she made the case known to the media for the sake of seeking social support. With the support of the media, she fought bravely for the public interest and won in the battle. The reason why Liu Shuwei was chosen as the Economic Person of the Year 2002 is that she has the precious quality of honesty.

Nowadays, the public is concerned about honesty, calling for it, and praising it. Once the honesty is lost, the consequences can be imagined. For example:

In 2001, more than 20 food manufacturers with the brand of Guan Sheng Yuan in China were almost destroyed due to the disclosure of the stala-filling mooncake incident of Guan Sheng Yuan in Nanjing, and even some manufacturers withdrew from the local market. It is estimated that the sales volume of mooncakes nationwide in that year dropped by about 40% compared with the same period in previous years and that the loss of the whole industry reached 16 billion to 20 billion Yuan.

In 2002, Enron Corporation, which used to be the world's largest natural gas dealer and the largest electricity dealer and known to have the most outstanding board of directors and the best corporate governance structure in the world, became one of the fastest collapsing enterprises in the history of the United States due to the lack of honesty. Arthur Anderson, one of the five best-known accounting firms in the world, came to an end at the age of 89 years old due to its engagement in the scandal.

On the contrary, those enterprises that can be rated as century-old brands, have been giving the top priority to honesty. For example:

Beijing Tongrentang Group Co.,Ltd. in China has been thriving for more than 300 years and continue as a going concern, because it can adhere to its enterprise tenet and business philosophy of "cultivating both noble morality and benevolence to do good to society and to keep people healthy," "operating with honesty and cheating no one neither the old nor the young" and that "though the processing of medicines was complicated, we must not save labors; though the medicinal materials were expensive, we must not reduce any of them."

Jack Welch, former CEO of General Electric Company (GE), emphasized the importance of honesty in his autobiography. He said, "we don't have police, we don't have prisons. So we have to rely on our employees' honesty. It is our first line of defense." And the market value of General Electric can soar more than 30 times in just 20 years, ranking from the tenth in the world to the second, which is closely bound up with its emphasis on honesty.

For a person, a noble character should be the highest goal, and the core and soul of a noble character is honesty. If you fail to do this, you won't be trusted by anyone, and you will have no true friends, not to mention any other achievements. As a result, honesty is your most important capital and the most important condition for you to achieve success.

In a society, honesty and trustworthiness are important factors that drive the development of society. If people from all walks of life are honest and trustworthy, observe social morals, and assume social responsibility, there will be no mutual suspicion and deception so that society will function properly. Enterprise is the cell of society. If enterprises are all healthy, society is bound to be healthy. Enterprises should repay society with their quality products, excellent services, and a high reputation, which represents that enterprises are fulfilling their corporate social responsibilities. On the contrary, if an enterprise engages in improper management, deception and production and sales of forged and fake commodities, it will inevitably damage the interests of the public and society, and such an enterprise will eventually lose all standing and reputation.

Examples of success

Honesty is my Bible

Feng Gensheng was born in 1934. At the age of 14, he became an apprentice in the Hu Qingyu Tang, a famous pharmacy of traditional Chinese medicine in Hangzhou. He once served as the chairman of China Hangzhou Qing Chun Bao Group Co., Ltd.

Feng Gensheng said, "Honesty counts a great deal. It is not too much to claim that honesty is a cornerstone of the market economy and the minimum standard for people to conduct themselves and handle affairs. Imagine that if the cornerstone is broken and the standard is gone, will the tall building collapse? In real life, if there are fakes and lies flying all over the world, if someone doesn't count, signs a contract but doesn't admit it, or even the court judges him to repay the debt, but he still repudiates the debt, how could the business go on? It will harm the interests of other people, ourselves, and society."

"As you know, there are plaques in almost every room of Hu Qingyu Tang, but only two of them are the most important, one is No Cheating, and the other is No Second Price. I personally believe that No Cheating means honesty, which is the treasure of Hu Qingyu Tang, as well as the Bible that I have been pursuing for 54 years in my career in the traditional industry and 30 years in a business management career. Hu Qinyu Tang can stand firm in the changing history, and now it can be rejuvenated 130 years after its birth. For the reasons, I believe that one of the critical reasons is its emphasis on honesty. People familiar with the development history of Qing Chun Bao and Hu Qingyu Tang know that when China Hangzhou Qing Chun Bao Group Co., Ltd. merged Hu Qingyu Tang in 1996, Hu Qingyu Tang had been already insolvent. At that time, I gave three prescriptions: shining the brand, transforming the mechanism, and clarifying the business. Among the three, I gave priority to the prescription of shining the brand."

The true meaning of shining the brand is to emphasize honesty. At that time, the operation and management of Hu Qingyu Tang was in chaos. Due to various reasons, the raw materials purchased are of poor quality, but high price, which is bound to damage the interests of customers ultimately, and the pharmacy will have no credibility at all. At that time, the wages of the workers were low, and even the pharmacy could not pay them. So the workers tried to get some medicine and even solicited customers at the door of Hu Qingyu Tang. These workers rumored that the pharmacy was selling fake medicine, but they were selling real medicine. And the employee in the pharmacy said those who sold outside were selling fake drugs. In the end, the customers were confused about what was true and what was fake. To shine the brand, the pharmacy should reform from the bottom, and eliminate these phenomena by strengthening management and straightening out relations, restore Hu Qingyu Tang's tradition of no cheating, and then recover its honest reputation.

No second price is one of the outcomes of honesty, as well as one of the foundations of honesty. The plaque of no second price is hung outside the hall to tell the customers, while the plaque of no cheating is hung in the pharmacy to warn the employee. The pharmacy has achieved the goal of no cheating, produced products with real materials and exquisite workmanship, and sell the products at a proper price. Therefore, the pharmacy does not cut the price at will to achieve the goal of no second price. It is the logical relationship between no cheating and no second price.

Feng Gensheng pointed out: “It's strange that Qing Chun Bao could be sold like hotcakes for twenty-three years, but it’s pretty good. Do you know why the health care product brands have been ever-changing like the trotting horse lamp? After a period of practical inspection by consumers, it turns out that it does not mean the products are really good, but the advertisement is well done. As a result, some health care brands have no market, and the following brands will lead the trend for three to five years.”

“Qing Chun Bao is refined from more than 100 ancient prescriptions, inheriting the tradition of no cheating and withstanding the test of time. Otherwise, it had been eliminated by the market earlier. In terms of technical progress, it has something to do with the characteristics of drugs. Generally speaking, before a drug goes on the market, it has to go through many years of clinical trials. Once the drug is determined, it can't be altered at will. Moreover, it is not a sign of slow technical progress. Qing Chun Bao has both the basis of ancient prescriptions and the experience obtained from modern pharmacological tests. More than 20 years ago, in order to test the therapeutic effects of Qing Chun Bao, more than 10,000 animals were used in the tests. Now, it has been tested in practice for another twenty years. Even though I don't say it out loud, you know what it is as a health care product. When it comes to honesty, I believe that honesty is reflected in what you do, rather than what you say. If every enterprise and manager treats people and handles affairs with sincerity and thinks for consumers wholeheartedly, consumers will never treat the enterprise and manager shabbily. On the contrary, if you cheat the consumers once, you may never change their bad impression on you all your life. It is a summary of my decades of experience."

Feng Gensheng stressed, "As is known to all in China's spirits culture, good wine needs no bush, and good doing, good drumming. In my opinion, it is an essential means for any kind of consumer goods to publicize and promote the products so as to seize a specific market share. As for the promotion of products, we have always believed in the concept that 90% of the sales of products depends on the effect and 10% depends on the publicity. Our goal in marketing is to build consumers' trust in the enterprise and the brand. The anti-aging tablets of Qing Chun Bao have been sold well for more than 20 years since they came out in 1978. It depends on its own quality and effect, and on the public praise. It turns out that modern economic laws do not like the title of the top bidder. The top bidder is indeed renowned, but it is not a good name. As an old saying goes, you reap what you have sown. We should not cheat the customers. My principle is no cheating. No cheating includes two aspects. On the one hand, we can not cheat our customers on product quality. On the other hand, we can not cheat our customers on product prices. If we think of everything for others and look at ourselves from the standpoint of others, everything will become very simple. It is the foundation of my business. In recent years, we have just begun to invest in an appropriate amount of advertising for Qing Chun Bao, but the advertising cost is far from proportional to our sales volume. In the past two decades, the unit advertising cost of Qing Chun Bao is the lowest among the similar health care products in China."

Data source: Zhang Yanning. A pioneering hero. (Beijing: Enterprise Management Publishing House, 2003.)

Honesty changed Zhou Dahu from a tramp to a billionaire

Zhou Dahu was born in Wenzhou in 1952. His father was a revolutionary veteran. Before his father was labeled as the Rightist and his mother was transferred to a rural post office, Zhou Dahu lived a warm and sunny life in his childhood and teens. After the misfortune came to Zhou's family, his life got into a dilemma all of a sudden. After graduating from junior high school, Zhou Dahu went to live and work in a production team in Wenzhou. Since Zhou Dahu had no way to support himself in the countryside, 17-year-old Zhou Dahu followed several fellow townsmen in Wenzhou to go out for work to make a living in 1969. "I first went to the suburb of Xi'an to work as a sheet metal worker. At that time, I did not have any national grain coupons. So it was a difficult problem in food, and I used to eat the dried persimmon for a month. Unexpectedly, the leader of our construction team was soon captured back to Wenzhou and shot for being an illegal contractor. And I was put in prison in Xi'an for a month."

Soon after he was captured back to Wenzhou, he began to wander in Jiangxi, Anhui, Hubei and other places to make a living. In 1976, Zhou Dahu took the place of his mother to work in the Wenzhou Municipal Post and Telecommunications Office. From then on, his wandering life came to an end, and he started his daily life by carrying postal parcels every day. "Maybe it's because of my previous wandering experience, I have cared too much about the job." When recalling the life during that period, Zhou Dahu said that he required himself to carry more parcels than others, better than others.

As early as around 1985, some people in Wenzhou began to produce lighters. Zhou Dahu was a latecomer of lighter production in

Wenzhou. He had no choice but to enter the industry. In 1991, the Wenzhou Soda Plant, where Zhou's wife worked, went bankrupt, and she received a settlement fee of 5,000 Yuan. Zhou Dahu found that it was easier to produce lighters because there were many manufacturers engaged in the production of lighter parts in Wenzhou at that time, and he could produce lighters by investing only a small amount of money. Based on the settlement fee, Zhou Dahu recruited three or five workers to vacate his home of more than 40 square meters and transformed it into a workshop. After work, he sold the products for his wife and found that the lighter market was highly lucrative. So he resigned a year later. In 1992, he formally started his business after renting a simple factory building of more than 200 square meters and recruiting more than 100 workers.

It was not long before he entered the industry that Wenzhou's lighter market came to a mad state. In the first half of 1993, the number of lighter manufacturers in Wenzhou increased rapidly from 100 to 200 to 3,000.

At that time, each lighter in Wenzhou was only 10 Yuan, while those made in Japan and South Korea were sold at 300 to 500 Yuan. Due to the huge price gap, Wenzhou was flooded with the foreigners who came to buy lighters. It's hard to believe that even if the box you send to the foreigner is filled with stones, the foreigner will take them away regardless of what it is.

At that time, in such a hot market, Zhou Dahu was on the verge of bankruptcy. The reason is that many lighter manufacturers in Wenzhou hold the idea of making quick money to produce lighters of poor quality. Zhou Dahu refused to fool customers and insisted on producing products of high quality. So the upstream supplier refused to supply him. As a result, except for a few core employees, more than 100 workers left the plant.

Zhou Dahu said: "At that time, according to my quality standards, workers could only make 150 lighters a day, while those manufacturers that produced lighters of low quality could make 500 lighters. Workers were paid by the piece, so if they worked for me, they would receive low pay, and then it is less attractive to them. Just at that time, I made a profit of about one Yuan for making a lighter, and even if I didn't make a penny, I couldn't pay them a high salary. This is also the case with suppliers."

In the face of the difficulty of the factory being shut down, Zhou Dahu was extremely depressed. In a week, he had three consecutive traffic accidents while riding a motorcycle. "That year, I had never had an accident when I drove the truck in the post and telecommunications office, but I had three traffic accidents in succession. It can be seen that I was under a lot of pressure at that time."

When the skilled workers left, Zhou Dahu decided to recruit a group of new ordinary workers and train them. "In the first half of 1993, I lost a lot. And I invested the profits of the previous two years in the production."

When Zhou Dahu was in a bad situation, his honesty ultimately played a role. In the second half of 1993, foreign businessmen who suffered a lot from the sales of products of low quality began to shift their focus to Zhou Dahu. Due to Zhou's honesty and trustworthiness, his orders soared in a short while. Originally, they had a production capacity of more than 5000 lighters a day, but they were able to receive orders for 50,000 to 60,000 lighters.

And nearly 90% of the 3,000 lighter manufacturers, which produced products of ow quality and thus fell into disrepute, went bankrupt suddenly, just like the autumn wind sweeping away the withered leaves. Since then, Zhou Dahu has become the spokesperson of the lighter.

In addition, Zhou Dahu has a strong desire to excel. It is his motto to only strive for the first place and the champion. Hirota Corporation used to be the largest lighter manufacturer in Japan. When being overwhelmed by the manufacturers in Wenzhou, Hirota Corporation decided to close its production line in Japan and conduct OEM production in Wenzhou. In order to fight for this opportunity, Zhou Dahu held the most positive attitude towards the company. In fact, it is more troublesome to make OEM than to produce by ourselves. Hirota

Corporation had highly strict requirements for lighter production. If a company had insufficient willpower and endurance, it would be difficult to persist. Two years later, Zhou Dahu finally met the technical specifications of Hirota Corporation.

Manufacturers in Japan, South Korea, the United States, and other countries wanted Zhou Dahu's factory as their 100% OEM manufacturer, but Zhou Dahu refused. He always insists on one principle that, no matter what the circumstances, 70% of the products must be branded with their own tiger lighter trademark, which means that the proportion between the production of OEM products and that of their own brand products is 3:7. “We must build our own brands,” Zhou said, “otherwise, as soon as the lighter market is in turmoil, other dealers will suspend trading at any time they like, and then we could only be exploited by others at will. In the past few years, China's clothing industry suffered a lot in this regard. Now, it's up to me to stop when I want to. It depends on what I think.”

In 2003, the lighter market in Wenzhou accounted for about 80% of the global lighter market, the annual output of Tiger Lighters accounted for about 50% of the global production, and Zhou Dahu's personal value exceeded 300 million Yuan. He has been firmly convinced that as long as he has willpower and endurance, and adheres to what he is doing to the last, he will win and become the world's king of lighters.

Data source: Jia Cheng. A Wenzhou businessman is better than a Jewish businessman. (Beijing: People’s Daily Press, 2011.)

Chapter 16 Develop A Good Habit

Maxims for Success

You have to control your habits. If you can develop a positive habit, the seeds it grows will be positive accordingly. On the contrary, if you develop a negative habit, the seeds it grows will be negative correspondingly.

—Napoleon Hill

Principles and Guidelines

Everyone is different from others because of their own habits. As the saying goes, Sow the seed of behavior, and you will reap the habit; sow the seed of habit, and you will reap the character; sow the seed of character, and you will reap a specific fate. Each of us is bound by habits. The more times we repeat our thoughts and experiences, the deeper the constraints our habits will impose on us. There are good habits and bad habits. There are many habits you know and some habits you don't know. The purpose of this chapter is to help you review all your habits and tell you how to change bad habits and cultivate good ones. In order to achieve this goal, you must first understand and be able to apply a universal principle, which I call the universal habitual force.

Universal habitual force

The universal habitual force is a force that makes all creatures, and all things submit themselves to the rule. Although the power can't be seen by the eyes, heard by the ears, and touched by the hands, it really is an objective existence that can not be changed by the will of any person.

The universal habitual force may be good for you or bad for you. The result depends entirely on your choice.

The best example to prove the existence of the universal habitual force is the operation of celestial bodies. As we all know, the planets cycle like clocks, and they don't collide or suddenly deviate from their orbits. The complex terrestrial gravity and inertia allow the planets to move very precisely so that human beings can predict the positions of the planets, the time of solar and lunar eclipses, and the laws of meteor showers. It is evident that the great invisible force that can control the accurate circulation of all celestial bodies is the universal habitual force.

The movement of all creatures and all things is affected by the universal habitual force, including the movement of human beings themselves. The movement of human beings is an integral part of the whole universe movement. Whether your movement is conscious or blind, it is carried out under the influence of the universal habitual force. The movement of man is first manifested in thought and action. When thoughts and actions are repeated many times, people will gradually develop a habit. In the same way, people's habits are invisible, inaudible, and intangible. However, it is also an objective existence and has great intangible strength.

Once a habit is fixed in mind, it will be accepted by the universal habitual force, which will automatically drive the person to take action. For example, if your mental habits are poverty, failure, and disease, the universal habitual force will make you fall into poverty, fail and suffer a disease. If your mental habits are affluence, success and health, the universal habitual force will enable you to live a wealthy, successful and healthy life. Therefore, whether the effect of habit is positive or negative depends fully on what kind of habit you will cultivate.

Therefore, you must first control your thoughts, then control your behavior, and finally develop a fixed habit. Then, in turn, you can control your thoughts and behaviors naturally and easily through your habits.

Give up bad habits and develop good habits

Once formed, people's habits are not only relatively independent but also have a great reaction to thoughts and behaviors. The nature of this reaction depends on the nature of the habit. That is to say, and a good habit has a good reaction while a bad habit has a bad reaction. Therefore, we must get rid of bad habits and develop good habits at the same time. So, what are the common bad habits?

Mankind has bad habits in many aspects, and the common bad habits include aimlessness, content with poverty, addiction to a lazy life, moaning without illness, oral envy, all talk and no deed, greed, arrogance, extreme vanity, grumpy temper, petty jealousy, dishonesty, revenge, sadism, etc. If you don't get rid of these bad habits, they will play a very negative role, and they may even destroy your life.

So, what good habits should we develop? Good habits are manifested in varied aspects. Here we focus on the following:

A clear goal

A clear goal is the most important habit, which enables you to become more alert, imaginative, enthusiastic, and willful.

Self-confidence

Self-confidence not only enables you to hold a positive mental attitude from the bottom of your heart and eliminate all the negative factors and fear but also allows you to develop a habit of self-discipline.

Personal enterprising spirit

You should take the initiative to do things well before being pressed by others. The indomitable perseverance will make it easier for you to achieve that.

Keep enthusiastic

The enthusiasm here refers to controlled enthusiasm. You should accept it on a voluntary basis and extinguish it as soon as you find that it is not behaving properly or that it will put you at risk.

Exercise strict self-discipline

It is a cyclical process. The more frequently you use it, the more you can have it.

Give a little more

You should start to do some work that has no return for the time being. In the beginning, you may have to force yourself to do this, but with the lapse of time, such a self-demand will turn into a habit.

Control willpower and develop good habits

Willpower is of great help for you to develop a good habit that can be accepted by the universal habitual force. The willpower stems from the sense of self-respect, which acts as the supreme judicial court in your mind. It has the power to judge, overturn, amend, change, and eliminate all other parts of the work. It can be seen that without the sense of self-respect, the influence of your willpower will go the wrong way, and without the willpower, you will not be able to get rid of bad habits or develop good ones. In this regard, the core of developing a good habit is to control and strengthen your willpower on the premise of defending your sense of self-respect. Here are the steps to control and strengthen your willpower:

Step 1: Take the initiative to reach out to the people who can help you achieve a clear goal, organize a mastermind alliance, and create a number of models for the universal habitual force to follow. It is the truth that one takes the behavior of one's company.

Step 2: Make your plan and seek knowledge, ability, and confidence from all members of the mastermind alliance so as to enrich and inspire yourself.

Step 3: The universal habitual force may make you highly vulnerable to the surroundings. Therefore, you should keep a distance from the people and environment that can make you feel inferior, because it is impossible to cultivate willpower in a negative environment.

Step 4: Learn to forget the past and cut off all the associations with the unpleasant experiences in the past. People with strong will should not always hold on to the past but should have a strong desire for the goals that have not yet been achieved all the time and have the vitality that will never collapse. If you have such a strong desire in your heart all the time, the universal habitual force will transform these strong desires into substantial benefits of equal value for you.

Step 5: Use all possible means to fill your heart with clear goals, such as hanging some creeds or mottos on the wall or posting the photos of your role models on the wall. You should form an image of a goal that can be achieved in your mind. The clearer these images are, the faster the universal habitual force can receive them and print them in your subconscious.

Step 6: Don't inflate your sense of self-respect. Otherwise, you may deviate from the goal you want to achieve.

Step 7: You must take action right now, repeat it, and give a little more. Repetition is the mother of habit. It is a decisive factor that affects the development of a habit. Only when you are driven by the sense of self-respect and willpower, and make unremitting efforts towards a clear goal, can you get rid of your bad habits and develop good habits and achieve the goal of success.

Examples of success

How did Benjamin Franklin develop a good habit?

Benjamin Franklin is a writer, printer, politician, diplomat, financier, educator, inventor, philosopher, humorist, and entrepreneur. He tried his hand at all sorts of professions and achieved great success in all of them. What's more, he has achieved so much because of his lofty morality and good habits. The formation of his noble morality and good habits comes from the plan of moral perfection and the self-examination book, which he made at the age of 22 and consciously abided by all his life.

Benjamin Franklin wrote in his autobiography, "it was during this period (1728) that I conceived a bold and arduous plan to achieve moral perfection. I hope that I will never make any mistake in this present life."

"I decided to overcome all my shortcomings, whether they were caused by my natural character, hobbies, habits, or bad friends because I know or I think I know what's good and what's bad. I thought maybe I could keep on doing good things and never do bad things, but I soon found out that what I wanted to do was much harder than I thought. Just as I was trying to do in all my power to overcome one shortcoming, another came out beyond expectation. Habit makes use of a moment's neglect, and the reason is sometimes no match for hobby. Later, I finally decided that it's just a theoretical belief that perfect virtue is not beneficial enough for me to prevent the mistakes that we have made because of our negligence. And we have to get rid of bad habits, learn to develop a good habit, and make it established. Only in this way can our actions be expected to be consistently correct from beginning to end. To this end, I have devised the following methods. I included under thirteen names of virtues all that at that time occurred to me as necessary or desirable, and annexed to each a short precept, which fully expressed the extent I gave to its meaning."

The names of virtues and corresponding precepts are as follows:

1. Temperance

Eat not to dullness; drink not to elevation.

2. Silence

Speak not but what may benefit others or yourself; avoid trifling conversation.

3. Order

Let all your things have their places; let each part of your business have its time.

4. Resolution

Resolve to perform what you ought; perform without fail what you resolve.

5. Frugality

Make no expense but to do good to others or yourself; i.e., waste nothing.

6. Industry

Lose no time; be always employed in something useful; cut off all unnecessary actions.

7. Sincerity. Use no hurtful deceit; think innocently and justly, and, if you speak, speak accordingly.

8. Justice

Wrong none by doing injuries, or omitting the benefits that are your duty.

9. Moderation

Avoid extremes; forbear resenting injuries so much as you think they deserve.

10. Cleanliness

Tolerate no uncleanliness in body, cloaths, or habitation.

11. Tranquillity

Be not disturbed at trifles, or at accidents common or unavoidable.

12. Chastity. Rarely use venery, but for health or offspring, never to dullness, weakness, or the injury of your own or another's peace or reputation.

13. Humility

Imitate Jesus and Socrates.

Thus, how can we meet the requirements described in the above names?

First, concentrate on putting virtue into trial use for a period. Franklin wrote, "My intention being to acquire the habitude of all these virtues, and I judged it would be well not to distract my attention by attempting the whole at once, but to fix it on one of them at time; and, when I should be master of that, then to proceed to another, and so on, till I should have gone through the thirteen; and, as the previous of acquisition of some might facilitate the acquisition of certain others, I arranged them with that view, as they stand above. Temperance first, as it tends to procure that coolness and clearness of head, which is so necessary where constant vigilance was to be kept up, and a guard maintained against the unremitting attraction of ancient habits, and the force of perpetual temptations. This being acquired and established, Silence would be easier; and my desire being to gain knowledge at the same time that I improved in virtue, and considering that in conversation it was obtained rather by the use of the ear than of the tongue, and therefore wishing to break a habit I was getting into of prattling, punning, and jesting, which only made me acceptable to trifling company, I gave Silence the second place. This and the next, Order, I expected, would allow me more time to attend to my project and my studies. Resolution, once become habitual, would keep me firm in my endeavors to obtain all the subsequent virtues; Frugality and Industry relieving me from my remaining debt, and producing affluence and independence, would make easier the practice of Sincerity and Justice, & c., & c."

Second, review the results of the trial use of virtue every day. Then he wrote, "Conceiving then, that, agreeably to the advice of Pythagoras in his Golden Verses, daily examination would be necessary. I contrived the following method for conducting that examination. I made a little book, in which I allotted a page for each of the virtues, ruled each page with red ink, so as to have seven columns, one for each day of the week, marking each column with a letter for the day. I crossed these columns with thirteen red lines, marking the beginning of each line with the first letter of one of the virtues, on which line, and in its proper column, I might mark, by a little black spot, every fault I found upon examination to have been committed respecting that virtue upon that day." The little book was his self-examination book, shown in the below table: Form of the pages.

	Sunday	Monday	Tuesday	Wednesday	Thursday	Friday	Saturday
Temperance							
Silence	-	-		-		-	
Order	-	-	-		-	-	-
Resolution			-		-		
Frugality		-		-			
Industry			-				
Sincerity							
Justice							
Moderation							
Cleanliness							
Tranquillity							
Chastity							
Humility							

At the bottom of the form, he added an inscription: Here, I will stick to it!

Third, give a week's strict attention to each of the virtues successively. So for the first week, you just need to make great guard and avoid every the least offense against temperance. As for the other twelve virtues, you may leave them to their ordinary chance, only marking every evening the faults of the day. In this way, if you can achieve no spot in the "temperature" line in the first week, it indicates that the temperance has so much strengthened. Then you might venture to extend your attention to include the next, and for the following week, keep both lines clear of spots. Proceeding thus to the last, you can go through a course complete in thirteen weeks.

Fourth, cycle four times a year to develop a good habit. After 13 weeks of daily examination, when you see that the spots on the form of the self-examination book are gradually eliminated, and finally, you see a clean book, you will feel the encouraging pleasure of seeing on your pages the progress you have made in virtue. But at this time, you have to move on, and you should not stop or go backward. As the saying goes, repetition is the mother of habit. It circulates 13 weeks at a time and four courses a year. After a few cycles, these requirements will develop into a good habit.

Data source: Benjamin Franklin. The Autobiography Of Benjamin Franklin (R. L. Shi & B. S. Song, Trans.). (Beijing: National Academy of Governance Press, 1998)

Zhang Xiuyu's "unshakable" and "second business"

I have insisted on two unshakable things. One is that I study for an hour every day to master the latest trends, theories, knowledge, and skills. And the other is that I walk for two hours every day (one hour in the morning and one hour after supper), and I keep on exercising to ensure that I can have a healthy body, full of physical strength and energy.

In the beginning, I was not used to it. I needed to control myself consciously every day so that I could insist on accomplishing the two things. After a period, I have gradually developed a habit, which is now a matter of common practice. If I don't read or take a walk for one day, I will feel sick all over. As I adhere to the two unshakable things, I am ahead of my time in my ideas, highly sensitive to new trends, theories, knowledge and skills, and faster than my peers in accepting the newly emerging things. And I'm physically and mentally healthy, full of physical strength and energy.

Therefore, I always want to make use of the golden period of my life (60-70 years old) to engage in my second business, so as to fully realize my own value and make my due contribution to others and the society.

To this end, I have formulated a plan for my second business, which mainly consists of the following contents:

First, I will carry out the centenary project and strive for physical and mental health and live to a ripe old age. For this reason, I will adjust my mental attitude, hold the goal in my mind, have a balanced diet for nutrition, take more exercise, ensure safety, take good care of my health, have proper rest, follow the rules, develop good habits and persist in them, etc.

Second, I have the intention to write two books and become a famous expert in this field.

(1) On the basis of the book strategic enterprise management published by Peking University Press, I edited and published another book Chinese Style Management, which was a companion volume of the book strategic enterprise management. This is my fist product, which is mainly used to help organizations and individuals do the right things.

(2) I've compiled and published the book The Science of Success in China, which is another major product of mine. This book should strive to combine the scientific principles of the science of success of the United States with the actual national conditions of China to make it a masterpiece if the science of success with Chinese characteristics. The main function of the product is to help organizations and individuals do the right things and hold on to the last until I finally achieve success.

Third, I will keep on my teaching, focusing on the teaching of strategic enterprise management, Chinese style management, and the science of success.

Fourth, I will found a consulting company to engage in the businesses of training and consulting in terms of business strategy, business management, and the methods of success. The purpose of the company is to provide the customers with the best consulting services of success and help the organizations and individuals achieve success.

Fifth, I want to help successful Chinese entrepreneurs sum up their experience in business management and help them write books and set up a theory.

Sixth, I want to cooperate with North American Business Press and complete the publication of the series of contemporary China (100 books).

Chapter 17 Make A Budget for Time and Money

Maxims for Success

Time and money are two precious resources. Few of those who aspire after success may say that they have too much time and money. As the saying goes, it is a crime to waste time. Time is your most valuable asset. If you can make the correct use of your time, it will be as useful as the money in the bank.

—Napoleon Hill

Principles and Guidelines

Time and money are valuable resources to achieve success. Understanding how you spend your time and money will help you assess the progress of your pursuit of success and analyze the factors that prevent you from moving forward. Once you can improve your use of time, you can focus on the management of your money.

Time is life; time is money

"Do you love life? Then don't waste time, because time is the component of your life." "Remember that time is money. If a man can earn 10 shillings a day, play for half a day, or lie on the sofa for half a day, he may think that he only spent 6 pence on entertainment. No, it's wrong! He also lost five shillings he could have earned. Money begets money, and its descendants will have more descendants. Whoever kills a pig that has a baby will destroy all its descendants, even its future generations. If anyone destroys five shillings of money, it destroys everything it can produce, which means that it destroys a mountain of pounds."

It is a famous remark of Benjamin Franklin, a famous American thinker. It expounds such truth in a popular and direct way that if you want to succeed, you must attach importance to the value of time.

Time is a special resource. It can neither be stored nor reversed nor can it be regenerated. At the same time, it treats all on the same footing. Time is absolutely fair to anyone. With 24 hours a day, people's life is accumulated by a limited time day after day. If a person's life is calculated at the age of 80, it will be about 700,000 hours, of which the person can have more energy to work for only 40 years, about 350,000 hours. Apart from the time for sleep and rest, there are about 200,000 hours left. To improve work efficiency in this period of time is to prolong life. Therefore, whoever wastes his time wastes his life, while whoever is able to make effective use of his time prolongs his life. From this perspective, it is above reproach that efficiency is life.

The Massachusetts Institute of Technology in the United States conducted an investigation on 3,000 managers and found that any excellent manager can do well in arranging their time so as to minimize the waste of time. Peter F. Drucker, a well-known master of management in the United States, wrote in his masterpiece The Effective Executive, “But everyone can follow the injunction ‘Know Thy Time’ if he wants to, and be well on the road toward contribution and effectiveness.” Napoleon Hill also pointed out that the boundary between success and failure often lies in how to allocate time and how to arrange time.

Doer and tramp

Your attitude to life determines your attitude toward time. From this perspective, we can divide people into two types: doer and tramp. The following is an analysis of the different characteristics of the two types of people:

Doer

- Set a clear goal.
- Be able to adapt to the environment and manage resources.
- Conduct a survey on each idea before accepting or rejecting it.
- Be bold to take a risk and bear the responsibility.
- Be good at learning from mistakes.
- Be able to give a little more.
- Be able to control your habits.
- Have a positive mental attitude.
- Be able to apply your confidence to succeed.

- Organize a mastermind alliance to expand your own knowledge and experience.
- Understand your weaknesses and be able to overcome them.

Tramp

- Have no goal in your life.
- Be unable to adapt to the environment or manage the resources.
- Let the idea slip away one by one, acting on a whim or according to the opinions of others.
- Don't take advantage of opportunities and envy other people's achievements.
- Make the same mistake again and again.
- Just do something that you can barely cope with.
- Be subject to your habits.
- Have a negative mental attitude.
- Do not take any action to improve the situation.
- Only know what they want to know from TV.
- Don't understand your weaknesses.

Think about it. Are you a doer or a tramp?

Make a schedule

The purpose of making a schedule is to allocate and arrange the limited time scientifically so as to do well in what is established in a fixed time. Making a schedule mainly includes the following aspects:

Manage your time properly

The requirements for proper management of your time are as follows:

1. Schedule the day

Each of us has 24 hours a day at our disposal, roughly distributed as follows:

(1) Sleep for 8 hours

Under normal circumstances, you should have eight hours of sleep a day. You should not spend too much time sleeping. Otherwise, it will damage your health. You may steal an hour or two from your sleep time to do other things occasionally, but it's a bad habit. Don't get into this habit.

(2) Work for 8 hours.

When you spend another 8 hours at work, you should focus all your energy on your clear goals and show the habit of giving a little more.

(3) Rest for 8 hours.

The last eight hours are your rest time, also called leisure time. Although you can take a rest in the eight hours, you still have to be careful. In real life, we often spend these hours inappropriately dealing with trivial matters at home or other things that have no actual harvest.

2. Make a schedule for a long period

It's critical for your success to schedule your day because doing so ensures that you are able to concentrate on doing what you should do at all times. In addition, it is also important to schedule a week, a month, a quarter and a year, because it will give you an overall direction so that you can see your grand plan and help you achieve your goals.

The precondition of making a schedule for a long period is that you must have clear goals in each period and work plans or arrangements to achieve them, including annual plan, quarterly plan, monthly plan, and weekly plan. The way to make a schedule for a long period is to make a work schedule and to do work according to the schedule. In this way, you will not forget a task or miss the time to complete the task.

Manage your working hours well

The key to making a schedule is to manage your working hours well. Experts in time control have proposed a lot of methods and skills to manage your working hours well. Several of them will be introduced below:

1. Prioritize your tasks

As shown in the figure below, draw four columns on a piece of paper, and divide the tasks into four categories, namely "important and urgent task," "important but not urgent task," "unimportant but urgent task," "other neither important nor urgent task." Then fill in the tasks to be done in the corresponding columns, and indicate the processing date and completion time of each task in proper sequence.

Task priority sequence table

Important and urgent task (A)	Important but not urgent task (B)
Unimportant but urgent task (C)	Neither important nor urgent task (D)

2. Make a priority sequence table for important tasks every day

Take out a piece of paper before work every day, or on the calendar, write down the important tasks (about five) to be done the next day, and arrange them in order of importance and urgency. After going to work the next day, do it one by one according to the arranged order. When you are completing the first task, do not care about other tasks until the first one is finished. Then do the second, third, and so on until all the tasks are done. In this way, it seems that although you only accomplish five tasks a day, what you do is the most important task.

3. Write down your goals

If you want to know the priorities of the tasks to be done, the most important thing is that you should make it clear whether what you do can help you achieve some important goals in life. So, the premise of managing time well is to write down your goals clearly.

4. Throw away useless paper

There are usually two kinds of paper on your desk, one is useful, and the other is useless. You should quickly throw away the useless paper and never put any more paper that is of no use on the desk.

5. Spend as little time as possible on the documents to be processed

If possible, you should immediately process the documents, read the latest materials, sign the letter of authorization, and write the reply.

As for the reading materials like newspapers and magazines, you should set aside a specific time to read them.

6. Mark the documents that can not be processed at one time

If a document cannot be processed at one time, you should mark a spot at the top corner of the document and mark another spot when you process it again. In this way, you can clearly understand how many times you have processed the same document and take this opportunity to make corresponding improvements.

Make good use of leisure time

In real life, besides sleeping time, work often takes up all your time, including your leisure time. But in your life, you have to do some other important things besides work and sleep. To do these important things well, you must make up your mind to spare some time.

By allocating your time in the following ways, you will be able to do a good job in all the important things you should do:

(1) Take a moment every day to think quietly about the following matters:

- Make a plan for a clear goal.
- Communicate with infinite intelligence and express your gratitude for the happy life now you live.
- Analyze yourself, identify the fears you have to control and make plans to overcome them.
- Find ways to achieve a harmonious relationship with the people and the environment.
- Other matters you expect to get.

(2) Spend two hours a day providing a little more service to your community and family, and do not ask for any return.

(3) Spend at least one hour a day learning.

(4) Spend an hour a day with the members of your mastermind alliance or your close friends, and the rest of the day resting, exercising, or doing other things.

When you are familiar with these activities, you can combine them with other things in an organic and harmonious manner. You only need to follow the schedule mentioned above for six days a week. Then, on the seventh day, you do not need to do anything but relax and spend more time with your family. I believe you will feel delighted with what you have done.

Make skillful utilization of the odd time

The focus of making a schedule should be on a longer period of time. However, you should not ignore those scattered short time, because the scattered short time can accumulate into a longer time. The common skills of utilizing the odd time are as follows:

1. Make good use of the waiting time and odd time

For example, if you have a book with you when you are waiting in line, you can study at any time.

2. Make good use of commuting time

You will spend a lot of time on the road every year, assuming that you spend one hour commuting every day. If you can do some reading or writing, organize your thoughts, listen to the recording, and so on at the commuting time, you can save a lot of time. But the precondition for doing so is that you go to and get off work by commuter bus or regular bus. If you drive yourself to and from work, the cost will be even higher.

3. Contrarian operation to save time

Contrarian operation is the term for stock trading, which refers to the act of buying and selling stocks in a different way from most people. The principle can be applied in many cases of our daily life. If you apply this principle to time control, it means that you can do something that someone else has not yet done. In this way, you can save a lot of time of crowding and waiting.

Budget your money

There are many books on how to manage money. And you can choose one or two. I won't go into too many details here, but I'd like to remind you of the importance of budgeting your money and provide you with a few principled opinions.

Like time, money must be spent for a clear purpose. You have to budget all of your expenses and actually abide by that budget by using your self-discipline.

The main principles of budgeting are:

First of all, pay off your debts

Poverty alone is enough to destroy one's enterprise, self-confidence, and hope. But if the person is impoverished and indebted, it may be impossible for him to achieve success. A person who is involved in debt must have no time or be in no mood to build or realize his dream.

Take part of your earnings as a deposit

Napoleon Hill pointed out that saving is one of the basic conditions for success for all people, and that saving is purely a matter of habit. Developing a habit of saving does not mean that it will limit your ability to make money. On the contrary, when you apply this rule, you will not only save the money you have earned in a systematic way to have a better chance but also enhance your aggressiveness, self-confidence, observation, imagination, and leadership, so as to truly increase your ability to make money.

Invest in a planned and focused way

It is an excellent habit to save money, but the money saved has a limited capacity of value increasing. In order to add a higher value of the money in a shorter time, you can invest in a planned and focused way, such as setting up enterprises, buying and selling stocks, and bonds. But it should be noted that stock investments are subject to market risks so that you should study harder and handle affairs cautiously.

Make donations to public welfare undertakings

If you make more money and become rich, you can pay back to the public and make some donations to public welfare undertakings. In this regard, rich people such as Bill Gates and Li Ka Shing are all examples.

Examples of success

Lu Guanqiu's schedule

In January 1945, Lu Guanqiu was born in Ningwei Township, Xiaoshan City, Zhejiang Province (now Xiaoshan District, Hangzhou

City). He dropped out of school at the age of 15 and worked as a metalsmith. In July 1969, he led six farmers and raised 4,000 Yuan to create an agriculture machinery repair factory alongside the Qiantang River. In the next 30 years, the company changed its name 10 times, from a blacksmith shop to Cardan joint factory, to a Cardan joint general factory and finally to Wanxiang Group. It eventually became the first township enterprise in China, one of the national first-class enterprises, one of the 520 key enterprises and one of the 120 pilot enterprise groups under the State Council.

In 1995, Wanxiang Group officially established a branch in Chicago, the United States. It became the first Chinese enterprise to enter the international host supporting market and the first designated manufacturer in China to provide parts for General Motors Company of the United States. In addition, it has successfully acquired or invested in 19 overseas companies, which has marked the beginning of the Group's expansion towards the international market on a large scale.

In 2001, the Group achieved an operating revenue of 8.636 billion Yuan, a profit of 706 million Yuan, and an earning of foreign exchange through export at 178 million US dollars. Lu Guanqiu ranked seventh on the Forbes Rich List in mainland China, with an asset of 4 billion Yuan. In the past thirty years, the Group has worked hard, undergone numerous trials and hardships and grown steadily. Moreover, Lu Guanqiu's entrepreneurial style has subdued many elites in the industry and is known as the evergreen tree of non-governmental enterprises in China.

Lu Guanqiu was once asked, "It is too common that the entrepreneurs have led the trend for three or five years in turn. But you have been running the enterprise for more than 30 years, and you have been a model for more than 20 years. You have not fallen down, but your business is getting better and better. What's your secret?"

"It lies in the outlook on the life for our career," he said, "If I don't work, it seems that I'm sick, and my life has not yet been activated."

In the past thirty years, Lu Guanqiu has been running the enterprise and constantly learning. He dropped out of junior high school and then engaged in agriculture, which made him develop an extremely strong desire for knowledge. In the 1980s, he signed up for a modern management training program at Zhejiang University. Every Wednesday, he went to Hangzhou from Xiaoshan to attend the class, and never missed one class. In that era, it was not easy to have such a sense of self-study.

In daily life, he has been making the best use of his time to study. In 24 hours a day, he spends one-third of the day on his work, one third on the rest, and the rest one-third of leisure time on the study as much as possible. For many years, he has been getting up at 6 o'clock in the morning, going to work at 6:50, returning home for dinner at 6:45 in the evening, watching CCTV News and Focus Report at 7 o'clock, handling the documents that were not processed in the daytime at 8 o'clock, and starting to read books, newspapers, and materials at 9 o'clock. By about 10 o'clock in the evening, he will take a shower when he feels tired, and then continue to study until going to bed at 12 o'clock. From this schedule, we can see that his spare time is almost spent on study and work. He believes that the key to improving his decision-making ability is to learn more and read more books. He has always adhered to the principle of reading ten thousand books, traveling one thousand miles, making friends with thousands of people and founding an eternal business.

Lu Guanqiu said: "our worst enemy is ourselves, and it is the most difficult to overcome ourselves. Controlling our material desires is conducive to honing our will. When an entrepreneur just indulges in enjoyments, and works around the automobile in the morning, around the plate at noon and around the skirt at night, he will never become an entrepreneur, but a loser. He is good at finding his own shortcomings and adhering to learning and improving himself. There is no doubt that the 21st century is an era of competition among talents and knowledge. If the enterprises and individuals are not good at learning, they will be bound to be eliminated by society."

Peter F. Drucker, the master of management, pointed out that "According to my observation, effective managers start not from their tasks, but from the mastery of their time. They don't start with a plan but start with the knowledge about where their time is spent. Then they manage their time and reduce the time they spend on unproductive work. Finally, they centralize the scattered time when they can spend freely into a continuous period. These three steps are the basis of the effectiveness of managers. The most remarkable characteristic of effective managers is that they are able to value their time highly."

Data source: Dang Ning. A Chinese billionaire talked about how he got rich. (Harbin: Harbin Publishing House, 2004.)

Li Ka Shing loves his third son most

Li Ka Shing once said that in addition to Victor Li and Richard Li, in fact, he has a third son. Moreover, no one in his family has a share in the property of the son, and no one is allowed to touch it.

Li Ka Shing said that he was not aware of the fact that he had "the third son" until he lost sleep one night. Li's third son is, actually, the Li Ka Shing Foundation named after him. Li Ka Shing Foundation was founded in 1980, by which Li Ka Shing fulfilled his desire to grant more systematic financial assistance for education, medical care, culture, and public welfare undertakings. Over the years, he has contributed more than 5 billion Hong Kong dollars, about 70% of which are funded by Li Ka Shing Foundation, and his enterprise group driven by him contributes the remaining 30%. Li Ka Shing joked that his third son is now responsible for a lot of affairs concerned. He said that, of the 5 billion Hong Kong dollars donated by Li Ka Shing Foundation, 400 million Hong Kong dollars are granted to foreign countries, and the remaining 4.6 billion Hong Kong dollars are granted to Hong Kong and mainland China.

Li Ka Shing disclosed that his Li Ka Shing Foundation had not had fixed funds before and that he would not inject the capital into the Foundation until a donation was needed. But in recent years, for the sake of the long-term development of Li Ka Shing Foundation, he began to invest in Li Ka Shing Foundation and make long-term investments so as to generate regular income as a source of the donation.

He also plans to inject part of his income into the Li Ka Shing Foundation on an annual basis, so that the Li Ka Shing Foundation will have a more abundant financial foundation and can engage in more and more public welfare undertakings such as education, medical care and the welfare of the elderly. Li Ka Shing said that he also invited many outsiders to work in the Li Ka Shing Foundation. In Li Ka Shing Foundation, the board of directors has the final say on which project to donate to via secret ballot, rather than any individual.

Although Li Ka Shing asked his sons Victor Li and Richard Li, to share the commercial risks with him, he was highly concerned about his third son. He not only spent 40% of his time on the Foundation but also didn't let him take any risks.

As for the reasons for the establishment of the Li Ka Shing Foundation, Li Ka Shing said, "I hope to do something meaningful with my own money, so I plan to save enough money for the next generation to develop their own business, and donate the rest for social welfare undertakings."

Data source: Chun Xiao. Loving the third son best, Li Ka Shing proposed to establish the ideal combination of the Shenzhen-Hong Kong Special Industrial Zone. (Beijing Youth Daily, 2003-09-30)

Chapter 18 Encourage Teamwork

Maxims for Success

Teamwork is a kind of spirit of voluntary cooperation and collaborative efforts to achieve the established goals. If the team members cooperate with each other on a voluntary basis, it is bound to produce a strong and lasting force. Teamwork can reconcile all resources and intelligence of team members, and automatically eliminate all disharmony and unfairness. At the same time, it will give appropriate rewards to those who make sincere and selfless donations.

—Napoleon Hill

Principles and Guidelines

Teamwork is an essential element for you to achieve the goals and ultimate success. All the people who have made great achievements at all times and in all over the world are good at rallying the will of the people and mobilizing the overall strength of the team.

What is teamwork?

Teamwork is a kind of spirit of voluntary cooperation and collaborative efforts to achieve the established goals. Its form is very similar to that of a mastermind alliance, but it is quite different from a mastermind alliance. Teamwork aims at all the members of an organization, while its starting point is to mobilize the efforts of all members of the team, but these efforts may not always be purposeful and mutually compatible. However, a mastermind alliance aims at a small number of team members who are directly involved in the consultation, planning, decision-making, and leadership of the team and takes clear objectives and mutual harmony among these members as an essential factor. Its starting point is to fully stimulate the wisdom of all members and integrate the wisdom into a joint effort to achieve the established goal.

Teamwork can generate some strength, but whether the cohesion of the strength is temporary or permanent depends on the motivation to stimulate cooperation among team members. If the cooperation among members is based on voluntary motivation, teamwork is bound to generate lasting power before this motivation disappears.

Real teamwork must be based on others' willingness to cooperate with you, and you should also show your motivation for cooperation and be alert to any changes in the cooperative relationship with your partners. Teamwork involves an endless process. Although the success or failure of cooperation depends on the attitude of each member, it is your inescapable duty to keep the members working together all the time.

Power of teamwork

In the process of team cooperation, each of the members can share the good aspects of another person, and integrate these good aspects into a powerful team force, so as to ultimately be able to achieve the goal of the team. That's why we all hold the belief that union is strength. Specifically speaking, the strength of team cooperation is concentrated in the following two aspects:

A combined willpower can be formed via cooperation

There is a fable that one day, an old man called for his ten sons, and gave each of them a chopstick and then asked them to break it. As a result, each of them easily broke it. Then the old man tied ten chopsticks together and asked his sons to break them, but as a result, no one could break them. Thus, the old man took this opportunity to educate them to unite and not to split. In this way, they can form a force to overcome difficulties, protect themselves, and live a better life. This fable is almost known to all ages, and it implies that we will generate great strength when we work together and that combined willpower can be formed via cooperation.

We can form a common willpower by putting the willpower of each member together, which is known as a combined willpower. If an organization wants to attain the goal and succeed in its career, it must first enable the willpower of each member in the organization to form a common willpower. In case that each member of the organization is engaged in their own affairs and acts in their own way, but they go in opposite directions, it is impossible for the organization to achieve success. Andrew Carnegie, the steel tycoon of the United States, attributes his huge wealth acquired in the steel industry to the combined willpower, which means that each member of the company, based on a clear goal, contributes their own experience and knowledge to jointly exploring the steel market. Carnegie is mainly responsible for asking the employee to act with united strength so as to achieve a common goal.

New and larger willpower can be generated via cooperation

Through cooperation, not only the combined willpower can be formed, but also new and larger willpower can be generated. The combined willpower is just the sum of single willpower, while the new and larger willpower may far exceed the sum of single willpower.

It is why we often say that one plus one is greater than two.

As we all know, the human brain is like a battery. When energy is lost, the brain will shrink, and the man will become listless and hesitate to press forward. At this moment, it is necessary to charge. There are many ways to recharge. The most effective way is to contact and communicate with those who are intelligent and energetic so as to cheer each other up. When two or more people work together to communicate with each other, each is able to absorb the knowledge and abilities of the other members subconsciously. It will get instant results, and it can inspire more wisdom, more power, more lively imagination, and the sixth sense. Through the sixth sense, new inspiration will emerge and combine with what you are thinking about naturally. If the entire cooperative organization focuses on the common theme, the inspirations will emerge in a steady stream, as if there is an external help. In this case, the hearts of all members of the organization will, like the magnetites, attract new ideas and thoughts, stimulate new wisdom and strength, and then generate the greatest willpower and cohesion.

How can we stimulate the spirit of teamwork?

It is the toughest task for an entrepreneur to make his employee have cohesion and centripetal force, and cooperate with each other. If he can do this, he must be the best of his peers. So, how can we stimulate the spirit of teamwork?

First, identify the traits of the team members you need. In order to stimulate the spirit of teamwork, the prerequisite is to organize a good team first. A good team is not a motley crew that gathers together rather casually, but an elite group in which the members are strictly selected and organized according to the necessary conditions so as to achieve a common goal. Therefore, determining the traits of team members and organizing a good team is the key and starting point to inspire the spirit of teamwork.

The traits of team members should mainly include the following aspects:

(1) Loyalty.

(2) Capability.

(3) A positive attitude.

(4) The spirit of giving a little more.

(5) Confidence.

(6) Willpower.

Second, select team members according to the above standards.

Here you should pay special attention to the fact that you must adhere to the standards and rather go without than have something shoddy.

Third, you must trust all members of the team, and all the members should speak frankly and sincerely, open hearts to each other, and thus they can be closely attached to each other without reservation.

Fourth, you need to work closely with every member of the team until all the members of the team can work closely with each other.

Fifthly, analyze the motivation of each member to complete the work, study their urgent needs, give them the benefits they deserve according to their motivation and needs, and enable them to gain as much as possible on the premise of not affecting the development of the team.

Sixth, make clear the time and place of the meeting, discuss the plan, and carry out the plan. Otherwise, it is doomed to fail.

Seventh, do a good job in communication and coordination among team members so that the whole team works in an orderly and harmonious way like a machine.

Eighth, be strict with yourself and play an exemplary role.

As long as you can keep the above principles in mind and implement them unswervingly, there will be nothing you can't do, and the spirit of teamwork will definitely be inspired.

Examples of success

How does the manager of Guangzhou Lima Company Limited make use of the personnel?

Human resources are the foundation for the establishment and development of an enterprise. It's said that talents are hard to find, but I always think that only those who can give full scope to their talents can be called talents. As far as small-sized enterprises are concerned, they are small in scale but are fully equipped. Although small enterprises can't distinguish each department as well as large enterprises, there are still many things to be done in each department, but the employee have to play multiple roles in many cases. And the employee should give play to their energy to the extent where their talents can reach. I'm afraid it's not enough to rely solely on a person’s ability alone. Every person has advantages and disadvantages. There is no doubt that the advantages are good, but it is impossible to evade the disadvantages. In terms of the use of personnel, a small-scale enterprise should focus on finding proper ways to give play to the strengths of the employee and keep away from their shortcomings. To a large extent, the survival and development of small enterprises depend on their sales performance. Therefore, establishing a marketing team with the spirit of teamwork should be the top priority among priorities for a small-scale enterprise to make use of personnel.

Guangzhou Lima Company Limited, established in July 2002, had only three employees at its initial stage. The system was well developed, but it was a new company rarely known to the public, so it had not received any customer for the first three months after its inception. After the SARS in 2003, the company was almost paralyzed. Only half a year later, Guangzhou Lima Company Limited had more than 100 customers and nearly 20 employees. And its business covers more than ten provinces.

The old system has been upgraded, and the rapid development of the system has made Guangzhou Lima Company Limited a new star in the anti-counterfeiting industry, while the company has not made any additional investments. Many friends asked me what made Guangzhou Lima Company Limited change so much. I told them that the development of our company depends on the spirit of teamwork.

When the SARS broke out in 2003, the market was almost at a standstill, so the company had enough time to consider its development, and then the employee of the company gathered together every day to study the reasons for the chaos in the early stage, and found some solutions to each step and every detail of the solutions, involving the links ranging from administration, finance, propaganda, promotion, production, cooperation, planning, and development. When the market began to recover, the company's system was gradually improved. In the end, the company won at a stable pace. It seems that the company has slowed down at work, but its efficiency was improved on the whole at the time of the year-end settlement. It is the spirit of teamwork that is carried out in the whole process.

The spirit of teamwork, in my opinion, means that all the members can center on one person, understand and help each other as a family, give full play to their respective advantages, and make up for their shortcomings gradually, and thus the team will develop into a perfect team.

First, it starts with recruitment. The employee we employ are not necessarily the most capable, but they must agree with our values, understand our entrepreneurial ideas, and be able to start from the grass-roots level in a down-to-earth manner. When we had interviews with many applicants, they asked for a base salary of 3,000 Yuan as well as a variety of subsidies. I had to tell them, "I am so sorry that I am too poor to support you. I'm sorry, I can only give you a base salary of 800 Yuan to keep you from starving and freezing. As for the other needs, you have to rely on your own efforts." At that time, we often couldn't recruit a suitable person, but I still adhere to my principles of recruitment. I told them, "The spirit of the company is to serve the public in good faith. Our project is to help enterprises solve their problems in anti-counterfeiting. Our goal is to make more consumers easily identify the authenticity of products. The money we have made is a reward for our hard work rather than a debt owed by customers. If you can't agree with our spirit, I will not accept your application even if you are very capable, or you are willing to work for us with a monthly salary of 800 Yuan. But if you can really accept our ideas and are willing to serve the people, you will not get a salary of 800 Yuan a month. If you can't find a customer, I will help you analyze the reason; if you can't achieve the designated performance, I will help you analyze the reason; if you can't accomplish the task, I will help you analyze the reason. There is a great demand for anti-counterfeiting products. Enterprises need it, consumers need it, and governments also need it. Our project is so excellent. As long as you put your heart into it, there's no reason you can't do it well. " Now, our sales employee can earn a monthly pay as high as several thousand Yuan.

Training starts after recruitment. First of all, we told the new employees about the history and current situation of the anti-counterfeiting industry and taught them about the previous anti-counterfeiting products and the current anti-counterfeiting products, and thus enabled the new employee to integrate into the industry gradually. Then I ask four old employees to train the new employee for a week. On the other hand, the new employees begin to cooperate with the work of the old employees, look for necessary information, act as assistants, and observe how old employees worked. Every time the new employee finishes the training course of an old employee, he or she will write a summary report to express his or her views on our work and on the old employee and must write out three strong points and three weak points.

The old employee must also give me a report to express their views on the new employee. In this way, all the new employees are trained, and the new employee will familiarize themselves with the team, while all the employees are able to have a preliminary understanding of the new employee. Finally, I will hold a meeting and ask the employee to vote to determine whether the new employee is suitable for the position by a show of hands. If all the employee agrees, this person can become a regular employee. I'll ask the one who does not think the new employee suitable for the position to teach the new employee for another week. In a week's time, I will ask them whether the new employee is suitable. If he does not fit the position, it will prove that the new employee is not suitable for our company and then I will pay him another month's salary. In this way, everyone can get along well with each other. All the employees can have an idea about the strengths and shortcomings of each other and know how to correct the shortcoming. In this way, the company makes slower progress, but we will lay a more stable foundation for the future.

Next, it is the internship. I will ask the new employee to choose one from the old employee and learn from the old employee in one month, and then assess the new employee one month later. The assessment is composed of two parts, written and verbal expressions. Written assessment requires new employees to write down their views on corporate culture, corporate spirit, and other items of corporate culture, as well as their opinions on the development of the company and their own experience. Verbal assessment requires new employees to write down their understanding of the company and its customers. And they have to meet a standard in the assessment. If the new employee fails to meet the requirements, it is deemed as the mistake of the master worker. Then the employee will have to practice for another month, but I will not pay him. The salary should be paid by the master because the apprentice is recognized by the master. Since the master has approved him, he bears the responsibility of teaching the new employee well. Otherwise, the master has to pay the new employee. As a result, my employees are growing very fast and they are on speaking terms with each other.

Then, it is the regular office hours. I don't require new employees to have orders in the first month, but they must complete the task of visiting customers every month. The new employees must have to learn how to visit customers from their masters. I do not set a high standard for the task, and the new employees are inevitably able to accomplish it. If new employees are unable to accomplish the task, there is only one reason that they do not work hard enough. When a new employee is on duty for the first month, the master should also play a role in supervising his or her work. If the new employee can't finish, I will pay him two months' salary before asking him or her to leave, and the extra monthly salary will be deducted from the master because it's his dereliction of duty. But my employees have done a good job, and even the worst employee has an order in less than half a month.

I will ask for a regular meeting every weekend to summarize the work of this week, but it's very short. In the meeting, anyone who has a question can say it to find a proper solution, while the meeting can be dismissed if no one has a question. It is like the imperial court session in the early morning, where any official can submit a memoria to the throne if he has something to say, while the session can be adjourned if all the officials have nothing to say. But if the employee doesn't say anything this time, there will be no chance next time. When I find out any problem, it will be his or her dereliction of duty. Every employee should take a notebook with them, and write it down immediately if any problem is found. I will check it every weekend. So, we have fewer and fewer problems, and the problems that can be solved will be solved immediately.

We have a monthly meeting once a month, which can not be easily dealt with. We will have a meeting on the day when the employees are paid, and the employees should first attend the meeting before collecting the salary. On that day, we should do nothing, but these two matters. The meeting is mainly used for communication, and the members of the marketing team must communicate with each other on their sales experience, and they should make clear how they sign for each order. In this way, it can promote the sales staff to exchange sales experience, enhance their skills and their overall strength. In addition, we will evaluate the suggestions made this month at the meeting, and everyone present at the meeting will rate each suggestion. We will give different rewards for the suggestions scoring different points, ranging from 100 Yuan to 500 Yuan.

Half of the rewards will be given by the company, and the other half will be borne by all other employees because this suggestion is not only beneficial for the company, but also for everyone in the company. Therefore, all the employees should be delighted to propose some suggestions. Suggestions can be made from every detail of the company, including financial affairs, personnel, publicity, development, and other affairs. After the meeting, the employees can have dinner together, which will be paid by the company, and then go back home early to write a report to summarize the work of this month. The report involves the personal experience of employees, their understanding of sales, suggestions to their colleagues, and suggestions to the company, which will be submitted to me the next morning. In this way, all the employees will grow up quickly and then they can learn a lot in a short time.

The company is small, so I have to undertake a lot of tasks and understand the ideas of our subordinates. Otherwise, I cannot make a budget, and I will have no idea about what the company's current weaknesses are when it needs to strengthen publicity, and what needs to be improved, let alone develop a larger market. All the matters of the company are made known to the company staff. Every employee can put forward some ideas to publicize the products or cooperate with others. Then we will decide by vote together at the meeting. As long as the employees who make suggestions can do it, and everyone thinks it is feasible, I will let them do it. If the employee makes a mistake, the company will bear half of the loss, and the employees will share the last half of the loss. If the employee succeeds, the company will get part of it, the employee who makes the suggestion will gain another part, and the rest will be shared equally by all the employees. Therefore, every employee holds a positive attitude.

There is no doubt that rewards cannot be separated from punishments. I don't think anything that affects team cohesion can be tolerated. I'm very strict in this respect. If an employee grabs customers or steals other people's materials, I will dismiss this person as soon as I find out. I don't prescribe any other punishments but only dismissal. As long as half of the employees agree to dismiss the employee, I will execute immediately. It goes without saying that the rotten apple injured its neighbors. Therefore, I have to be cruel.

Now our company doesn't have to worry about basic revenue, but we just need to focus on system development and market development. Small companies cannot compete with big ones. We are unable to afford huge investments, so it is better for us to be down-to-earth. When the work is well scheduled, we have to pay attention to the personal problems of employees. Many employees are not local, so we try to help them rent their houses closer to the company. In addition, many of the employees are single, so we often organize some activities or associations. We need to know that a person will inevitably feel lonely when he works alone away from his home. If our company organizes relevant activities, it not only increases the emotional communication between employees, but also relieves their work pressure, and it can also avoid other unnecessary incidents.

It is not difficult to look for a proper project to start a business, but the difficulty lies in how to carry out the project. As mentioned above, small companies can not afford huge investments like large companies. Staff management cannot rely on the system alone but must be humanized. Team spirit is the pillar of the company as a whole. Of course, every company has its own special place. It is merely a macro policy to give full play to the team spirit of small companies, but the details need to be arranged according to their own situations. Data source: Ce Ya. How does the manager of a small enterprise make use of the personnel: Teamwork (Hc360.com, 2004-02-28)

Pony Ma and his entrepreneurial team of five members

This is a rare story of brothers' entrepreneurship, where Pony Ma's reason can be rated as a sample. Many years ago, Pony Ma and his classmate Zhang Zhidong jointly invested and registered Shenzhen Tencent Computer Systems Company Limited. Then they absorbed three shareholders, Zeng Liqing, Xu Chenye, and Chen Yidan. It is said that the QQ account numbers of the five founders are 10001, 10002, 10003, 10004 and 10005, respectively. In order to avoid competing for power with each other, Pony Ma and his four partners agreed at the initial stage of Tencent that they should each give full play to their strong points and perform their duties. Pony Ma serves as CEO (Chief Executive Officer), Zhang Zhidong serves as CTO (Chief Technology Officer), Zeng Liqing serves as COO (Chief Operating Officer), Xu Chenye serves as CIO (Chief Information Officer), and Chen Yidan serves as CAO (Chief Administrative Officer).

The reason why we say that the five founders of Tencent are a rare team is that until 2005, the founding team of these five people basically maintained such a cooperative structure and had never left. Even if Tencent has grown into an empire today, four of them are still on the front line of the company. Only the COO Zeng Liqing retired as a life-long consultant.

As the saying goes, two tigers cannot live on the same mountain. Especially in the process of rapid growth of the enterprise, it is not easy to maintain the stable cooperation of the founder team. Behind the cooperation, Pony Ma, who is an engineer, made great contributions to the rational design of the cooperative framework at the initial stage.

From the perspective of share composition, the five founders raised a total of 500,000 Yuan, including 237,500 Yuan from Pony Ma, accounting for 47.5% of the shares; 100,000 Yuan from Zhang Zhidong, accounting for 20% of the shares; 62,500 Yuan from Zeng Liqing, accounting for 12.5% of the shares; 50,000 Yuan from Xu Chenye and Chen Yidan, respectively, accounting for 10% of the shares. The principal part of the funds was invested by Pony Ma, but he voluntarily reduced his share to less than half, or 47.5%. "The sum of their shares should be slightly more than mine because we do not want to form any monopoly and dictatorship." At the same time, he must make the most capital contributions as the substantial shareholder of the company. "If we did not have a backbone and divided the shares equally, there would be definitely some problems arising, and the company would be ultimately be doomed. "

Another key factor for the stability of the team lies in the right combination of the partners. According to Lin Jun, the author of the book The History of China's Internet Industry, Pony Ma is very smart but very stubborn, and he attaches great importance to user experience and is willing to check its products from the perspective of ordinary users. Zhang Zhidong has a very active brain and indulges himself in technical research. Pony Ma is excellent in technology, but he is good at simplifying a lot of things, while Zhang Zhidong is better at doing everything to its perfection.

Xu Chenye, Pony Ma, and Zhang Zhidong are classmates in the Department of Computer Science of Shenzhen University. Xu Chenye, a well-known yes man, is very easygoing. He has his own opinions, but he does not express them easily. Chen Yidan was a classmate of Pony Ma when he studied in Shenzhen Middle School. Later, he was also admitted to Shenzhen University. He is very rigorous, but also very swanking. Moreover, he can arouse all people's passion for different circumstances.

If the other partners are regarded merely as partners, only Zeng Liqing is the most fun, open, passionate, and inspiring one among the five founders of Tencent. Compared with the mild Pony Ma and Zhang Zhidong, who is keen on technical research, Zeng is another type. Zeng Liqing's easygoing personality is more aggressive and he is more like the decision-maker. However, it may be his character that led him to be the first to leave the team and start his own business.

Later, in a joint interview with multiple media, Pony Ma admitted that he initially considered the way to share the shares equally with Zhang Zhidong and Zeng Liqing, but he finally chose the founding team of five founders. Even if someone intends to make additional investments for a larger shareholding ratio later, Pony Ma refused, "according to my judgment on your ability, you are not suitable for taking more shares." In Ma's point of view, the potential of shareholders in the future should match the shares they should have, and if not, some problems may come out. If some shareholders who hold large shares do not do anything useful while the shareholders who perform practical tasks hold a small number of shares, conflicts will arise.

After several times of stock dilution, the proportion of shares they held in the IPO was only 1 / 3 of the original, but even so, each of the founders is worth billions of Yuan, which is a happy ending. It can be said, in private enterprises in China, it is rare to find an entrepreneur like Pony Ma, who can tolerate and rope in talents like what Pony Ma has done, who can choose the persons with different personalities and specialties to form an entrepreneurial team, and who can maintain long-term tacit cooperation after successfully developing the market. The success of Pony Ma lies in that he has well designed the responsibilities, rights, and interests of the entrepreneurial team from the very beginning. The more capable the person is, the greater responsibilities he will assume, and the higher power he will possess, and then the more the profits of his company will be. Data source: Anonymous. The story of Pony Ma and his entrepreneurial team founding Tencent (Asian Business Leader, 2015-01-09)

Author's Remarks: Overcome Fear and Head Towards Success

"Fear is the biggest obstacle to success," warns Napoleon Hill, "from time to time, people may be controlled by their fear to make all the decisions and take all the actions in order to seek a stable life. Fear is just a state of mind. You can control and direct your state of mind towards the right track. "

Before you apply any of the principles in this book to the practice of striving for success, you must be prepared to accept this set of success philosophy in your mind. The core of the preparatory work is to overcome the fear in your heart, the greatest and most vicious enemy for mankind. It is the first step for you to head towards success and achieve your goal.

What is the fear?

What is the fear? What is its root? In fact, the fear is purely a psychological phenomenon, an erroneous assumption of a disaster that can not be foreseen or coped with properly, and a monster in our imagination. It is nothing but this. Its root lies in our ignorance. If we have received formal education or training, and we have a broad horizon and a large stock of knowledge and keep a cool head all the time, fear will have no effect on us. However, in real life, fear is not only found everywhere, but it is also in varied forms.

Basic forms of fear

A magazine, in the interview with 2,500 people, found that the respondents have a total of more than 7,000 types of fears. However, there are six kinds of fears that do the most harm to people, as follows:

The fear of poverty

Although the fear of poverty is just a kind of mental attitude, it is enough to destroy the chance for a person to make some achievements in any industry. The fear of poverty is undoubtedly the most destructive of the six basic forms of fear. There is nothing like poverty that makes people suffer from countless hardships and injustice. As the saying goes, the well-fed don't know how the starving suffers. Only those who have experienced the taste of poverty can fully understand the bitterness of poverty.

The fear of criticism

People who have a fear of criticism tend to lack the ability to express their own opinions accurately, and they are used to avoiding topics and easily agree with others' opinions before pondering over them. The fear of criticism is as common as the fear of poverty, and its negative impact on personal development is as deadly as that of the fear of poverty. It will make you lose motivation, destroy your willpower and imagination, limit your personality, and then make less believe in yourself and conduct yourself with less dignity, as well as do harm to other people in other ways.

The fear of losing love

Here, the fear of losing love refers to the fear of losing the love of a person, which is mainly manifested in the following aspects:

(1) Jealousy. The jealous may be filled with suspicions, apprehend danger in every sound, suspect those they love without any conclusive evidence, and accuse the other party of its unfaithfulness without any reason.

(2) Pickiness. The picky are accustomed to finding trouble and making mischief endlessly when they are slightly offended by their loved ones or have no reason at all.

(3) Gambling. People who love gambling believe that they can buy love with money, puff up their faces, and buy gifts for their loved ones. In order to get money, they may resort to fraud, stealing, and even gambling.

The fear of losing love has more severe damage to the human body and mind than other bears. It is evident to everyone that a setback in love hits a person far more serious than that in the career.

The fear of illness

The fear of illness is closely bound up with the fear of old age and the fear of death, but their specific manifestations are diverse from each other. The main manifestation of the fear of illness is a suspicious frame of mind.

The patients who suspect that they are sick are used to talking about diseases, always imagining those terrible symptoms, focusing on their diseases every day, and imagining that they may become less charming due to their diseases. What follows is that they will suffer endless pain and torment until they are completely collapsed in their minds. They have been suspicious that they are ill. With the lapse of time, it will affect their appetite, lead to malnutrition, and thus lower their bodies' resistance to diseases. It is exactly an opportunity for those diseases that they feel anxious about to come to them.

One famous doctor estimates that about 75% of all the patients seek medical advice from the doctors due to their suspiciousness. Even in the parts where it is the least likely to fall ill, as long as you are always afraid of getting sick, you may tend to get ill in the parts, which has been confirmed by numerous cases. There is no remedy for this disease, because it comes from a negative attitude, while it can only be cured when you hold a positive mental attitude.

The fear of old age

The fear of old age slows your pace and makes you feel inferior. No matter how old you are, this kind of fear will make you convinced that you have let the opportunity slip away and that the golden time of your life has been gone.

You will acquire invaluable experience in every period of your life. You should express your sincere thanks to the wisdom and ability you have gained in each period of your life. A majority of the achievements made in the history of human beings are created by wise people who have experienced the baptism of the years.

The best way to overcome this fear is to grind it beneath your heel and laugh at it, "get out! Don't bother me anymore, damn it! I don't need you! Get out of here!" Whenever a fear of old age comes out in your mind, you might as well try to do like this, which will protect you from this kind of fear.

The fear of death

The fear of death is the cruelest among all the fears. No matter what you believe in, it is absolutely impossible for you to evade death. Since death is a universal phenomenon that cannot be changed, it is quite difficult to drive out the fear of death.

In fact, the fear of death may make it more likely for you to stop working harder than any other fear. When you are always in the shadow that all people will inevitably die, you may easily feel that all that you have done is of no vain and that all your efforts go for nothing.

However, a primary fact is neglected in the idea that every moment of your life is valuable and that based on your actions, it is possible to achieve far more positive results than your current situation. Even if your life is about to come to an end, the lives of those who you love and those you don't know have not ended yet, and your efforts are the contributions you have made to the universal well-being of mankind.

You should know that no one can escape from death. Therefore, it makes no sense that you are terrified of death. Since death can't be avoided, it's better to accept the fact simply. Only the most stupid people will worry about something inevitable all day long.It is precisely the way to overcome the fear of death.

Fear is the worst enemy of mankind

Fear is the worst enemy of mankind. Uneasiness, anxiety, jealousy, worry, anger, and timidity are all fear in disguised forms. Fear will deprive people of their happiness, turn many people into cowards, and make many people fail to achieve success and fall into a humble situation.

Fear is enough to destroy the courage and creativity of a person. It will do great damage to a person's ambition, personality, and self-confidence. Moreover, it will make him melancholy and weak so that he will not dare to do anything. People who have a fear when they are in trouble, who are dominated by the fear in their work, and who have a sense of foreboding in everything, must be very inefficient at work. From ancient times to the present, the fear has destroyed the causes of countless people as a devil.

Fear has the power to wither the life of mankind. With the help of the power of fear, we can change the circulation of blood and the production of some other secretions in our bodies in a short time, as well as lead to some physiological and chemical changes in our body. It may even cause our hair to turn white, our faces to grow old, and our feet to be difficult to take a step forward in a few hours or overnight. Anything that makes us feel happy can make us feel excited and delighted, relax the capillaries, and thus make the blood circulation smooth. And those things that make us feel depressed, painful, sad, and anxious can constrict the blood vessels and block the circulation of blood. That's why people's faces often turn white when they are frightened.

Fear can have a significant impact on the nervous system. When people feel fear or face a sudden blow, some of them may suffer a nervous spasm all of a sudden, or become paralyzed with a stroke, and even die suddenly.

Fear will cut short a person’s normal span of life. It can make people anaemic and reduce their physical and mental vitality. It will destroy the physiological balance and weaken the physiological function of the human body. When you feel fear, the blood in your body will immediately change its chemical composition, which will invisibly exert an extremely adverse impact on your body.

People who are prone to a fear tend to age easily and may even die prematurely

The antidote to banish fear

The great destructive power of fear is often realized through our imagination, as we always keep imagining all kinds of terrible things. As a result, our natural spiritual antidote is the most effective drug to banish our fear. So, what are these antidotes? They are brave spirit, firm belief, a positive mental attitude, and optimistic character. Once you fill your mind with a brave spirit, firm belief, a positive mental attitude, and optimistic character in advance, the thought of fear can no longer intrude into your mind.

First of all, you must be possessed with the spirit of courage. In short, you have to be brave.

As the saying goes, the brave is the conquerer. Fear is the worst enemy of mankind. If we want to defeat the fear, we must first dare to despise it and overwhelm it in spirit. The primary reason why many people fail in the world is that they lack courage. On the contrary, for those who are fearless and resolute, no difficulty or obstacle can stop them from moving forward.

Then, what is courage? Courage is the conviction of our power that comes from deep in our consciousness, a firm belief that we have overwhelming capabilities, as well as the belief that we are able to face all emergencies, deal with all obstacles, and control all situations.

Among the personality elements, courage is a synthetic quality. Courage does not mean the ability to deal with a thing itself, but the attitude towards it. It is this attitude that determines success or failure in many cases. The boundary between the best and the mediocre among the people from all walks of life lies in that the best have done or are doing something that is impossible for ordinary people.

Therefore, no matter what happens, don't be discouraged or drift with the current, but always believe in yourself and smile at everything you encounter with courage.

Second, have a firm belief.

Regardless of what you need, have faith in it first. Do not ask how to do, why, or when to do it, but remember to go to all lengths and have faith in it, because faith is the creator of the great miracles of all times.

Many people fail because they like to stop and ask what the final result will be and whether they can achieve success in the future. Such constant inquiry about the result of the incident tends to lead to doubt and fear, which are fatal threats to success.

The secret of success is to concentrate on what you are doing, and any kind of doubt or fear is not conducive to concentration and will destroy your courage and creativity, leading to failure.

Third, hold a positive mental attitude.

In order to protect you from fear, you must keep a positive mental attitude, overcome the negative mental attitude, and use a positive mental attitude to dominate your thoughts and guide your actions. There is nothing in common in the performance of people with different mental attitudes. Those who hold a negative mental attitude must be pessimists. They are full of fear and are used to lowering their heads. And they usually only look at the bad in everything. On the contrary, those who hold a positive mental attitude must be optimists. They are full of confidence and are used to raising their heads. And they can find the good in everything all the time. The pessimist always predicts failure, while the optimist always expects success.

There are two different results for the two types of mental attitude. Those who hold a negative mental attitude may grow old before their time, with deep wrinkles on their faces. There is no hope or vigor in them, and they are far older than their years. On the contrary, those who hold a positive mental attitude must be dynamic, optimistic, and lively and agile. They look much younger than their years. And what a contrast emerges here.

Finally, have an optimistic character.

The optimistic can always look on the bright side of things and are ready to turn a losing game into a winning one at any time. They feel delighted themselves, but they will also make others find some pleasure. Therefore, they are always welcomed everywhere.

As long as you have an optimistic character, you ca ultimately eliminate your fear. Then, how can we develop an optimistic character? Like optimists, you should take the idea of being happy all the time as the most important creed of your life. Like optimists, don't predict the misfortunes that might happen to you. You should believe that everything has a bright side and try to find it out. You need to believe that the best things are bound to happen, but if something unfortunate happens, you can also minimize its negative impact, and even strive to find the joy in the bitterness when a disaster hangs over you.

The secret and formula of success

The secret of success

After summarizing the research results of his whole life, Napoleon Hill concluded that the secret of success lies in two aspects:

First, all achievements and all earned wealth originate from one thought. That is to say, the original source of all achievements comes from your own thoughts. Therefore, in order to succeed, you must first have an idea to succeed. Only in this way can you strive for success in action.

Second, there is no such thing as a free lunch. The secret I put forward is that success can only be achieved at a price. That is to say, and there is no doubt that the idea of success is the original source of success, but it must depend on your actions and efforts to achieve success. If you do not take action or make efforts, you will undoubtedly achieve nothing, in the end, no matter what you imagine.

The formula for success

Based on the above two secrets of efforts, we can get the formula for success, idea + effort = success.

An idea is the prerequisite of success, and effort is the guarantee of success. And success is the outcome of idea and effort.

Reflection and action

I hope that after learning each principle of success, readers can seriously reflect on the following four questions:

(1) What are the primary standards for us in this principle of success?

(2) What are your deficiencies compared with these standards?

(3) Why do these deficiencies arise?

(4) How are you going to make up for these deficiencies?

After reflection, you should act immediately and continue to act. You should never give up until you achieve the goal. As long as you can make unremitting efforts to achieve a clear goal, you will succeed in the end.

Finally, I would like to have some words for you. We all want to succeed, and everyone can be successful. I can help you succeed! We can all succeed! I sincerely wish you success!

References

Bian, Siguang (2002). Application of Napoleon Hill's Success Intelligence. Changchun: Changchun Publishing House.

Carnegie, Dale (2001). Dale Carnegie's Lifetime Success Book (S. Liu et al., Trans.). Beijing: China Commercial Publishing House, 2001.

Carnegie, Dale(2001). Dale Carnegie's The Art of Eloquence (T. J. Gao, Trans.). Yanji: Yanbian University Press.

Carnegie, Dale (2001). Dale Carnegie's Training for Interpersonal Skills (X. Jin, Trans.). Yanji: Yanbian University Press.

Carnegie, Dale (2001). Dale Carnegie's Way of Business (G. Z. Gao, Trans.). Yanji: Yanbian University Press, 2001.

Hill, Napoleon (1999). A Lifetime of Riches (Z. Q. Zhong & S. Li, Trans.). Haikou: Hainan Publishing House.

Hill, Napoleon (1999). My Own Journey (S. F. Zhang & M. H. Wang, Trans.) . Haikou: Hainan Publishing House.

Hill, Napoleon (1999). Napoleon Hill's Road To Success (S. F. Zhang, Trans.). Haikou: Hainan Publishing House.

Hill, Napoleon (1999). Success Through a Positive Mental Attitude (Q. Q. Ding, Trans.). Haikou: Hainan Publishing House.

Hill, Napoleon, Pierre, N. V. (2000). The Power of Positive Mental Attitude (J. Liu, Trans.). Chengdu: Sichuan People's Publishing House.

Hill, Napoleon (2001). Everyone can be successful. Wuhan: Hubei People's Publishing House, 2001.

Hill, Napoleon (2001). Rebuild Your Life: Manage Your Better (T. Liu, Trans.). Beijing: Jiuzhou Press.

Hill, Napoleon (2002). Collection of Napoleon Hill's Maxims on Success (Stankin, Trans.). Hulun Buir: Inner Mongolia Culture Press.

Hill, Napoleon (2002). Collection of Napoleon Hill's Maxims on Success (Stankin, Trans.). Hulun Buir: Inner Mongolia Culture Press.

Huang, Helang (2002). Tutorial of Napoleon Hill's Science of Success. Haikou: Hainan Publishing House.

Li, Jie, Dong, Shubao (2002). The Application of Dale Carnegie's Success Wisdom. Changchun: Changchun Publishing House.

Lin, Yutang (1996). An Inspirational Life. Chengdu: Sichuan Literature and Art Publishing House.

Mandeno, Auger (1996). The Greatest Salesman In The World (L. An, Trans.). Shenzhen: Haitian Press.

Marden, O. S.(2000). Lifelong Capital (G. S. Bao & L. J. Li, Trans.). Beijing: China Archives Publishing House.

Marden, O. S. (2001). Fundamentals of Success (C. M. Zhang, Trans.). Beijing: China Development Press, 2002.

Marden, O. S.(2001). Noble Personality (X. Y. Lin, X. Li & G. S. Bao, Trans.). Beijing: China Archives Publishing House.

Marden, O. S.(2001). Pushing to the Front (Q. F. Wu, X. Yu & G. S. Bao, Trans.). Beijing: China Archives Publishing House.

Marden, O. S.(2001). Qualities for Success (H. L. Luo, Y. J. Liu & G. S. Bao, Trans.). Beijing: China Archives Publishing House.

Marden, O. S.(2001). Thinking and Successful (Q. F. Wu, Z. M. Liu & G. S. Bao, Trans.). Beijing: China Archives Publishing House.

Marden, O. S.(2002). The Personality of Genius (W. B. Jiang, X. M. Tian & G. S. Bao, Trans.). Beijing: China Archives Publishing House.

Marden, O. S.(2004). Life can be better after this lesson (M. Xia, Trans.) . Yinchuan: NingXia People's Education Press.

Stone, Clement (2002). The Success Law that Never Fail: PMA is Your Winningest Trump Card (Y. Zhang, Trans.). Changchun: Jilin People's Publishing House.

Tian, Ye (1997). Complete Works of Napoleon Hill's Science of Success. Beijing: China Economy Daily Press.

Tian Yuan, Ouyang Yun, Yang Xiyue (1997). Time Management. Beijing: China City Press.

Wei, Jie (2002). Planning for your success step by step . Beijing: Haichao Press.

Wellman, George (2003). Success Begins with Method: 10 abilities of explosive power from weak to strong (C. Ma, Trans.). Beijing: China Zhigong Press.

Wu, Mei (2001). 22 rules for wealth and success: from rags to a millionaire. Beijing: Chinese Overseas Publishing House.

Index

D

E

F

G

H

I

J

K

L

M

N

T

W

X

Y

Z

About the Author

Zhang Xiuyu is a Professor, the founder of the science of success in China, and a renowned expert in management consultancy, business strategy, and management science in China. He is the former director of the Department of Business Administration of Beijing Institute of Economic & Management. After retirement, he founded Beijing Chenggong Zhiyao Consulting Co.,Ltd. as chairman and general manager. He is also a visiting professor of Peking University, Tsinghua University, Renmin University of China, China Europe International Business School (CEIBS) and many other famous universities, a postgraduate supervisor of the leading cadres of the Party School of the Central Committee of the Communist Party of China, a member of the Beijing SMEs Expert Advisory Committee and the management consultant and strategic consultant of many medium- and large-sized enterprises.

Made in United States
Orlando, FL
04 November 2026

90206782R00207